'824

MW01226771

SAFE HAVEN

Ben Barman with the Penrose family, January 1943: left to right, Ben, Margaret, Oliver, Roger, Jonathan, and Lionel

SAFE HAVEN

*The Wartime Letters
of Ben Barman and Margaret Penrose,
1940–1943*

Edited by
Roderick J. Barman

McGill-Queen's University Press
Montreal & Kingston · London · Chicago

ISBN 978-0-7735-5505-1 (cloth)
ISBN 978-0-7735-5612-6 (epdf)
ISBN 978-0-7735-5613-3 (epub)

Legal deposit fourth quarter 2018
Bibliothèque nationale du Québec

Printed in Canada on acid-free paper that is 100% ancient forest free
(100% post-consumer recycled), processed chlorine free

Funded by the   Financé par le
Government   gouvernement
of Canada   du Canada

Canada Council   Conseil des arts
for the Arts   du Canada

We acknowledge the support of the Canada Council for the Arts, which last year
invested $153 million to bring the arts to Canadians throughout the country. Nous
remercions le Conseil des arts du Canada de son soutien. L'an dernier, le Conseil a
investi 153 millions de dollars pour mettre de l'art dans la vie des Canadiennes et
des Canadiens de tout le pays.

Library and Archives Canada Cataloguing in Publication

Safe haven (Montréal, Québec)
Safe haven : the wartime letters of Ben Barman and Margaret Penrose, 1940–1943 /
edited by Roderick J. Barman.

Includes bibliographical references and index.
Issued in print and electronic formats.
ISBN 978-0-7735-5505-1 (cloth).
ISBN 978-0-7735-5612-6 (epdf).
ISBN 978-0-7735-5613-3 (epub)

1. Barman, Ben – Correspondence. 2. Penrose, Margaret, 1901–1989 – Correspondence. 3. World War, 1939–1945 – Children – Canada – Correspondence. 4. Children
– Canada – Correspondence. 5. World War, 1939–1945 – Evacuation of civilians –
Great Britain. 6. World War, 1939–1945 – Personal narratives, British. 7. Children
and war – Canada. 8. Canada – Social life and customs – 1918–1945. 9. Personal
correspondence. I. Barman, Roderick J., 1937–, editor II. Title.

D810.C4S24 2018   940.53'161   C2018-903315-0
                                          C2018-903316-9

Contents

Illustrations

Preface

This is the story of my oldest brother, Adrian Benjamin Barman, known as Ben, and of the years he spent as an evacuee or "war guest" in Canada during the Second World War in the household of Margaret Penrose, her husband, and three sons in London, Ontario. The story is told through the letters that Ben and Margaret wrote at the time, Ben's memories of his experience, the recollections of and letters written by others involved, and visuals from the period. Ben's mother, and mine – Penelope Spencer Barman – wrote regularly to him and to Margaret, but only two letters from her exist. Not all of Ben and Margaret's letters survive, but those that do are compelling, telling a graphic story. Ben was one of the several thousand children sent to Canada from Great Britain during the fraught months of June to September 1940. Children began to return from Canada long before the war ended in Europe in May 1945. Ben himself came back to his family in September 1943, after three years' absence.

Most of the written materials appearing here were collected by our mother and held by her until, when clearing out her possessions in old age, she offered the papers to Ben. Supplementing these materials are Ben's own memories of the war years together with information, both oral and written, gathered from members of his family and from others, including the Penroses, with whom he lived in Canada. The unpublished reminiscences written in old age by Margaret Penrose and the papers of her husband, Lionel Penrose, held in the Science Library of University College, London, have provided useful information. Ben prepared two draft transcripts of the materials, together with some reminiscences. At Ben's request, I have reworked the various materials into a text, drawing on my background as a historian and as Ben's youngest brother (who remained in England throughout the war).

The experience of each child evacuee was shaped by particular circumstances. What made Ben's experience distinctive was that, as he himself states, "I am, like my father, dyslexic, that is, I have severe difficulties with spelling and writing." During Ben's childhood, dyslexia had been identified as a condition by medical specialists, but, despite this, it was not generally recognized and treated, especially not by educationalists, who dismissed those suffering from dyslexia as either lazy or dim witted. To give the reader an idea of what Ben was experiencing, the spelling and phrasing of his letters have been left unchanged from the original text, with some emendations given in brackets.

The intent in presenting these letters is twofold. Ben's scrawls, as the images show they were, make real and drive home the difficulties and barriers faced by children affected by dyslexia and also demonstrate the ways in which the young met the challenge. It was extremely hard for Ben to convey on paper what he was experiencing in Canada. On the other side, Margaret Penrose's letters, those of an intelligent and imaginative woman, give a graphic account of the evolving condition of a well-to-do family as the exigencies of the war pressed home.

For the reproduction of copyright material, I must give warm thanks to the following: Shirley Hodgson and her brothers, Oliver, Roger, and Jonathan Penrose, as the heirs to Margaret and Lionel Penrose; Christopher Barman and Blair Barman, as heirs to Ben's uncle and aunt, Ross Barman and Orion Barman; Dan Flanagan, as heir to his mother, Elizabeth Randall Baile Flanagan; and Martin Dewey for his written account of the Atlantic crossing. I am also grateful to the late Eric Avebury and his cousin Flavia Ormond (both war guests) for information about Kate Rigling, the long-time nanny to the Lubbock family, who in 1943 accompanied Ben back to England. It has not been possible to trace the heirs of Mrs Elsie Hart, her son Beverley Hart, Ms Aileen Wallace, and Mr Hugh Lawson in order to request permission to reproduce their letters.

The illustrations, and the letters, are courtesy of my brother Ben Barman, with the following exceptions: the photograph of Melchet Court formerly Pinewood School (figure 1.4) is © Peter Stacey (cc-by-sa/2.0); the photograph

of the ss *Antonia* (figure 2.5), is taken from http://www.clydemaritime.co.
uk/HMS_Antonia; the photograph of the Kagawa family (figure 8.1) is reproduced by permission of the archives of the Nikkei National Museum and Cultural Centre.

Dan Mitchell, the archivist at the Science Library of University College,
London, very kindly gave me access, on quite short notice, to the papers of Dr
Lionel Penrose. I have also to thank Tom Belton, archivist at Western University, London, Ontario, for supplying material, and to Linda Kawamoto Reid,
researcher at the Nikkei National Museum and Cultural Centre, located in
Burnaby, British Columbia, for finding materials on the Kawaga family. Thanks
are also due to Jonathan Barman, Blair Barman, Oliver Penrose and Rosemary
Wilson for sharing their memories. The book owes its existence to the warm
welcome given the project by Philip Cercone, executive director of McGill-
Queen's University Press, and it has greatly benefited from the skills of Ryan
Van Huijstee, managing editor. Finally, I must thank my spouse, Jean Barman,
for her excellent and unstinting participation in the preparation of this work.

SAFE HAVEN

Introduction

The impact of the Second World War on the peoples of Great Britain and Canada was both profound and diverse. The war particularly affected British and other children, often very young in age, who were sent across the Atlantic to find a safe haven in Canada. These "war guests," as the Canadian press termed them, formed but one part of a flow of children who in the early years of the war left Great Britain for the British Dominions and the United States. A 1950 study, still not supplanted, calculated that, between 1 July 1939 and 31 December 1940, 16,237 individuals under the age of sixteen left the United Kingdom.[1] A work published in 1988 estimated that 253 children had been sent privately to Canada in 1939, nearly 5,500 arrived under various auspices the following year, and a further 451 in 1941.[2] Dr Claire Halstead, in her 2015 doctoral dissertation, sets the number of private evacuees (defined by the Canadian government as those children travelling without their mothers) arriving from June to December 1940 at 5,118. The children travelling in 1940 included a further 1,529 sponsored by the British government's evacuation scheme, known as CORB (Children's Overseas Reception Board), and sent in nine parties between its start on 21 July 1940 and the torpedoing of the *City of Benares* steamship on 17 September 1940. The death of seventy-seven children in that disaster brought

---

1 The under-sixteen age group comprised one quarter of all emigrants; see Titmuss, *Problems of Social Policy*, 246–7.

2 Bilson, *Guest Children*, 9–10, 61. No sources are given for these figures, probably owing to the author's death before the book was completed and published.

the official scheme to a halt. The British prime minister, Winston Churchill, had never favoured child evacuation, and by September 1940 he held an unchallengeable authority over governmental affairs.[3] Some evacuations under private auspices continued, but the German assault on the Soviet Union in June 1941 removed any danger of invasion and so any need to send offspring abroad.

Individual "war guests" encountered a diverse range of experiences in Canada.[4] Further, the way in which these experiences combined was so different and so distinctive that their impact on that particular war guest came close to being unique. A synthesis, laudable as it is for many scholarly works, does not suit or do justice to the experiences of the war guests. To make this point is not to deny the reality that most of Canada's war guests underwent a similar trajectory of life during the evacuation. This trajectory can be divided into six distinct phases that were diverse in their nature and impact: decision, transit, reception, living, going home, and reintegration.

The first phase encompasses the factors – human, material, and social – that led to a decision to send a child out of Great Britain. In human terms, those involved in this decision were not just the parents or parent but the child, the state bureaucrats sanctioning the departure, and adults on the other side of the Atlantic able to provide a safe haven. The role played by the child depended a great deal on the individual's age and gender – older boys probably having the most input. In material terms, the decision turned on the command of immediate financial resources and on access to transport. Social factors included suitable host families in Canada and access to decision makers for the granting of passports and visas. The initiative for making the decision did not invariably lie with the parents or parent. Family or friends in Canada might trigger action by offering hospitality. Similarly, the decision by a number of private boarding schools in England to move their pupils *en bloc* across the Atlantic to Canada allowed parents to avoid active choice and planning.

3 Halstead, "From Lion to Leaf," 24, noting that in 1942 three children already in Canada entered the CORB program, making a total of 1,532; and Fethney, *The Absurd and the Brave*, 130–45, 300.
4 The Canadian government did not keep records on the children who came to Canada in the company of their mothers. Given that Ben Barman travelled to Canada with his uncle, this study does not consider the experience, significant as it was, of those "war guests" who came with their mothers.

Transit, the second phase of the war guest experience, involved considerable challenges. While the first flights across the North Atlantic – a once-a-week flying boat service – had begun in June 1939, they ceased upon the outbreak of war. Travel by ship was the only possibility. In the last full year of peace, several hundred thousand passengers crossed the Atlantic in around thirty-three liners, which were configured to attract the wealthy. The outbreak of the war drastically reduced the number of sailings, with a British blockade confining German and Italian ships to their home ports, many neutral boats laid up at the docks of New York, and the British government requisitioning nearly half of the nation's liners. The torpedoing on 3 September 1939 of the *Athenia* steamship, killing ninety-eight passengers, provided a grim warning that disaster at sea might preclude reaching safe haven.

It is within these constraints that the transit of evacuated children should be viewed. Scholarly research has focused on the transit of children, drawn from all classes, arranged by the official CORB, which was established in June 1940, but in fact the considerable majority of war guests came from the upper echelons of British society. The high costs of the voyage, the intense competition to secure berths, and the need for adult supervisors all favoured the well to do. A Canadian diplomat sardonically noted in June 1940 that "people would rather let their children run the risk of being bombed than send them on a sea voyage without their Nanny," the reality being that the offspring of the upper classes were often emotionally closer to their nanny than to their parents.[5] Further, the upper-class custom of sending children to boarding school from the age of eight onwards meant that children were used to separation from their parents for months a time – and vice versa. Regardless of such practices, separation was difficult, and the trauma probably hit adolescents (those aged over twelve) and infants (those five and under) hardest. Adolescents might refuse, when push came to shove, to be evacuated. Infants had no such option. It is hard in this age of jet travel, when the sea serves only for cruise ships in calm water, to appreciate how alien and disturbing transit was. The strangeness of the sea, the tossing waves, the ship's décor, and the crowds of strangers must have been stressful and frightening, for many, perhaps most, children. The zigzag course of the ship, the lifeboat drills, and the uneasiness and tension ev-

5 Ritchie, *Siren Years*, 58.

ident among the adults on board contributed to the trauma of transit, often with long-term effects.

If transit were traumatic, the third phase – the reception of the war guests in Canada – could be equally harrowing for the children. The lack of precise data as to the number of war guests, their destination and so their distribution across Canada, the length of their stay, and the socio-economic standing and psychological outlook of the families hosting them complicates analysis. Nonetheless, one thing is clear: the children suddenly came face to face with what was, despite many similarities to Great Britain, an alien culture, with unfamiliar accents, vocabulary, dress, food, and scenery. The war guests were outsiders, many of them of upper-class origin and now confronting a far more egalitarian society. Compounding this challenge was that entry into the new setting made starkly evident the child's loss, in psychological terms, of her or his parents and family. Canada was not invariably a safe haven.

At this moment in the reception process, the attitudes and actions of the host family were critical. Unfortunately, these are perhaps the least investigated elements in that process. Taking care of a war guest laid great burdens on foster mothers, causing Margaret Penrose, the foster mother whose letters are reproduced in this volume, to comment on "the poor neglected foster parent and how her reactions vary – and no one cares about that!"[6] Familiarity on the part of some host families with the British way of life may have acted to ease the child's adaption to his or her new existence. Neither residence with blood relatives nor living with a wealthy family guaranteed happiness. Of course, even in the most "normal" of circumstances, neither a secure parent-child relationship nor a settled home life necessarily ensure a happy childhood or a fulfilling maturity. In sum, a multitude of factors, not easy to assess, influenced just how the individual child responded to the shock of reception, determining whether he or she ultimately flourished, endured, or rebelled.

Reception merged into the fourth phase, that of living for months and years as a war guest in Canada. A central aspect of that life was schooling, which took up much of the year. Some of the war guests had crossed the Atlantic as part of evacuated boarding schools, and most of these children were housed in Canadian private schools. In these cases, living was, for the pupils, a fair simulacrum of their previous existence in Great Britain. However, for the vast majority of

6 Margaret Penrose to Penelope Barman, 7 April 1942.

the war guests, going to school meant attendance at their local public school. Public education in Canada, drawing on the philosophy of John Dewey, differed sharply from that prevalent in England. It was concerned less with the inculcation of knowledge than with the formation of good citizens. Given these assumptions and the prevailing admiration in Canada for the British people, the children escaped much of the prejudice usually experienced by newcomers and outsiders. In many ways, school provided an alternative setting for those who were not comfortable in their new homes.

School was, of course, out in the summer months, but that vacation time included, in most cases, some weeks at summer camp. War guests found summer camp to be quite unlike, and psychologically distinct from, anything that life had to offer in Great Britain. At camp the participants were encouraged to build up their physical and practical skills along with others of their own age group. Summer camp exemplified freedom of action and egalitarianism, so different from the conformism and class ranking intrinsic to Great Britain, qualities that could make life in Canada attractive to those old enough to appreciate the difference.

How much war guests thought about going home, the fifth phase, is difficult to tell. Homesickness probably made them consider return as an eventuality but one that, being remote from their daily existence, did not engage their attention. The summons to come home could be unexpected and so unsettling, although for many adolescents, return represented a chance to embark on life on their own terms. The factors that made parents, or their equivalent, decide to call their offspring home are not clear. The British victory at El Alamein in October 1942 banished all possibility of a German invasion. By that date, most war guests had been absent for two or more years, making parents fear that memories of home had started to fade, affective bonds to weaken, and, most of all, physical appearance to change. A further concern for parents was that life in Canada was making their children culturally different from the British norm, with their experience steadily "declassing" them.

To desire return was one thing, to achieve it quite another. Although May 1943 finally saw the Allied navies dominating the German U-boat wolf packs, the torpedoing of ships did not end, and travel across the Atlantic remained dangerous. Return to Europe could be made on Portuguese ships, which were neutral and thus safe, but berths available on them were few and very expensive. Further, because these ships docked at Lisbon, the last leg of the journey had still to be arranged. Securing a seat on the flights across the Bay of Biscay was not easy, and these ran the risk of being attacked by Luftwaffe patrols. This danger was eliminated when, late in the war, flying boats carried returning children from Lisbon first to Foynes in Ireland and then on to England. Also late in the war, the British government arranged for a fairly safe method of travel by allowing boys, appointed "ship's messengers," to sail on warships travelling from North America to the United Kingdom. Securing such appointments depended on one's influence, to the advantage of upper-class children. While the pattern of return has not been much investigated, it is clear that, by the start of 1945, most war guests were back in the United Kingdom.

The reintegration of the evacuees into British society, the sixth and final phase, aroused at the time no concerns and commanded no attention. The prevailing attitude was that children were returning to their families and their familiar way of life, ending a long period of what was perceived as deprivation. Notwithstanding the hardships and losses imposed by the war, the British way of life, opinion held, continued to be infinitely superior and preferable to anything North America had to offer. (Typical of this outlook was the belief among the upper classes that the failure of the Canadian school curriculum to teach Latin demonstrated its inferiority.) In consequence, it was for the returnees to adapt, without protest, to the status quo, not for the British to offer understanding or make allowances for the children. The transatlantic experience of the children had simply no relevance for the British. When the CORB suggested in 1945 to various government departments that a survey be undertaken to ascertain the effect of evacuation on the children involved, the minister of education responded that "any enquiry such as is suggested would involve a great deal of labour which would not be commensurate with the results that would accrue."[7] For British bureaucrats, such an investigation, with its diversion of limited resources from the task of postwar reconstruction, could not be justified, but the minister's brusque dismissal of the request also demonstrates the absence of any concern about the children's reintegration into society.

The assumption that the Canadian experience had no significance, beyond the need to remedy the defects that absence from British society had caused, makes it very difficult to evaluate what the impact of being war guests was on

7 Fethney, *The Absurd and the Brave*, 279n21, citing Dominions Office 131 (CORB records) 70, Ellen Wilkinson, minister of education, to CORB, n.p., n.d.

the children and how the experience shaped their subsequent lives. The existing literature devotes considerable space to how many war guests returned – or desired to return, without actually doing so – to the host country. Children who had come over with private schools were perhaps the least likely to go back to Canada, since they had, essentially, continued to live within a British cultural milieu while abroad. The final report of the CORB provided statistics on how many of the children it had sponsored had decided to remain in Canada or would remain if their parents came out to join them.[8] The factors that led to a decision to remain are not easy to establish but the age of the child at the time of possible return probably played a considerable role. Those in mid- to late adolescence, thoroughly attuned to the culture of the host country, were more likely to stay, although families were probably more likely to let sons remain while insisting that daughters return. Younger children, particularly those either below or approaching puberty, had not integrated so thoroughly in the host society and further did not perceive themselves as capable of resisting a return to England.

The lack of interest in Great Britain about the returnees during the postwar years does much to explain the lack of contemporary accounts, whether in the United Kingdom or Canada, of war guests' experiences. Not until the fortieth anniversary of the war's end, the moment when the immediate past comes into focus and so becomes history, did scholarly studies begin to appear. Those studies, though limited in number, contain many of the personal accounts available on the subject. These reminiscences have, it should be stressed, both the advantage and the drawback of being retrospective. The narrator's subsequent life course shapes and colours what she or he recalls of their experience as a war guest.

The present study, while it does draw on personal retrospective memories, is based on the contemporary correspondence of one war guest and of the woman who took care of him. Canada did in this case provide for the two of them the safe haven that so many sought. Both of them would return to Great Britain and spend the rest of their lives there. This study may not be representative, since no single account can be such, but it provides a graphic insight into the war guest experience.

8 Fethney, *The Absurd and the Brave*, 300. The final report was presented in February 1946.

1

Beginnings,
1931–1940

To get away from people I used to go and hide in the foundations
of the new classrooms then being built.
~*Reminiscences of Ben Barman*

Adrian Benjamin Barman, known as Ben, was born at a nursing home in Belgravia, London, on 22 May 1931, the first of the three sons of Harry Lowis Barman and Penelope Spencer. The social standing of Ben's parents played a major role in shaping his life. They were more than secure in financial terms and possessed the cultural attributes that marked them as belonging to the lower echelons of what may be termed the upper classes. In the interwar years, the British upper classes were still composed of three elements: the aristocracy, that is, the titled nobility and their families; long-established families often identified as the "gentry"; and wealthy industrialists, as were Ben's parents, who together with merchants, bankers, and professionals constituted the lower end of the upper classes.[1]

Indicative of the class standing of Ben's parents was their employment of a nanny to take care of their three sons. They held a long lease on a flat in Queen's Gate Gardens, Kensington, London, and they also leased a house called Hollybush at Newdigate, near Dorking, Surrey, to the southwest of London. Both Ben's parents were offspring of families newly established in the upper middle class. Ben's paternal grandfather, Harry Drummond Dawson Barman, who was orphaned as a baby, had worked his way up in the world as an industrialist. His great good looks had gained him the hand of a woman who was the granddaughter of a governor of the Bank of England and the cousin of an earl.[2] Ben's

---

1 Only in the later part of the nineteenth century were titles of nobility conferred on men in this third group.

father, Harry Lowis – "Lowis," as he was usually called – had been educated at Repton, a private boys' boarding school, and at King's College, Cambridge University, both of which he attended because his mother's brother had done so. On Penelope's side, her father, Leonard James Spencer, the son of a school teacher, had also made his way in life, gaining a doctorate at Cambridge University and eventually rising to be Keeper of the Minerals at the Natural History Museum in London and a fellow of the Royal Society. Her mother, Edith, the daughter of a tenant farmer, ran a well-regarded private primary school attended by the children of the eminent, including the offspring of the philosopher Bertrand Russell, maverick and subsequently fascist politician Sir Oswald Mosley, and bohemian painter Augustus John (Fig. 1.1).[3]

Ben's parents were kind, generous, and well intentioned, but they very much subscribed to, and lived within, the conventions of their time and class. This trait was particularly notable in Lowis. As a young woman, Penelope Spencer had shown originality and flair in creating and performing solo dances on the stage: she was probably best known for her "Funeral Dance on the Death of a Rich Aunt," set to the music by Lord Berners, prominent in artistic circles in the 1920s (Fig. 1.2). Her broad circle of acquaintances included Dame Sybil Thorndike and Sir Lewis Casson in the theatre and Dame Ninette de Valois and Sir Frederick Ashton in the dancing world. Familiar with and little troubled by the ways of the artistic world of the interwar years, Penelope outwardly became, after her marriage in 1930, a dutiful wife, following her husband's views and assumptions. These assumptions included what may be termed "the eldest son and heir" syndrome, by which the first-born son received preferential treatment as the bearer of the family name and guardian of its fortunes. In return, he was expected to excel in all respects. The weight of these expectations fell on Ben, born in May 1931, and they were intensified by the birth of his younger brothers Jonathan in September 1934 and Roderick in January 1937.

2 Harry Drummond Dawson Barman (1861–1933) was married in 1896 to Lilian Palmer (1866–1934), the granddaughter of John Horsley Palmer, a director (1811–57) and governor (1830–33) of the Bank of England and the first cousin twice removed of Roundell Palmer, the 1st Earl of Selborne, twice lord chancellor. The couple had three children – Ursula, Lowis, and Ross.
3 Leonard Spencer (1870–1959) made his career as an official in the Natural History Museum, also serving as editor of the *Mineralogical Magazine* (1900–50). In 1899 he married his first cousin, Edith Mary Close (1872–1954). They had three children – Penelope, Philip, and Sylvia.

Figure 1.1 Pupils from Edith Spencer's school in about 1907. Edith Spencer is in
the centre, with her daughter Penelope (later Barman) the second girl on her
right and Margaret Leathes (later Penrose) on the far right of the top row.

On reaching school age, Ben entered his grandmother's school. The school,
located at "11 Brechin Place, which backed onto the Old Brompton Road," was
in walking distance of his parents' flat in Queen's Gate Gardens. He recalls his
time there with some pleasure, although he had traumatic memories as well.
"I remember playing outside in the small back garden when I heard a screech
of car brakes. My mother had been hit by a car and was carried into the house
through the back gate. Fortunately she wasn't killed or crippled." Ben remained
at his grandmother's school until world events intervened.

Bitterness over defeat in the First World War and the deprivations of the
Great Depression had in 1933 brought Adolf Hitler and the Nazis to power in
Germany. Remilitarization and aggression followed, culminating in the annex-
ation of Austria and the destruction of Czechoslovakia in 1938 and 1939, respectively. By then, it was clear both that Hitler was bent on further expansion

Figure 1.2 Penelope Spencer as dancer, late 1920s

Figure 1.3 Lowis Barman, on the far right, with the other management staff
of Production Engineering Ltd, about 1939

and that his word could not be trusted. Great Britain finally abandoned its policy of appeasement and gave guarantees to Poland, the next target for Nazi aggression. Refusing to give the assurances the British demanded, the Germans attacked Poland on 1 September 1939.

In Ben's own words, "In September 1939 when war was declared we lived at Hollybush in the country. I remember that my parents were installing blackout, my mother at the sewing machine making curtains and my father constructing panels, since German bombers were wrongly expected to strike next night." Blackout, usually made of black cloth, was affixed to all the windows of a house to prevent any light escaping. The panels made by Ben's father, probably out of cardboard, served the same purpose. Streetlights were dimmed and the headlights of automobiles covered with black tape, leaving only a narrow slit through which light could escape. The intent was to make the whole country dark and so provide no targets for enemy bombers.

An immediate consequence of the war was to disrupt existing livelihoods. Ben's grandmother, Edith Spencer, by then in her late sixties, found it impossible to keep her school open.[4] Many parents were not willing to expose their children to the risk of bombing, which everyone expected to happen, and moved their offspring to schools in the countryside. Ben's parents thus had to look elsewhere for his education. Jonathan and Roderick, aged four and two, respectively, had not yet reached school age and continued to be cared for by the family nanny.

Among the conventions governing the family life of the upper classes was the expectation that sons would, sooner rather than later, be sent away to boarding school, starting with what was known as a "prep" school, so termed because it "prepared" pupils for entry into a "public" school, which educated boys (girls having separate schools) from the ages of thirteen to eighteen. Boarding schools, both preparatory and public, had three terms: autumn, from late September to early December; winter, from January to late March; and spring, from May to late July. Parents therefore did not have their offspring at home for nine months out of twelve in the year. Most parents made occasional visits

---

4 Prior to my maternal grandmother's death, I saw among her papers a demand from the local government authority for the payment of rates (property tax) on 11 Brechin Place. On the letter was a draft reply from Edith Spencer stating that the closing of her school had deprived her of the means to make an immediate payment.

Figure 1.4 Melchet Court, formerly Pinewood School, now
St Edwards School (© Peter Stacey (cc-by-sa/2.0))

to the school, visits during which their conduct could, as a letter in this chapter shows, cause acute embarrassment to their offspring.

Preparatory schools were, in general, private ventures offering minimal facilities and employing masters whose qualifications to teach were often as scanty as the salaries they received. Many schools operated in old country houses that had been adapted only slightly, and sometimes not at all, to their new purpose. Facilities were often not updated, as Lewis, with Penelope in tow, discovered when visiting his own prep school with an eye to enrolling Ben there. Their inspection revealed that the outdoor earth closets, in use in his own youth, had not been replaced by modern sanitation. The stench, which was, Penelope later told her son Jonathan, nauseating, decided them to look elsewhere. Pinewood School, on the borders of Hampshire and Wiltshire, met their expectations. In 1940 it enrolled almost seventy boys, several of whom were, judging from their surnames, born in to the upper classes.[5] No information survives as to when the school was founded or how long it was in existence.

5 A printed list of pupils includes a Hanbury-Tracey, the surname of Baron Sudeley; a Cozens-Hardy, the surname of Baron Cozens-Hardy; and a Aubrey-Fletcher, which is the surname of a baronet.

Ben's Reminiscences about Pinewood School

In January 1940 at the age of eight I was sent to Pinewood School. It was a boarding school near Romsey in Hampshire and was housed in Melchet Court, a large Victorian building [Fig. 1.4]. I was desperately unhappy there, being bullied probably because I started in January rather that at the beginning of the school year in the autumn. I remember playing chess in a competition with some of the boys. I was winning the game when I needed to go to the lavatory very badly. Of course when I returned they had tipped the board over. To get away from people I used to go and hide in the foundations of the new classrooms then being built.

Pinewood School had only recently (probably in 1939) moved to Romsey from Farnborough, Hampshire, where it had existed at least since 1929 at a locality named Pinewood.

Melchet Court, constructed in the late nineteenth century, was later owned by Sir Alfred Mond and his wife. That it had not previously served as a school is indicated by the building of the classroom wings that Ben refers to.

Contributing to Ben's unhappiness was his dyslexia, his inability both to perceive the printed word and to reproduce it in writing. The condition, which adversely affected his class work, was regarded by the other boys at Pinewood as proof of stupidity and childishness. He received no sympathy or remedial aid from the teachers at the school in respect to his reading or writing, nor did they protect him from harassment by other boys. Ben's unhappy life is evident from his letters, correspondence that reflect the practice of requiring pupils to write home on Sundays [Fig. 1.5]. One or more of the masters oversaw the writing and, even more importantly, vetted each letter's contents for suitability. I recall that, some years later, in 1946, when I wrote my first letter from prep school (not Pinewood), I commented on the poor quality of the food. It was questioned whether I could make such a comment, but the passage was ultimately permitted.

At both prep and public schools, the masters were addressed as "Sir." The few female teachers at my prep school were also addressed as "Sir," in order, it was explained to parents, "to avoid confusion." The pupils were known by their surnames, not just by the masters but by the other boys as well, even when in

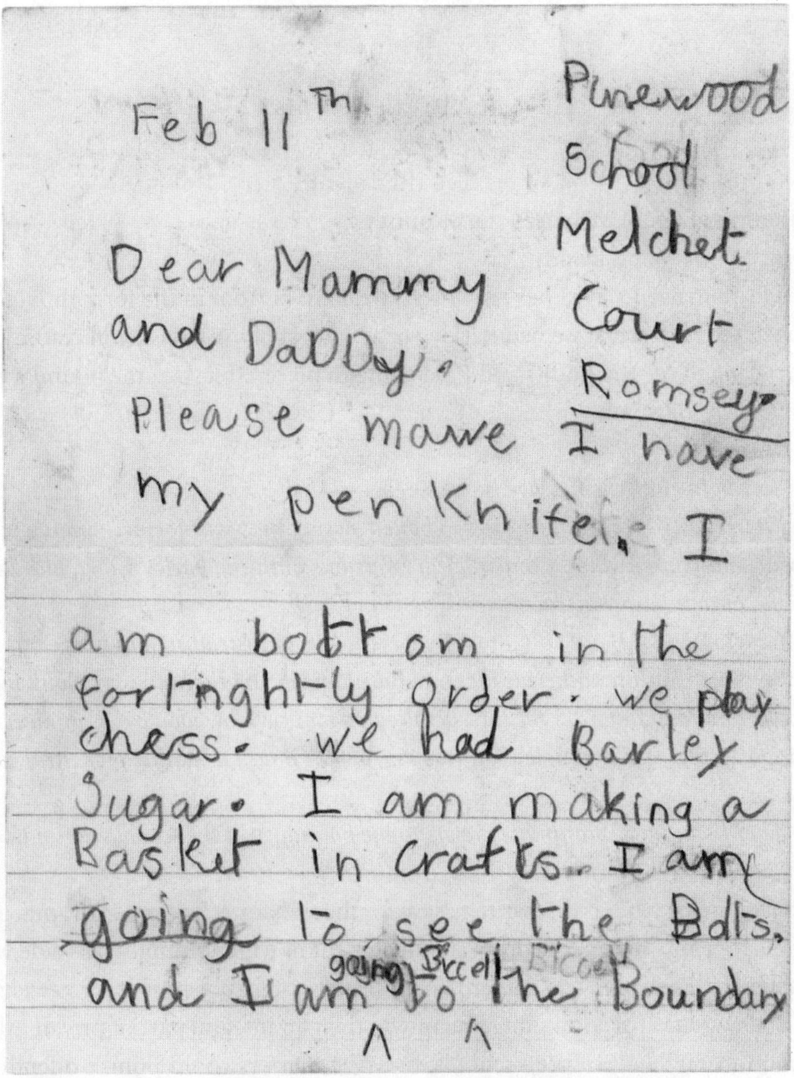

Figure 1.5 Ben Barman's letter to his parents, 11 February 1940

private. If two brothers attended the same school they were known, as was the case with Jonathan and myself, as "Barman ma" and "Barman mi," from the Latin *maior* (bigger) and *minor* (lesser).[6]

6 The youngest of three brothers was called "min," from the Latin *minimus* (smallest).

Ben to His Parents

Feb 11th [1940]

Pinewood School Melchet Court Romsey

Dear Mammy and Daddy

Please mawe [may] I have my penknife. I am bottom in the fortnghtly order. We play chess. we had Barley Sugar. I am making a Basket in crafts. I am going to see the Bodlts and I am going to biccell [bicycle] the boundary. Love form Barmam

A "fortnight" in British usage is two weeks.

"Barley sugar" is a hard candy (boiled sweet) that was formerly made with sugar and barley water. Contemporary versions omit the barley water, although some contain barley extract.

Cedric Randal Boult (1853–1950), a prosperous industrialist, had been married to Ben's great-aunt, Katherine Florence Barman, who had died in 1927. Boult lived at Northlands, Lanford, Wiltshire, being cared for in widowhood by his unmarried daughter, Olive. The couple's son was Sir Adrian Boult, a leading orchestral conductor.

The "boundary" presumably refers to the boundary of the school's grounds.

The following letter is typewritten, save for the signature. It refers to the practice of "slippering," a form of corporal punishment in which a pupil's backside was beaten with a slipper – a standard and unquestioned punishment for perceived misbehaviour. Corporal punishment was then an integral part of private education in England. In prep schools, only the masters could punish offending pupils, but in public schools "prefects," the most senior boys, usually those in their final year, possessed to right to use the slipper. Serious offences entailed visits to the housemaster or, in exceptional cases, to the headmaster, who used a cane to beat the offender's backside.

C.A. Ranger to Penelope Barman

Printed heading: C.A. Ranger, Pinewood School, Melchett Court, near Romsey, Hants Telephone: Whiteparish 48

February 15, 1940

Dear Mrs. Barman,

Many thanks for telling me the exact point of difficulty in Benjamin's mind. It looks as if somebody had been "pulling his leg." I will take an early opportunity to relieve his mind of this bother. So far nobody this term has been slippered, and is only an occasional event in any case usually after a boy has had half a dozen warnings from various people.

I do wish this snow and the cold winds would vanish.

Yours sincerely
C A Ranger

C.A. Ranger had been the headmaster of Pinewood School since at least 1929.

Ben to His Parents

Undated Pinewood Melchet court Romsey

["18/2/40" added in another hand, probably that of Lowis Barman]

Dear Mommy and Daddy,

The snow is 6 inches deep. Thank you for the pen-knin[f]e. We have 2 hare and hounds. I will till you when I come home. We are having the exans soon. I con not go to the Boults Because of the weather is to bad.

Love form Barman

"Hare and hounds" was a sport in which "the hare," one or two speedy individuals, carrying a large bag containing scraps of paper, would run ahead of "the hounds," leaving behind a paper trail. The object of the hounds was to follow the trail and eventually catch the hare.

Ben to His Parents

Fed 25 [1940] Pinewood Melchett Court Romsey

Dear Memmy and daddy,

We are haveing no exams. please may you right [write] every day. We have films every Wednesday. The sowdrops are beautiful. Are yours to? The pictures are up. please right not much.

I have mabe a basket and too trays. I hop Bampa won't be a nuisanc.

Love form Barman

Ben's use of "right" for "write" is a good example of his dyslexia.

Schools often possessed home film projectors, with sound, on which they showed "suitable" films rented from agencies existing for this purpose.

Bampa, or BP, was the familiar name used by Ben and his brothers for their maternal grandfather, Dr Leonard James Spencer. Retired from the Science Museum, he paid visits to Hollybush, where he gardened and planted fruit trees. I recall reading in our parents' guest book (which included the names and dates of visits along with observations made by those who stayed at our house) entries by my grandfather from 1939 recording his activities.

Ben to His Parents

March 3rd [1940] Pinewood School Melchiet Coirt Romsey

Dear Mammy and Daddy,

pleese will you right a short letter. We had filns on Wednesday. do not come on easter saw [stay?] at home. please do not pot in the litter this [two small squares] o. The play shed [is] up. ight in the evening and when nanny go[es] for a walk she will post it.

Love form Barman

"Nanny" was a Miss Collinson, who looked after the Barman sons until 1940; see her letter of 25 June 1940 to Ben in the section "Going to Canada" below. Her first name, which would, in any case, never have been used by her employers, cannot be retrieved.

Ben to His Parents

March 10 Pinwood School Melchet Court Romsey

["1940" added by Lowis Barman]

Dear Mammy and Daddy,

Thank you for your letter. We had a lecture on Africa by Miss Newbury. We are in quadrant[ine] for Germen Measles. We went for a nature walk. We had no films. When you came here you call me Ben the holde [whole] time instead of Barman.

Love form Barman

[Added at the bottom of the page:]
W[h]ich one is the litter av [sic]

Since only surnames were used by pupils, even among themselves, Ben's parents addressing him by his first name was but one of the many causes for intense, if un-witting, embarrassment that parents could inflict on their sons when visiting them at school.

Ben to His Parents

Sunday 17th March [1940] Pinwood Shool Melchet cort Romsey
Dear Mammy and Daddy.

We have hab films. we are haveing a chess coupetition. how is Sally? how long is there to the end of term? when are you going to see me? we want for a walk to the tuck-shop and I hab too wine gums. which one is the litte doy is? I want to now How is the famay? Have PB gon home? Plees can I have some pensuls [pencils]? I am all right are you? I am not rannig out of tuck. I am gette i sitit of cuming home.

Love form Barman

"Sally" was the family cat.

"Which one is the litte day is　?" is not comprehensible but the words are a par-tial repetition of the phrase at the bottom of Ben's letter of 10 March.

"Tuck" was candy and other supplementary food. Schools often had a tuck shop where the boys could buy such treats at specific times on specific days, provided they had the necessary pocket money. "Tuck boxes" were used to store food such as cake sent from home.

"PB" is switch for "BP," a shortened form of "Bampa," Ben's maternal grandfa-ther.

"Gette it stit of" is probably "getting excited at."

"Wine gums" were, and are, a translucent candy made in various colours and flavours.

Ben to His Parents

Dear Mammy and Daddy,

I hope you are all right. I am. We want for a bic[yc]le ride wich I like it. we want 18 miles. I have not open[ed] my Easter egg yet. We hade two Services on Good Friday. We hade a Chapel collection. I am gtting excited about Easter. When are we caming home?

Love form Benjamin.

Ben to His Parents

March 31 [1940] Pinewood School Melchet court Romsey

Dear Mammy and Daddy,

We had Films but I misst one Film. I [my] marks are 141. I am all right. how is the cat? I was going to right a litter to BP. I have got to the last piece of paper of my righting paper. I have Been to Olive and I saw Katy once. I have paayed [played] 5 conpetion [competition] case [chess] games. and to o o mar games to play. how loing is there to the end of the term. How long is the holidays. I have had 6 wine gums through this term all together.

Love form Barman

Olive was Ben's cousin Olive Boult, and Katy was probably a long-time servant with the Boult family.

The spring holidays, lasting the month of April, now intervened. Ben went home, where he clearly made his intense unhappiness known to his parents, who must have written to the school to express their concern. Ben's letters resume at the start of the summer term. A missive – typed, save for the signature – from the headmaster arrived first.

C.A. Ranger to Penelope Barman

From C.A. Ranger, Pinewood School, Melchet Court, Near Romsey, Hants.
Telephone: Whiteparish 48
May 1, 1940

Dear Mrs Barman,

I am very glad that Benjamin is happy in spite of difficulties; he really is a very wise little boy in many ways; I think his habits with other boys quite likely have their origin in trying to keep his end up; may he be wise enough to see that if he will just be his quiet natural self, that is what the other boys will always like best.

It is good that those tonsils etc. are out; please remember the late Dame Mary Scharlieb's saying that it took a year to get the full benefit of the operation, not that initial benefit should not begin to come much sooner of course.

This 2½d postage is no fun!

Yours sincerely,
CA Ranger

Dame Mary Scharlieb (1845–1930) was a pioneering English surgeon, known for her very conservative views on contraception and divorce, which made her opinions on other subjects acceptable to many males.

The standard rate for mailing a letter had recently risen from 2d (two pence) to 2½d, an increase of 25 percent, hence the complaint.

The above letter presents the classic argument that the victim of bullying, not those who do the bullying, has to change his or her conduct. In case Ben's experience is thought to be unusual, the following are comments by a British evacuee to the United States in 1940 about bullying at his preparatory school in England. "Is there any situation where a previous 'record' is more damning than in an English boarding school? Being a marked man seemed to typify most of my British school days. On that very first day, my fellow students were given an excuse to take it out on me – and, during all the three years I was at Eastacre, never once did they let up."[7] Incapacity to play sports was an instant invitation to be bullied.

7 Horne, *Bundle from Britain*, 84.

Ben to His Parents

May 12th [1940] Melchet Court, Romsey, Hants

Dear Mammy and Daddy,

will you send me a ship. We have hade 3 a.r.p. There is a new boy. I saw a grass sanke. how is Jonathan and Roderick. how is the school. I have not got a tennis racket. The rhododendron are over. we played cricket. The swimming bath is full. We want for 2 nature walks. will you tell me when you are come-ing down. The gardens are very nice. I [am] all right. Will you send me a dar-wing book.

Love from Barman

"a.r.p." refers to the Air Raid Precautions network created in 1924 to meet the threat of aerial bombing. The network was staffed by wardens wearing dark blue uniforms with tin hats. By 1939 the system would have involved the holding of rehearsals that taught civilians (in this case, children) to remain calm during air raids and to take refuge in cellars and other protected places.

The "school" presumably refers to Edith Spencer's Brechin Place School, which was by then closed.

Cricket was the defining sport of the private school system, encapsulating all the values that such schools prized, as Henry Newbolt's 1892 poem, "Vita Lampada," with its refrain, "Play up! play up! and play the Game," proclaimed. Until 1962 an annual cricket match was played, usually at Lords Cricket Grounds in London, be-tween the Gentlemen (upper-class amateurs) and the Players (lower-class profes-sionals).

Ben to His Parents

May 19 [1940] Melchet Curt Romesy

Dear Mammy and Daddy,

The azaleas are fading. The classrooms have ben painted. June we will begin swimming. The board hase a staircase. The rhododendrons are over. A prast [priest] came to capel. We have had 3 or 4 cames of cricket. To bay it is a nice day. Will you send me some ? in your letter.

Love form Benjamin

By a priest, Ben meant an ordained clergyman of the Church of England, the form of Christianity to which most private schools subscribed.

The illegibility of the above letter, probably the result of emotional distress (as its being signed "Benjamin" indicates), caused the headmaster to send Ben's parents the following note.

C.A. Ranger to Ben's Parents

Memo From C.A. Ranger, Pinewood School, Melchet Court, Near Romsey, Hants. Telephone: Whiteparish 48

I'm afraid Benjamin's letter is not a very grand one this Sunday, but it will miss the post if I hold it up, & we will try for a better one next Sunday!

CAR

19 May 40

The final document related to Ben's time at Pinewood School is a printed list of the pupils, organized by their forms (grades) and, within the forms, by their marks. The list is undated but, since its contents give the final marks for the school year, it was probably produced in June 1940. Ben stood at the very bottom of the First Form. His marks in arithmetic were respectable but those in history, geography, and English pulled him down.

At this point, the Second World War exploded into its most critical and threatening phase. Ben's entire life was now disrupted.

2

Going to Canada,
April–July 1940

Two torpedoes had been set just too deep and exploded on a timer
on the other side of the ship.
~Martin Dewey, 17 January 2007

On 3 September 1939, the prime minister of Great Britain, Neville Chamberlain, announced, in a plaintive, almost pathetic broadcast, that the Nazi regime had failed to guarantee that they would withdraw their troops from Poland, which they had invaded on 1 September, and "consequently this country is at war with Germany."[1] Immediately afterwards, the air raid sirens went off across London, their long undulating wail announcing a coming raid. But no German bombers appeared to rain down destruction. This anticlimax set the tone for the conflict during the months from September 1939 to early April 1940, termed at the time "the Phoney War."

The most immediate and significant consequence of hostilities was the British government's ordering on 1 September 1939 the immediate evacuation into the countryside of a million and a half people, over half of them children, from London and the other urban areas deemed most exposed to aerial attack. In 1932, Stanley Baldwin, a leading member of the cabinet, had stated that "the bomber will always get through," and this belief commanded general acceptance. Nonetheless, many ordinary families resisted the government-arranged evacuation, as it disrupted their lives and removed their children into the unknown.[2]

---

1 For the entire speech, listen to "Britain Declares War."
2 On the September 1939 evacuation, see Inglis, *Children's War*; Jackson, *Who Will Take Our Children*; and Wicks, *The Day They Took the Children*.

Families in the upper classes possessed both the means and the connections to move themselves and their offspring away from the danger zones. "We were on holiday in Coverack [Cornwall] on September 3rd when Chamberlain made his announcement," Sir Anthony Laughton, a leading hydrographic scientist, recalled. "My brother and I were standing in the street listening to the broadcast through open windows of people's houses on the sea front and my parents realised immediately that it was perhaps not sensible to go back to London."[3] After extending their vacation for a month, the Laughton family moved in with friends at Marlborough, Wiltshire, deep in the countryside. Some parents began, even at this early stage, to send offspring to live with relatives or friends in North America.[4]

The German conquest first of Denmark and Norway in April and then of the Low Countries and France in May 1940 ended the Phony War and turned what had been a trickle of children sent overseas into a flood. The German victories made abundantly clear that no part of the country was secure from bombing and that an invasion of Great Britain was imminent. In the dominions, public opinion, aghast at the crisis, now forced governments to offer safe havens and financial assistance. The response of the newly formed Churchill cabinet was to approve on 17 June, the very day that France requested an armistice, the creation of the Children's Overseas Reception Board (CORB).[5]

By that date, families with wealth and influence were already busy making private arrangements to send their children abroad; indeed, many had already done so. Canada was the preferred destination, due in part to its relative closeness (compared to Australia and New Zealand) and in part to its being perceived, in contrast to the United States, as reassuringly British (if colonial). The second secretary in the Canadian High Commission in London noted on 11 June "several exhausting days during which the office has been flooded with people trying to arrange for their children to get out to Canada." What impressed him was "the unnatural coolness of English parents – no broken voices

3 Sir Anthony Laughton, "Interview."
4 Some child migration occurred prior to the outbreak of the hostilities. For example, the three Penrose children accompanied their parents to North America in April 1939 and the family remained there, expecting war to break out.
5 Fethney, *The Absurd and the Brave*, 38–9.

or tear-filled eyes."[6] That was the attitude of Chips Channon, a British member of Parliament, who on 24 June took his son and heir to Euston Station for travel to Liverpool and onward to the United States. His diary entry makes plain the class nature of the exodus: "At the station there was a queue of Rolls-Royces and liveried servants and mountains of trunks. It seemed that everyone we knew was there on the crowded platform."[7]

Prior to the creation of the CORB, the upper classes alone possessed the means and influence needed to send their children overseas. Several considerations led them to this decision. The first stemmed from an instinct of self-preservation in terms of both race and class. They agreed with the views of a Vancouver, British Columbia, matron that their offspring would, if the worst came to the worst, form "the nucleus of a new Britain founded on British stock."[8] For others, a justification for immediate evacuation lay in ensuring the preservation of their particular family through safeguarding their son and heir and thereby, by extension, protecting their class and race. Chips Channon, on learning that his son had safely reached Montreal en route for the United States, commented in his diary: "Now I care less about what happens; my life is over, the rest is residue. I can live on in my dauphin who looks, acts, re-acts, and thinks, just like me."[9] A third, and quite common, justification, was related to scarce resources. As recalled by the two youngest children of Kenneth M. Bell, dean of Balliol College, Oxford, their mother told them how "Father has the idea of sending you and some other children to Canada," believing that "you ought to be out of the way, because you are only a nuisance in wartime and eat food the soldiers need."[10] The evacuation of children would both save resources and enable their parents to devote themselves unstintingly to the war. A fourth reason was the least avowable. Evacuation provided a convenient way to shuck

6 Ritchie, Siren Years, 57.
7 Entry for 24 June 1940, in Rhodes James, ed., Chips, 259.
8 Mrs Emma Wilson, chair of the North Shore Council of Women, British Columbia Archives, Add Mss 499, North Shore Council of Women fonds, scrapbook, as cited in Bilson, Guest Children, 2, 263.
9 Entry for 5 July 1940 in Rhodes James, ed., Chips, 260.
10 Bell, Thank You Twice, 9–10. In fact, the scheme, by which the Bell children went to Canada, seems to have been initiated not by their father but by a group of faculty of the University of Toronto where he had previously taught; see Bilson, Guest Children, 11, 256–7.

off parental responsibility, especially when a marriage was collapsing or one parent had died, leaving the survivor unable to cope with bringing up offspring. Allan Horne, an elderly widower burdened with a son he saw "perhaps one day in ten," dispatched young Alastair to live with a female acquaintance in New England, although he did also invoke the second justification: "But you are my only son – and my most treasured possession. I just want you to come through it, even if I don't."[11]

The decision by Ben's parents to send their eldest son to safe haven in Canada was not made, it would appear, in response to the German triumphs. Plans were already on foot for his departure by at least in early April 1940. As Ben recalls, "During the Easter holiday I can remember being 'softened up' by my father about how wonderful Canada was, reading me cowboy stories, which made little impression. On being asked if I wanted to go to Canada I jumped at the opportunity – I would do anything to get away from the detested [Pinewood] school."

Sending their eldest son to Canada presented few problems for Ben's parents. They commanded the necessary resources and both of them possessed close connections in that country. Lowis's younger brother, Ross Barman, had late in 1927 migrated to Canada, where, two years later, he married Orion Thompson from a well-established Montreal family. The couple and their two sons, Christopher and Blair, were then living in the village of St Bruno de Montarville, on the east side of the St Lawrence River across from Montreal. After the outbreak of the war, Ross Barman received a military posting, overseeing the production of heavy artillery at factories in Longueil and Sorel (now Sorel-Tracy) in Quebec. In the early months of 1940, Ross was sent in England as a member of a Canadian military supply mission. As Ben recalls, his uncle had already agreed that, when he returned to Canada, he would take with him, as their legal guardian, Martin and Rosemary Dewey, the younger children of Lowis and Ross's sister, Ursula. Ben would make the journey with Ross and his two cousins but, after his arrival, would move to London, Ontario, to live with the Penrose family.

Penelope Barman had a separate Canadian connection, which stemmed from her long friendship with Margaret Leathes, later Penrose. As children, the two girls, born at the turn of the twentieth century and separated by less than a year

11 Horne, *Bundle from Britain*, 119–20.

Figure 2.1 Benjamin Barman, May 1941

in age, resided on the same street, at 68 and 111 Albert Bridge Road, facing Battersea Park in London. Both had attended Edith Spencer's school (Fig. 1.1). Margaret's father, John Beresford Leathes, was a distinguished physiologist, a professor first at the University of Toronto (1909–14) and then at Sheffield University (1914–33). He had met Margaret's mother, born in Russia, when studying at Bern University. Penelope and Margaret's friendship was so close that it had survived Margaret's sojourn in Canada when her father was teaching at the University of Toronto in 1909–13 and the very different trajectories taken by their subsequent careers. Whereas Penelope left school at the age of twelve to become a dancer and actor, Margaret entered Bedales School in 1914, and then Newnham College, Cambridge, later qualifying as a medical doctor. During these years, Margaret had become good friends with Frances Marshall and Julia Strachey, friendships through which she came to know Julia's brother

Figure 2.2 Margaret Penrose, London, Ontario, July 1942

Lytton Strachey as well as Dora Carrington, who were central figures in the Bloomsbury circle.[12]

In 1928, Margaret married Lionel Penrose, whom she had first encountered on a trip to Germany two years earlier. Penrose had been born into the upper middle class, his maternal grandfather, a very successful banker, having been created Baron Peckover in 1907. However, Penrose's Quaker upbringing and often unconventional outlook (he was a conscientious objector in the First World War) meant that he did not quite fit in. His father, a successful painter, enjoyed a wide acquaintanceship in artistic and intellectual circles. Financially independent and well connected, Lionel Penrose did not embark on a viable

12 According to Margaret's reminiscences, Lytton Strachey liked her but not Lionel Penrose. Carrington, who did not like Margaret but who described Lionel as "the wild lion faced boy," had a final love affair with Bernard (known as "Beakers" or "Beakus"), the youngest of the four Penrose brothers; see Garnett, *Carrington*, 352, 379–80, 385–6.

career until his acquaintance with Margaret Leathes served as a catalyst, inspiring him to obtain a medical degree and then undertake pioneering research in medical genetics.

Following her marriage, Margaret did not practise medicine or pursue an independent career. As her second son, Roger Penrose, stated at her funeral service in 1989, "She largely sublimated what must have been her early ambitions in a deep pride and appreciation of those who were close to her, particularly her children."[13] Like Penelope, Margaret devoted herself to being a support and adjunct to her husband, who in 1930 took up a post with the local health authority at Colchester, Essex. In common with Penelope, Margaret gave birth to three sons – Oliver in 1929, Roger in 1931, and Jonathan in 1933. Lionel Penrose established his scientific reputation with the publication in 1938 of the "Colchester Survey," an innovative clinical study of the genetic dimensions of what was then called "mental retardation." The end of his post at Colchester, invitations to give lectures in the United States along with his private means allowed Lionel Penrose to remove himself and his family from Britain, where war was already on the horizon.

Early in April 1939, the Penroses sailed for North America on the *Aquitania*, a Cunard liner. The family spent three months in Philadelphia before vacationing in Ontario, staying with a friend made during an earlier sojourn in Canada. Lionel looked for employment, finally accepting the post of physician at the Ontario Hospital in London, Ontario, a city of nearly 80,000 people, situated two hundred kilometres southwest of Toronto. His success in this position led to his subsequent appointments as acting director of medical statistics for Ontario and finally as director of psychiatric research for the province.[14] The family moved into a rented house in London on 3 September 1939, the very day that Great Britain declared war on Germany. The Penroses settled into a comfortable existence at 1000 Wellington Avenue, paying a monthly rent of $65.[15] As their eldest son remembered, "We were lucky to be in a safe place and the Canadians

13 "Obituary: Margaret Penrose," 207.
14 In September 1940, the board of governors of the University of Western Ontario, London, approved his appointment as an instructor in psychiatry in the Faculty of Medicine; Western University, London, Archives, Board of Governors Minutes.
15 University College, London, Science Library, Special Collections, Penrose Papers, 1/16 Bank Statements at the Bank of Montreal, 1942–43.

made us feel very welcome."[16] Margaret, generous and welcoming by nature, received, according to her reminiscences, many requests from England to take in evacuee children.[17]

The first surviving piece of correspondence relating to Ben's Canadian experience is a postcard from Margaret Penrose to Ben's mother, Penelope (Fig. 2.3). It shows that, by the middle of June 1940, plans for Ben's move to Canada, where he was to be taken in by the Penrose family, had already been fixed.

PARK AVE., LONDON, ONTARIO, CANADA. -3

Figure 2.3 Postcard view of a residential street in London, Ontario

16 Oliver Penrose, "Lionel S. Penrose."
17 In her "Reminiscences," composed in old age, Margaret Penrose asserted that "nineteen English children of friends were offered to us as refugees, and we were preparing to rent a summer hotel for them," n.p. She attributes the non-arrival of all of these (save for Ben Barman) to the sinking of the *City of Benares*. However, Ben reached Canada four weeks before that disaster occurred.

Figure 2.4 Postcard from Margaret Penrose to Penelope Barman, 13 June 1940

Postcard from Margaret Penrose to Penelope Barman

1000 Wellington St
13th June 1940

This is what the place <u>looks</u> like. I've tried to get Stella Black to send you a photo of the children by our house – now out of print. Of course when I say blue flannelette, grey flannel is <u>O.K.</u> (better in fact). My letter was just to minimise your packing difficulties. <u>Please</u> let it be all 4 of you not only B. I can't write about what is on everyone's mind as the ink would blush & anyway all will be changed before this reaches you. Roger is thrilled at the prospect of B.

Stella's address, Aldgord, Aldham, Essex. She might be of use to you with school. She's out of a job I believe.

Margaret

1000 Wellington Street still stands on a broad tree-lined boulevard in a pleasant neighbourhood lying to the east of the River Thames and the University of Western Ontario.

Stella Black, who was perhaps an acquaintance of both Margaret and Penelope from school days, cannot be positively identified.

Grey flannel was the cloth used to make the school clothing for both boys and girls, being a marker and visible sign of their superior social class.

The postcard, brief as it is, reveals salient features of Margaret's character. She was energetic, ebullient, and direct in manner (Fig. 2.2). She showed much intelligence, but, as the mix-up between blue flannelette and grey flannel showed, she was not always adept when it came to handling the mundane aspects of life. She was capable of inspiring great affection: to this day, Benjamin remains deeply attached to her memory and grateful for her treatment of him during his years in Canada.[18]

The reference in the postcard to "all four of you not only B" (Fig. 2.4) suggests that the original plan had been for Penelope and her three sons to be evacuated together. Many years later, when I asked her why Ben alone went to Canada, Penelope responded that the idea was that he should go first, to be followed later by her and his two younger brothers. This statement is confirmed by a passage in Ben's letter to our parents dated 26 December 1940: "I hope you will be able to come over to Canada soon." The realities of the war and the dangers of submarine attacks on shipping made the project impossible.

The day after Margaret Penrose wrote her postcard, the German army occupied Paris, and on 22 June 1940, France signed an armistice that gave Germany control of three-fifths of that country including all the channel and Atlantic ports. At the end of June the German armies seized the Channel Islands, lying off the western shores of France but for centuries a part of Great Britain. The invasion of the British Isles seemed imminent and perhaps inevitable.

The course of events made the two Barman family homes unsafe. The house at Newdigate, Surrey, lay in the probable path of a German invasion, while the flat in London was likely to be bombed from the new German air bases in France. So the family downsized. The Barmans eventually moved to a small semi-detached house at Buckland Common, Buckinghamshire, in the Chiltern

18 This assessment is based in part on my encounter with Margaret in about 1957 at the Penrose house in London, when I brought their daughter, Shirley, back from a stay with the Barman family, then living in Derbyshire.

Hills.[19] The new location meant that Lowis had to get up very early every morning and commute by both automobile and train to his office at British Overseas Airways (BOAC) in London. As the ensuing letter shows, Nanny Collinson was dispensed with, forcing Penelope to take on total care of her two younger sons. It was a time of change and goodbyes.

Nanny Collinson to Ben Barman

c/o Wishart
4 Charmers Street Clydebank Glasgow 25-6-40

My dear Benjamin,

I was very sorry I could not say "goodbye" to you before I went home to Scotland.

Mummy wrote and told me that you were going to Canada very soon with Uncle Ross.

It will be a great thrill for you, going on such a big ship and I hope you enjoy every minute of the voyage.

I am sure you will love Canada. It is so big and everything will be is so new and exciting for you. Won't it be fun seeing your two boy cousins?

I had a letter from Jonathan and he said that he and Roderick remembered to wash their hands and brush their hair before meals! Wasn't he funny?

I was very happy to be in Arbroath again and to meet all my friends.

I hope you will send me a postcard from Canada.

I expect your two little brothers are thrilled to be staying so near your cousins? Do you go to Uncle Cedric's house to see them?

I miss you all very much and hope to see you all again someday. You will all be big boys next time I come to England.

Bye bye, Bennie, and the best of luck for your journey to Canada.

Please write to me sometime.

With lots of love and kisses
from Nannie XXXXX

19 The house was rented at least by early July 1940, since Ross Barman's letter mailed on 19 July 1940 was addressed to "Cholesbury Road, Buckland Common, Near Tring, Bucks, England" and forwarded on to "Hollybush." I have a clear memory of the family's first visit (probably one of inspection) to Twin Oaks.

Ben's "two boy cousins" were Christopher and Blair Barman.
  "Staying so near your cousins." I have not been able to identify these cousins.

The time of departure had arrived, as Ben recounts. "I was to go to Canada with Uncle Ross, my father's younger brother and with Rosemary and Martin Dewey, my cousins, the two youngest children of Aunt Ursula, my father's elder sister." Ursula Barman was married to Norman Dewey, a steel industry specialist who, in 1940, was working for the government. They had three sons and a daughter. The Dewey parents decided that their elder children, Thomas and David, then aged fourteen and thirteen, were old enough to participate in the defence of their country, while Rosemary and Martin, aged nine and seven, were best sent to the safe haven that was Canada.

Ben's recollection continued: "We said goodbye to our parents at Euston station in London and travelled by train to the port of Liverpool with Uncle Ross. The train pulled right up onto the quay next to the boat. As we stood beside the boat waiting to board, I was most impressed by the armed soldiers guarding men with small trolleys wheeling heavy wooden crates off the train up the gangplank and into the ship. I was fascinated to be told that the crates contained gold." The Bank of England physically transferred all its gold reserves to Canada for safekeeping by the Bank of Canada. Possibly Ben witnessed part of the transfer.

The ship Ben boarded with his uncle and two cousins on 10 July 1940 was the ss *Antonia* of the Cunard White Star Line (Fig. 2.5). Built in 1922 to carry emigrants on the Liverpool–Montreal run, it had 500 cabins and space for 1,200 steerage passengers. In Martin Dewey's words, "the *Antonia*'s upper works had at some time been painted cream but it had become rather dirty. Mounted on the aft deck, like a sore finger, was an anti-aircraft gun in full field camouflage (probably a standard 5.5 inch gun). Running round the edge of the deck was a thick 'degaussing' cable to negate magnetic mines and also down each side of the bow, lines ending in paravanes, ready to throw in the water, which were designed to cut floating mine cables if necessary."

Of the passengers embarking on the *Antonia* that day, almost one-third were child evacuees, all of them privately sponsored. One source states that 106 of the children were travelling under the auspices of Yale University. The CORB was not to send its first party of children to Canada until 21 July 1940.[20] Having carried refugees to Canada and Canadian troops to England, the *Antonia* was

Figure 2.5. ss *Antonia*, Cunard White Star Line, late 1930s
(http://www.clydemaritime.co.uk/HMS_Antonia)

in October 1940 taken over by the British Admiralty and converted into a repair ship for the Royal Navy. The ship survived the war, to be broken up in 1948.

Ben remembers: "Uncle Ross and I shared one cabin and Martin and Rosemary another. We hung around for a day or so and one morning we awoke to find ourselves on our way in a convoy of other ships, one of which I was told contained Italian prisoners." Martin Dewey adds: "Naval escort left for England after a day or so, leaving us alone with the other similar ship which we were told had Italian prisoners on board. A couple of days later the ship had disappeared during the night."[21]

The following day, the realities of the war struck home. In Ben's words, "I was wandering around the deck when I heard some people were saying that

20 See Cooke, *Safe Keeping*, 2. On the first group of CORB children travelling to Canada, see Fethney, *The Absurd and the Brave*, 296.
21 Martin Dewey to Ben Barman, 17 January 2007. It is not clear if the implication was that the second ship had been sunk. However, according to the website "U-boats.net," none of the sixteen ships sunk by U-boats from 10 to 19 July 1940 was a passenger ship.

they had just seen a torpedo crossing our stern and just missing the ship. In order to avoid torpedoes the ship would sail on a zigzag course suddenly making sharp turns. Later that evening I was tired and went to bed early when there were two loud bangs. Uncle Ross rushed into the cabin, got me out of bed, into a life jacket, and onto deck ready to get into lifeboats should we be told to do so. We waited for about an hour, whilst the ship was being checked for damage, and we were then given the all clear and we all returned to bed." Martin Dewey has his own memories of this brush with destruction: "We had just gone down to our cabin to prepare for bed when there was a colossal bang, followed several seconds later by another. Almost immediately the alarm sounded and Uncle Ross dashed in and got us all up on deck to our lifeboat station, where we were in the cold for about an hour. Uncle Ross later said that the bangs were just like slamming a heavy, insulated, refrigerator room door, and everything shook. As a government (Canadian) armament inspector, he suggested that the two torpedoes had been set just too deep and exploded on a timer on the other side of the ship. Soon after that we reached the Straights of Belle Isle, which was dotted with icebergs and so on to Quebec."[22]

Ross Barman's explanation as to why the *Antonia* survived the attack was probably correct. At this stage of the war, the German T2 torpedo ran six feet (1.83 metres) below its assigned depth and the pistol mechanism detonating the T2's warhead was untrustworthy in performance.[23] The northward course taken by the *Antonia* following the attack was in no way unusual, since narratives by evacuee children indicate that, for greater security, passenger ships entered the Gulf of St Lawrence not from the south, through the Cabot Strait (between Newfoundland and Nova Scotia), but from the north, through the Strait of Belle Isle between Labrador and Newfoundland, a course that took the boats quite close to Greenland.

Uncle Ross sent an account of the voyage to Ben's parents. Censorship restrictions meant that the letter included no mention of the torpedo attacks.

22 Martin Dewey to Ben Barman, 17 January 2007.
23 See the analysis and explanation in Nedelchev, "Norwegian Operation"; also "G7e Torpedo."

Ross Barman to Lowis and Penelope Barman

Cunard White Star

Thursday 18th July 1940

Dear Lowis and & Penelope,

We are now entering the St Lawrence River so I think I can consider that we are safely over. I don't expect that we will get to Montreal till Saturday though. The trip has been a long and cold one. Having been anchored all day Wednesday after being aboard at noon Tuesday we actually started Wednesday night and didn't get to Belle Isle till the following Wednesday (yesterday).

Benny was sick for a day and a half but quickly got used to the motion after that. I think we must have gone close to Greenland because it was so desperately cold and we all caught colds. I took Benny down to the doctor just to make sure that there was nothing more than an ordinary cold. He gave him some pills and some stuff to sniff and Benny seems to be none the worse for it and the cold disappeared. All are behaving very well – you see out of 828 passengers on the ship there are 287 children over 1/3rd of the total so there is pandemonium all day long and they have all more or less picked their own friends. Even Rosemary has a crush on a red haired boy. I'm afraid the food is not all that it might be and it is made more difficult in that I have to choose it from a very long menu at each meal. Potatoes are usually black and soggy, the milk is nearly always frozen and doesn't taste very good, poor Benny is loud in his protests but I can't get him to take anything else – well it won't be long before we are ashore now.

Best wishes to you all,

Yours Ross

The account of the voyage that Ben gave his parents was understandably much briefer (Fig. 2.6). The exceptionally poor handwriting and wildly incorrect spelling attest to the physical and psychological distress that the near disaster inflicted on him.

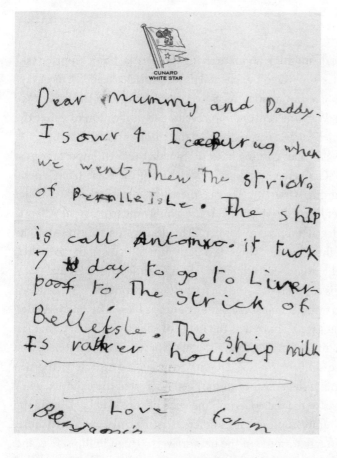

Figure 2.6
Ben's letter to his
parents, undated
[18 July 1940]

Ben to His Parents

Undated [18 July 1940]

Dear Mummy and Daddy,

   I saw 4 iceburug when we went through the Striats of Belle Isle. The ship is call Antonio. It took 7 day to go to Liverpool to the Strick of Belleisle. The ship milk is rather horrid.

Love form Benjamin

The envelope containing these two letters was addressed "Mr. and Mrs. H. L. Barman Cholesbury Road, Buckland Common, Near Tring, Bucks, England" and readdressed "Holly Bush, Newdigate, Surrey." It bears a 2 ½ stamp, which was over printed "Paquebot Posted at Sea" and a postmark "Quebec Jul 19 9.00pm 1940 P.O."

Ben does not recall anything about arriving in Canada, but a reporter sent by the *Montreal Gazette* covered the event. His long article, headed "400 Evacuees Join Children Safe in Canada," received pride of place on the front page of the 20 July issue. Wartime censorship prevented identification of either the ship or the port (Quebec), but surprisingly let the reporter reveal that the "First passenger ashore was a man coming back to Canada to fill an important post – Major-General D.G. Crerar D.S.O. new vice-chief of the Canadian General Staff." Under the subtitle "Dramatic Arrival," the article told its readers, "Smaller than most passenger liners the vessel had taken a long time to cross the Atlantic but she did so under a competent skipper." The description continued: "The drab liner slipped into her moorings as a light rain fell. She came to a shed being guarded by the military and the Royal Canadian Mounted Police."

As for Ben and his counterparts, the *Gazette* article continued: "The children on board reacted to Canada in just the same fashion as those who had preceded them. The older ones were amazed at the lights of the city. When a Canadian soldier, a few moments before docking, shouted: 'There's no blackout here,' the youngsters on deck, set up a roar of delight." As might be expected, "the two Mounties who stood at the entrance to the shed fascinated the children. They stared with wide eyes at the red coats and the wide brimmed hats." During the confusion of the disembarkation, with soldiers assisting children to get ashore, the reporter tried to talk to some of the new arrivals. "Hugh Phillips, five, and his sister Christine, four, when they were asked where they were going, replied 'Canada.' They were off to Montreal but they didn't know that. They just knew they were going to Canada." Like the others, Ben had reached a safe haven but he too had no idea of what living in Canada meant.[24]

---

24 John Cooke, travelling at the age of five, has left a brief description of the *Antonia*'s arrival, recalling the "enthusiastic crowds thronging the quayside to welcome us," and identifying the soldiers as "a contingent of the King's Own Yorkshire Light Infantry waiting to embark for the homeward journey." See Cooke, *Safe Keeping*, 2.

3

Reception and Settling In, July 1940–December 1941

B is so absurdly like you! I keep on calling him Penelope!
~Margaret Penrose to Penelope Barman, 23 September 1940

"We were made welcome at Uncle Ross and Aunt Orion's nice home at St Bruno just outside Montreal. One of the first things Ross did was to introduce us to Canadian ways. We were shown Poison Ivy by the ancient gardener who could handle it without being affected. We were told about skunks and how if you are squirted the odour lasts, which was an entirely new phenomenon since we had been brought up on a similar animal, a badger. Life was carefree during that summer and we have cine film of us all swimming in a nearby lake." As his recollection shows, Ben and his two cousins had entered a world markedly different from the one they had left behind in England. They were in the midst of reception, the third phase of the war guest experience, and had embarked on the long, slow process of settling in, one that was challenging both for the children and for their host families. Ben was meant to travel to London, Ontario, to live with the Penrose family, but Margaret decided to delay his arrival. In a letter dated 8 August, enclosing one to Ben from Penelope, Margaret informed him that the presence of visitors in the Penrose house meant that there was no space for him. Leaving Ben with his uncle and aunt for a month solved the immediate problem of space.

Margaret Penrose to Ben

1000 Wellington Street
London, Ontario
8th August 1940

Your mother sent this letter in one to me because she thought you were
here with us. For the present I think you will be happier with your uncle, as it
<u>can't</u> be as hot there as it has been here. We have been roasted, stewed, baked,
boiled and fried till we sizzled but now it's better. Our house is very full up
this month as we have four visitors staying here. I think they will soon settle
themselves somewhere else and then we will have a space for you.

Roger can hardly wait he wants you to come so badly. It is his birthday
today (9th) and he would have liked to have you for a birthday present. So I
shall have to get him a kitten instead to amuse him till you come. You will
have lots of interesting things to tell us about your voyage and about what
England is like now. Perhaps you would write some time and say whether
you want to come here and when. Schools are to begin later than usual this
year – in the middle of September.

Tell us how you feel about it all. We shall probably hear of someone
travelling from Montreal to London who could bring you as the journey
is a long one.

Love from Margaret Penrose

*In respect to the comment "till we sizzled," summers in London, Ontario, usually
range from warm to hot and humid.*

The kitten was acquired and given the name Pushkin.

The four visitors noted in Margaret Penrose's letter were Professor Lancelot
Hogben, his wife, Enid Charles (who, unusually for the period, continued to
use her maiden name after marriage), and their two younger children, Clare
and Julian.[1] Hogben, a distinguished British scientist and the author of the
highly popular *Mathematics for the Million* and *Science for the Citizen*, had been
on a lecture tour in Norway at the time of the German invasion. He had managed to escape to Sweden and then had travelled, via the Soviet Union and
Japan, to the United States, where he arrived in July 1940. His wife and the two

children, sponsored by Lionel Penrose, had sailed from England to Canada late in June. The family reunited in London, Ontario.

The Hogbens were not easy guests. As Margaret Penrose recalled in her reminiscences, "Enid threw herself onto the sofa as soon as she came into the house saying, 'Well, at any rate, this will be cheaper than a hotel.'" Late in August, Hogben left Canada for a temporary teaching post at the University of Wisconsin at Madison, while Enid Charles secured a job with the Bureau of Statistics at Ottawa. Initially, both Clare and Julian remained with the Penroses, but the latter, as Oliver Penrose recalled, "had rather a stormy passage with us and kept going on strike and would retire to bed for no obvious reason." Julian soon moved to Ottawa to be with his mother. In November, Hogben promised to pay, as soon he received the half of his salary promised by the Rockefeller Foundation "the modest contribution you agreed to take for the children's food" and asked Margaret to "please tell Clare I forgot to say how pleased I was with her marks." In January 1941, Hogben, about to return to his permanent post in Scotland, wrote to the Penroses: "I do not know how to thank you adequately for the kindness you have shown to us all. So cannot say more than that – especially you Margaret. Clare seems to be happier than she has ever been."[2]

It was not just the war guests and their host families in Canada who had to adjust to a new situation. Parents who remained in England came face to face with the realities created by their offspring's absence, which might be permanent, given the course of the war. The following two letters, the only ones from Ben's and his mother to survive, show what a void Ben's departure had made.

1 On the Hogbens in Canada and the United States, see Hogben and Hogben, *Lancelot Hogben*, xv, 176–7, and Wargon, "Enid Charles." In 1939, Enid Charles had secured a visiting post with the Dominion Bureau of Statistics in Ottawa, although, with the outbreak of war, she decided not to take it up. In June 1940, Lionel Penrose sponsored the entry into Canada of Enid with Clare (frequently spelled Claire, but standardized here as Clare) and Julian (also called "David," his second forename).
2 University College, London, Science Library, Special Collections, Penrose Papers, 2/35/6/12, Lancelot Hogben to Lionel Penrose, Memorial Union, Madison, WI, 12 and 25 November 1940 and 24 January 1941.

Penelope Barman to Ben

July 23 [1940] Holly Bush

Dear Benjamin,

How are you? We are back at Holly Bush. Sally's kitten is huge now and runs about all over the place. There is a big tank camp near and we often see them dashing about the lanes at about 40 miles an hour. Bampa does not think it is at all safe!

Lowis' red car has been mended it is lovely to drive after the little Ford. Are the Canadian cars very big? I wonder if you went to M^rs polite Beresford or did you come to London Ontario. It must have been a very long journey. Did you go alone? There are 100000000 things I want to know. <u>Do</u> write all about it. There is no news here, except we all miss you very much.

Love my darling, Mummy

As to the "big tank camp nearby," on 16 July Hitler authorized "Operation Sealion" for the invasion of Great Britain. The British, who had lost most of their tanks and artillery in the fall of France, began to organize the defences of their island. A "thick defence" ran along the south coast, with, stationed further inland, two mobile reserves, including the few remaining tanks, the first being based in the county of Surrey. Penelope is clearly referring to this reserve.

From the context, "Sally's kitten" must refer to the family cat and her offspring.

"Mrs polite [sic] Beresford" was Helen Lawford, married to Brigadier Tristan Massy Beresford. The Massy Beresfords were obviously good friends of Ben's parents, given that in 1941 and again in 1942 Helen sent Ben a Christmas present. She and her three children were living in Quebec during the war. When Singapore fell in February 1942, her husband was among those captured by the Japanese.[3]

Ben's absence also troubled me, his youngest brother, then aged three and a half, as the following letter shows.

---

3 See Imperial War Museums, Massy-Beresford private papers, n.p.

Roderick Barman, as Written by Penelope Barman, to Ben

[Twin Oaks, Buckland Common August 1940 added by Penelope Barman]
Dear Benjamin,

We come to the new little tiny house. We saw some lambs. When you going to come back? Will you come at Xmas? I play with your aerodrome. What? Yes I do. I throw the ball for the kitten. Come back at Xmas. Sally's baby has grown up, she can walk. Johnny is in London with Edie. We can't box each other now. We can't be cross.

Come back to me and us and bring your puffer trains. Love from Roderick
X X X X

Roderick told me what to say in this letter. He talks about you such a lot and says "keep Benny safe" at night in his prayers. We are in the brickworks today. Do you remember watching the men make bricks at Radlett?

[At the top of the letter, Ben later sketched a steam train and a boat.]

"Johnny" was the pet name of Ben's brother Jonathan, and "Edie" the name the boys' maternal grandmother preferred, refusing to be called "Edith."

"Box each other" and "can't be cross" refer to Roderick's appalling temper tantrums, of which his brother Jonathan was often the victim.

The "X X X" were large crosses made by Roderick.

The Barmans had lived at Radlett Hertfordshire prior moving to "Hollybush," their rented house in Surrey.

Twin Oaks was, indeed, a "tiny little house," one of a row of five or six semi-detached houses put up by a local builder as a speculative venture. It had three small bedrooms upstairs, and downstairs a hallway led to the living room on the right while on the left were the bathroom and the kitchen. A free-standing stove, burning coke, in the kitchen provided hot water. There was also a garage and a small back garden that opened onto a wheat field. The front bedroom upstairs was used by Lowis Barman as his workroom until Ben, on his return late in 1943, took it over as his bedroom.

By the time Ben received his youngest brother's letter, he was on the eve of another dislocation in his life. Labour Day, which in Canada traditionally marks the end of summer, fell in 1940 on 2 September. The moment when Ben was to take leave of his uncle Ross and his cousins was approaching. Rosemary had already begun to live with Dr and Mrs Struthers, who also resided in Saint Bruno. Chris and Martin departed for two different boarding schools. Ben finally left for London on 16 September, a few days before the school year opened. He recalls: "I was put on a night train to travel to London Ontario a distance of just under 500 miles and put in the charge of the large black steward who was a kindly man but I did not really have much conversation with him. He ensured that I got out at London. I was a bit worried about finding Margaret since I had not seen her for some time. I had stayed with the Penrose family at Thorington Hall, their country home near Colchester, now owned by the National Trust, but had little idea what Margaret Penrose looked like. She was there, recognised me immediately and all was well."

With respect to "in the charge of the large black steward," placing children in the charge of a railroad porter seems during the interwar period to have been quite usual in North America when train travel was the norm. In 1928, the writer Ernest Hemingway, about to go to Florida with his son John, had to leave the train on learning of his father's death but entrusted his child to the steward, who delivered him safely to Florida.

"Thorington Hall" was the name of a large farmhouse, built in the seventeenth century, north of Ipswich, which Lionel Penrose purchased in 1937 and restored from its decrepit state. In 1940, he transferred the property to the National Trust, retaining the right of residence during his lifetime.[4]

In her reminiscences Margaret recalled that "Benjamin aged nine, arrived with a label around his neck." However, writing in old age, she was probably mixing her memory of meeting Ben with her recollection of the newspaper pictures of the CORB evacuees who wore an identity number disc.[5]

The city of London, in which Ben was to live for the next three years, was in 1940 an archetypal example of Anglo Canada. Founded in 1793 by the governor of Upper Canada, it lay on the confluence of two rivers almost 200 kilometres west of Toronto. The city's name and that of its main river, the Thames, asserted and indeed glorified the link to Great Britain. The 1941 census recorded the population as 78,000. London's streets were generally broad and its neighbour-

4 See "Thorington Hall."
5 Fethney, *The Absurd and the Brave*, 304.

hoods well maintained (Fig. 2.3). The existence of the University of Western Ontario, established in 1878, gave the city a certain cultural standing.

The Penroses did not, accordingly, feel out of place during their residence in London. They established a wide circle of friends who shared their "progressive" views, and Margaret found sufficient activities, including public speaking, to occupy what time she had free from housework and raising her sons. Her husband, Lionel was, as his second son Roger later recalled, emotionally distant. "Within the family, it was very hard to relate to him about actual personal matters – almost impossible, in fact. (Anything of a remotely personal nature had to be attempted through the intermediary of Margaret, my mother.)"[6] Ben had the same experience: "I did not have much impression of Lionel," he later recalled, "He did not take much interest in my life."[7] In any case, Lionel was increasingly away from home, occupied with commissions across the province of Ontario. In the summer of 1940, for example, he travelled to Orillia, where undertook an assessment of conditions at the Ontario Teaching Hospital (originally the "Orillia Asylum for Idiots").[8]

The home (Fig. 3.1) in which Ben was to spend the next three years lay several blocks to the north of the London railroad station. Ben explained:

"The Penrose house at 1,000 Wellington St. was a typical Canadian home with steps up to the front door so that in heavy snow one could get into and out of the house, with a fly screen on the outside to keep out mosquitoes and black fly. In retrospect, it was small and cramped for the number of people Lionel and Margaret had to stay. On the ground floor immediately to the left of the entrance, the stairs ascended, curving around leaving a space underneath in which the telephone was situated. In front of the telephone was a chess table. Since calls were not charged by their duration, Margaret would play chess with Mrs. Gilinski, one of her friends, talking for an hour or so. On the right was the sitting room leading into the dining room through an open plan space. The kitchen and stairs down to the cellar were on the left of the dining room." Leading off from the dining room was a large sunroom, which served as a bedroom.

6 Roger Penrose, "Lionel Penrose: Colleague and Father," p. 5.
7 Ben Barman, communication to Roderick Barman, 19 August 2014.
8 This report, dated 18–20 June 1940, is in the Penrose Papers, University College, London, Science Library, Special Collections, 2/11.

Figure 3.1 1000 Wellington Street, London, Ontario,
with Ben and Jonathan playing baseball

Ben remembers his first entry into the house. "On my arrival I was made very welcome. Roger who is three months younger than I, was busy building different solid shapes out of cardboard (known as *polyhedra*) – if you have a cube (with six sides) and half cut off the corners the result is a twelve-sided solid. At the same time he was very slow at eating his meals and the only way his parents could get him to eat up was to invite him to cut his slice of corned beef into a square eating the bits he cut off, then cutting off the corners to get an eight sided figure and eating those bits."

The two boys rapidly became friends. "Roger and I were very close because we thought alike." They did everything together, so much so that, Ben remarks, "I did not make other friends." "Roger and I shared a large extension to the very right [that is, the sun room mentioned above]. In winter the room could be cold and I remember testing the temperature with a glass of water finding how far away from the door it had to be before ice formed on top. We did not seem to mind and became acclimatised to the cold." Ben recalls Roger's bed being closer than his to the heater.

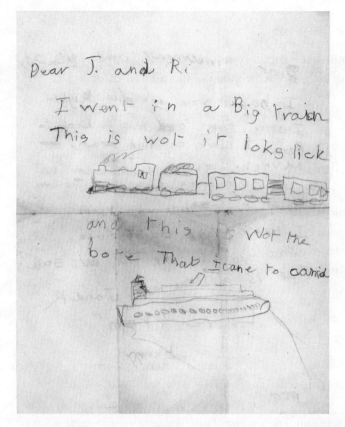

Dear J. and Ri

I went in a Big train
This is wot it loks lick

and this is wot the
bote That I cane to canid

Figure 3.2
Ben's letter to his
brothers, undated
[September 1940]

All these new experiences might have provided material for long descriptions in Ben's letters to his parents had it not been for his dyslexia, which precluded any extensive and informative narrative. Two letters Ben composed soon after his arrival have survived. Both lack dates but appear to have been written at roughly the same time and perhaps sent together, since only a single envelope exists. The post mark on the envelope containing the following letter reads "London Sep 23 10 pm 1940 Ont." The address was written by Margaret Penrose, who added on the back, "B is so absurdly like you! I keep on calling him Penelope!"

Ben to His Parents

Undated [September 1940]

Dear Mummy and Daddy,
    I hope you are all Right I am. Pleas sed me a book to Read. I have not had

any I only had 1 and that is coming down in the train to Lonbon Onterer. I have had los of fun are you. On the uv sid[e] there is a letter for and R.

PTO   Love from Benny

[Written on the reverse side of the letter (Fig. 3.2):]

Dear J. and R.

I went in a big train. This is wot it loks lick. [Image of a train] And this is wot the bote that I cane to Canid. [Image of a boat]

"Advanchc," a prime example of Ben's dyslexia, seems to mean "adventure" and to refer to his recent journey.

To this day, the Penrose offspring, when talking of Benjamin, call him "Benny," which his family rarely, if ever, did after his return to England in 1943.

Ben to His Parents

Undated [23 September 1940]

Dear Mummy and Daddy,

I hope you are all right and here is a picch [picture] for you. I am at 1,000 Welington st London Ont. I wayea 80 £. I am having a nice time here – her is a puzzly for you and the family.

Love form Benjamin

The picture is a newspaper clipping from the London Free Press, *evening edition, 23 September 1940 (Fig. 3.3).*

"A puzzly for you and the family": Lionel Penrose and his sons were fascinated by and spent much time creating puzzles, mazes, and visual challenges. In 1958 Lionel and his second son Roger would publish Puzzles for Christmas.

The clipping offers graphic proof of the warm welcome given to Ben and other war guests and of the zeal with which the Canadian population rallied to the support of Great Britain, particularly after the Fall of France in June 1940. This support did not mean the abandonment or dilution of Canadian identity, as the flags held by Ben and Yvonne Bowerman attest.[9] School children were rallied to the cause by direct participation, principally through the drives to collect paper, rubber, metal, and other materials. The money raised by the sales of

Figure 3.3
Ben and schoolmates,
London Free Press, 23
September 1940

these items was donated mainly to the Red Cross but also to other charitable organizations involved in the war effort.[10]

Ben and the two younger Penrose sons attended Ryerson Elementary School. Oliver, with his notable intelligence, had moved almost immediately following the family's arrival into the "advancement class" at Empress Avenue (now Jeanne Sauvé) School; after an unsatisfactory year there, he was placed, despite being only eleven, in Grade 9 in London Central Collegiate Institute (now London Central Secondary School). Ryerson School was situated at 940 Waterloo

9 Born in 1931, Yvonne Bowerman came to Canada with her mother and four siblings on the *Duchess of Atholl*, leaving Liverpool on 17 August 1940. She returned with her family to England in August 1944 from New York.

10 For a good, if determinedly downbeat, survey of the impact of the Second World War on Canada, its population, society, and culture, see Keshen, *Saints, Sinners, and Soldiers*, 199.

Figure 3.4 Ryerson Elementary School,
London, Ontario

Street, a block away from the Penroses' house. It was an ample, recently constructed building. As Ben recalled, "in the middle there was a large auditorium
where we gathered for assembly. Around the edge were the classrooms." He was
placed in Grade 4, the level appropriate to his age, and he was happy from the
start, in good part because, as he has remarked, "I have tremendous admiration
for the teachers at Ryerson School. They spent a lot of time with me." The presence of girls was a striking difference from what he had experienced at
Pinewood School. Further, his being a "war guest from England," as the newspaper article termed him, meant that he was both a centre of attention and
treated with respect.

Just as important as the school was his home life with the Penroses. Ben
rapidly established a warm relationship with Margaret. In his own words, "she
was very, very good and very caring." Lionel did not figure largely in Ben's life.
Not only was Lionel frequently away from home, but his sense of self did not
encourage intimacy. Ben recalls an occasion when Lionel, visiting Ben's school,
found that one of pupils was affected by Down Syndrome. Lionel expressed his

outrage that he, the leading expert in the field, had not been informed of the child's existence prior to his visit. While Margaret's character did contain, as her reminiscences suggest, elements of drama and imprecision, these was more than offset by her intelligence and by her medical training, which, Ben recalls, "was very useful" with four young children. The care and concern that Margaret Penrose gave to her new charge, are evident from the contentment and enthusiasm expressed in a letter written by Ben in November 1940. A Remembrance Day card, signed "Mummy love form Benjamin," sent at around the same time, was an earnest expression of Ben's love.

Ben to His Parents

Dry Stamped: 1000 Wellington St London Ontario
10 Nov [1940]

Deary Daddy and Mammy

I hope you are all right I am. Has are [our] Flat been bonbed? On the 10 off Nov it was 30°F and we had snow. I was in a choir on remembrance day. I went to a party. I went to the Dentist and I had 3 fillings and 2 teeth out. Schall I sund some stamps and here is a mase design Here.

[Pencil drawing of a maze designed by Ben]

The flat at 42 Queen's Gate Gardens was never bombed.

The school report Margaret forwarded in November 1940 (Fig. 3.5) shows her commitment to keeping Ben's mother informed of his activities.

Postcard from Margaret Penrose to Penelope Barman

Benjamin's School Report Ryerson Sch. London Ont. Nov. 14 1940. "Benjamin's work is showing improvement. He needs to study his reading, writing & spelling each night. He is an asset to our class & is always interested in our discussions.

(signed) A. Wallace"

(Of course he does study lots every evening). M.P.

If you should ever feel like writing to Miss Wallace I am sure she would be pleased to hear from you. She is B's form mistress. I send this p.c. really to let you know that Benny thrives – in case some of our missives do not reach you. He wrote last Sunday himself. He has been to parties & dentists & singing in church choir! etc. etc. Love M.

Uncle Ross very kindly settled the nurse's acct. I wrote too soon – to you.

"I wrote too soon to you" refers to a letter to Penelope from Margaret Penrose that has not survived.

This postcard is stamped "Passed T. 30" with a royal crown (Fig. 3.6), the first evidence of the censorship of all the correspondence crossing the Atlantic. What impact the censors' viewing of letters, packets, and postcards had on writers – how conscious people were of the oversight and how it shaped what they wrote – is not clear. Margaret Penrose's avoidance of any discussion of the war situation may be related to her being conscious that the censor's scissors would cut out anything deemed sensitive or unsuitable.

The following letter shows how a friendly school environment intersecting with a warm home life combined to foster Ben's contentment and a sense of confidence.

Ben to His Parents

20th [December 1940]

Dear mammy and daddy.

Here is a picture that I drew. Margaret sens her love. I Drew the picture at Ryerson. I can near[ly] spell. What date is Daddy birthday? It is snowing here the temperature is 20°F.

Love from Benjamin

The envelope in which the letter and the picture were sent is postmarked "London Dec 29 10PM 1940."

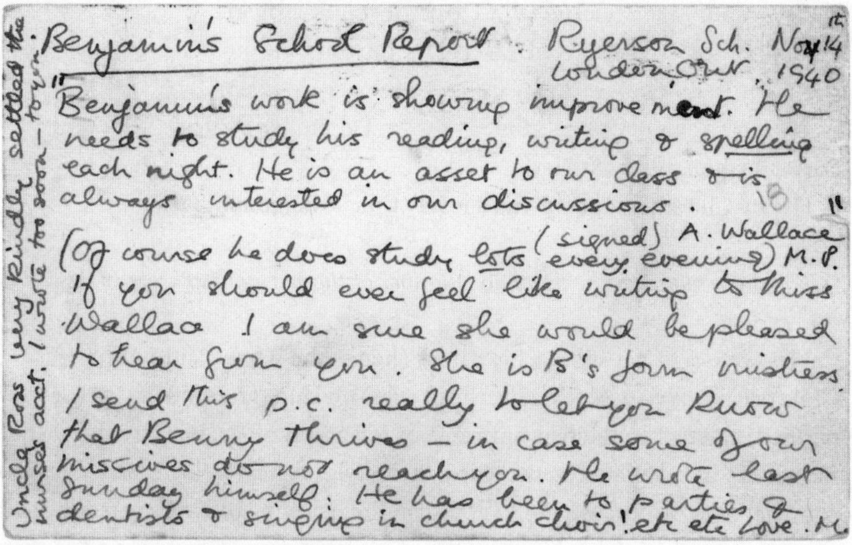

Benjamin's School Report . Ryerson Sch. Nov 14th
London Ont. 1940

"Benjamin's work is showing improvement. He
needs to study his reading, writing & spelling
each night. He is an asset to our class & is
always interested in our discussions .

(signed) A. Wallace
(of course he does study lots (every evening) M.P.
If you should ever feel like writing to Miss
Wallace I am sure she would be pleased
to hear from you . She is B's form mistress.
I send this p.c. really to let you know
that Benny thrives — in case some of your
missives do not reach you. He wrote last
Sunday himself. He has been to parties &
dentists & singing in church choir! etc etc love . M

Uncle Ros very kindly settled the
missed acct. I write too soon - to...

CANADA POST CARD

NOV 14
11 PM
1940
ONT.

PASSED
T.30

2 CENTS

Mrs Barman
Cholesbury Rd
Buckland Common
nr Tring
ENGLAND Bucks or ? Herts

Figure 3.5 *Top* Ben's school report, copied by Margaret Penrose, November 1940

Figure 3.6 *Bottom* Front of postcard stamped "PASSED T. 30"

Cable (via Commercial Cables)
Ben to His Parents

December 23, 1940

Barman Cholesbury 283 Herts
  Happy Christmas and having a lovely time = Benjamin Barman.

"Cholesbury 283" was the telephone number of the Barmans at Twin Oaks

Cables were sent via submarine cables (hence the name) laid on the seabed, while telegrams were sent via overhead wires on land. The sender took (or telephoned) the text to the relevant cable or telegraph office. Because the cost of messages was calculated by the word, their style, termed "telegraphese," was so compact as to be distinctive. On arrival at the receiving office, the message was printed on a teletype machine and the resulting strips of text were pasted onto a form, which was then delivered in an envelope to the recipient's address.

  The cable indicates that Ben, having lived with the Penrose family for over three months, was rapidly adjusting to their way of life. As the following letter makes clear, he had no desire to undergo any further changes.

Ben to His Parents

Undated [26 December 1940]

Dear Mummy and Daddy.
  I hope you are very well. Thank you for the £5. I got the £5 pounds on Xmas Day and I got a tractor, an Bow and Arrow and some outh[er] things.
  Ryerson has 8 teachers. The teacher that teaches me is Mis Wallace. I lick it very much better than any outh[er] school in English school. I do <u>not</u> want to go to <u>any</u> outher pearson. I like to <u>stay</u> with Margaret all the time. I am <u>very</u> happ[y] here. I hope you will be eventul come over to Can[ada] soon.
                                                    Love from Benjamin

"Come over to Can. soon" may refer to the original plan that Penelope and the two younger sons would follow Ben to Canada, leaving Lowis alone in England.

The five pounds sterling (then worth about $21.90, a very considerable sum for that period) that Ben received for Christmas is the first mention of finances in the surviving documents. This silence is somewhat surprising, since the cost of maintaining an evacuee child was by no means small – about $250 a year, according to the Canada Welfare Council.[11] Lionel occupied, as his surviving bank statements from 1943 show, a well-paid post, earning around $225 a month. The grandson of Baron Peckover, a wealthy banker, he also enjoyed a private income, including dividends from North American corporations. The cost of keeping Ben did not therefore impose a noticeable burden for the Penroses.

As Ben's letter suggests, Lowis Barman found ways of sending money to Canada. Although the British government did not authorize payments to evacuee children until January 1942, Lowis's post at BOAC, which maintained many agents abroad, probably gave him opportunities of funnelling (legally or no) money to Canada. Despite generally conforming to the accepted social and cultural norms, Ben's father took a certain delight in subverting inconvenient rules and regulations. Late in the war, after Ben's return to England, Lowis flew to Canada on BOAC business. His journey back took place at night in an unpressured aeroplane. "You aren't meant to sleep while wearing an oxygen mask," I recall him subsequently telling me, "but I was able to take several naps."

I celebrated my fourth birthday on 16 January 1941. It would be interesting to know whether the sending of a birthday card to me was Ben's own idea or that of Margaret as his surrogate mother. No envelope survives and the card, with the words, "Roderick love from Benjamin," may have been included with the picture in the letter dated "20th" and sent on 29 December 1940.

Although Ben lived with the Penroses, Ross Barman (Fig. 3.13) continued to be Ben's guardian and so was legally responsible for him. The following cable shows that the Montreal Barmans and the Penroses kept in touch, although there is no evidence that a close or easy relationship developed between the two families.

11 See Keshen, *Saints*, 199.

Cable (via Cable and Wireless)
Ross Barman to Lowis and Penelope Barman

Montreal 3 January 1941
Thanks for letters Penrose report Benjamin well and happy best luck for
New Year Barman

Beyond this telegram, no correspondence survives for the first three weeks of
January 1941. However, a letter to Penelope from Ben's Grade 4 teacher more
than makes up for the lack, as it tells us much about Canadian attitudes towards
the war as the conflict dragged on. For Aileen Wallace, the unchanged life of
ordinary Canadians contrasted sharply with the challenges and deprivations
faced by the British people. Her hope was for "a final British victory."

Letter from Aileen Wallace, Ben's School Teacher,
to Penelope Barman

889 Adelaide Street
London Ont. Canada
Jan 21 1941

Dear Mrs. Barman:

I am Benjamin's teacher at Ryerson School and I felt that you would be interested in hearing from me and learning how Benjamin is getting on.

I find him a very likeable little fellow who does his best to cooperate in
every way. We get on very well indeed together. I have noted greatest improvement in his Arithmetic. He topped the class in his last paper with 80%.
His reading and spelling are showing some improvement, though this is slow.
He seems to be very happy here and enters into our games very heartily. It is
indeed interesting to me, to have him in my class. I am enjoying it im-
mensely. I have one other war guest – A little girl of Benjamin's age.

We are all praying and working for a final British victory in this awful war.
Our own school has raised $600 in the past six months which we turned over
to the Red Cross Society. The news of the wonderful morale of all the English
people at home is a source of great inspiration to all Canadians. Our part is
so small when we compare it with the sacrifices you are all making.

I hope you will feel how interested I am in your boy and how I trust you may be re-united in the near future. In the meantime, I am only too glad to do all I can for him.

Sincerely, Aileen Wallace

No additional information can be found about Ben's teacher.

The "$600" was obtained by the collection and sale of old telephone books and other paper materials.

The other "war guest" was Yvonne Bowerman, pictured with Ben in the press clipping of 23 September 1940.

The emphasis in the literature on war guests has, quite understandably, been on the influence of evacuation on the children themselves. What has been less studied or considered is the impact of evacuation on the host families, or, more precisely, the mothers who took war guests into their homes. In this period, the vast majority of women, upon marriage, gave up any previous careers in order to take on the entire responsibility for running the household and raising the children. The gendered division of labour was so absolute that most husbands did not even think about participating in these tasks. The only intellectual occupation that a mother could expect was what she could improvise in whatever spare time she could find.

As the following letter shows, Margaret Penrose was caught in this situation. She not only had to run a household by herself and manage her own three sons but also had to look after an adolescent girl (Clare Hogben, who continued to live in the house into 1941) and a young boy (Ben). Very different in personality from Margaret's own offspring, Ben needed to receive separate attention, affection, and reassurance, in part to compensate for the absence of his own parents. Despite these demands, Margaret found the time to write long letters to her childhood friend Penelope, with the intent of easing the distance between Ben and his mother and also of having a means to express her own feelings.

Figure 3.7 Children in the Penrose household, winter 1940–41: Roger,
Clare Hogben, Ben, Oliver, and Jonathan

Margaret Penrose to Penelope Barman

1000 Wellington St, London Ont Can. 21st Feb. 1941

My dear Penelope,

In your letter of 26 Jan (which arrived a week or more ago) you say how
you hoped "intelligence was catching." All I can say is that I hope generosity
of disposition and <u>good nature</u> is infectious! Your son puts us all to shame in
this respect. Personally, I get exhausted & irritable & I can just hear myself
carping & nagging whenever the children are around. I have so far discovered
no other way of keeping them to their time-table but that of yelling myself
hoarse & using language unsuitable for anyone short of a sergeant major.
(They don't seem to <u>hear</u> anything else!) So on St Valentine's Day what
should I receive but an elegant card from Benny (depicting a young lady sitting in a teacup) with the motive "Quit your 'TEA-SING', let's be Valentines"!
Really it put me so much to shame that I can pride myself on having behaved
noticeably more patiently for the past week. But I've come to the conclusion
that I'm of a disgustingly sarcastic & spiteful disposition. I have difficulty in
curbing my tongue & so sound much angrier than I actually feel! This of

course was my mamma's technique with me & earned her my near-hatred for some 35 years. Now that I feel I am developing the same kind of symptoms myself & she is 3000 miles away my feelings towards her have softened considerably! (They would).

But Benny seems to have spotted the insincerity of my annoyance much more readily than my own children do or than I ever did myself as a child. I suppose it's easier when it is not a real parent. But I think perhaps the fact that he <u>does</u> may help my own three to be more tolerant of that kind of thing in me (& others).

Benny had <u>dozens</u> of Valentines himself from his little schoolfellows, so did Jonathan. O & R only had a few. But our mantelpiece is completely covered with decorated cards. I suppose it's about time I cleared them off & washed the paint. But my public speaking seems to have become so much the rage that I hardly have a spare moment. I've a grand luncheon to address next week & I seem to have brought down a house again the night before last on (what amounted to) "the psychology of race feeling." God knows what I shall be up to next. I feel that I'm quite out of my own control. Stepping into Ma's shoes again you observe.

My charwoman is in hospital but this moment someone has just telephoned & said that she knows of a neighbouring Hungarian short of a job. So I shall now visit her & post this en route.

MUCH LOVE Margaret (Benny thrives)

PS Give my love to Mr Bradley if you see him, please. He comes to mind continually as I repeat his perpetual refrain to me (over Latin) & mine to Benny (over spelling). "THINK man THINK." It's quite absurd how one reiterates what one has heard in childhood!

Lancelot Hog[ben]. "isn't <u>my</u> cup of tea" either if it comes to that. But one can't worry about tea these days can one? He's said to be en route for Britain. Claire has been broadcasting as an "evacuee" discussing England.

(No, I never saw B's letter saying that he liked being here and wanted to stay with us. I'm <u>delighted</u>.)

Margaret Penrose's "mamma" was Sonia Marie Natanson Leathes (1871–1964), born in Russia. A large part of Margaret's written reminiscences is focused on her mother, her treatment of Margaret and of her husband, and her peculiarities both in personality and in behaviour.

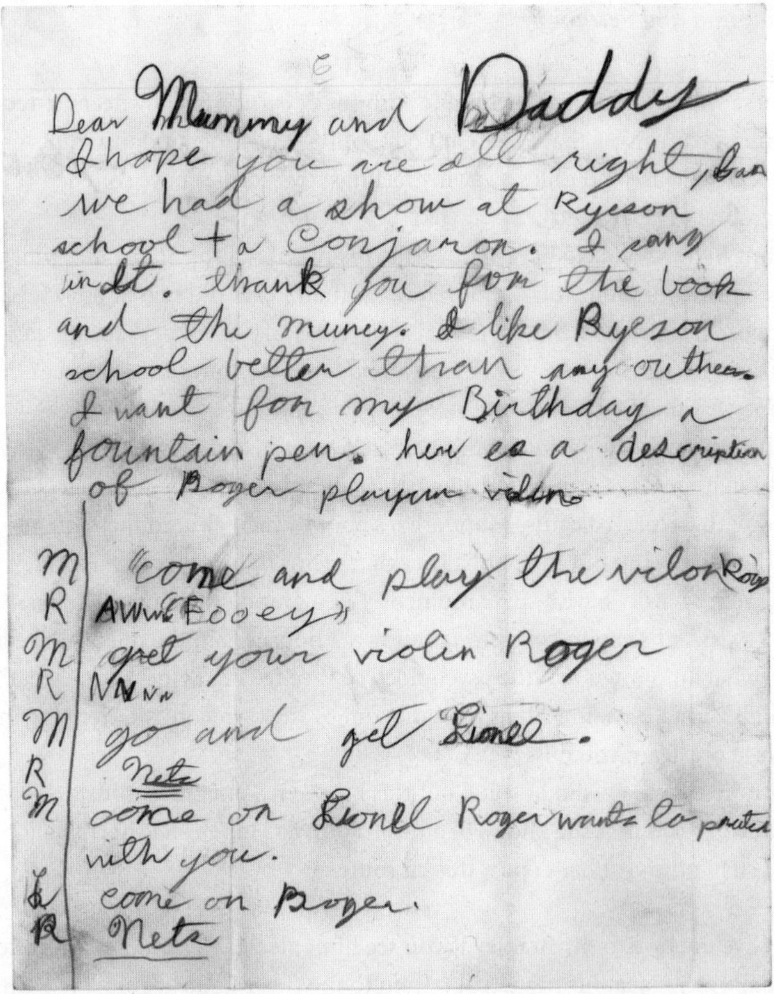

Dear Mummy and Daddy
I hope you are all right,
we had a show at Ryeson
school + a Conjaron. I sang
in it. thank you fom the book
and the muney. I like Ryeson
school better than any outher.
I want for my Birthday a
fountain pen. here is a description
of Roger playing violin

M "come and play the vilon Roger
R Awwe Fooey"
M get your violin Roger
R Nnnn
M go and get Lionel.
R Nets
M come on Lionel Roger wants to practice
with you.
L come on Roger.
R Nets

Figure 3.8 Ben's letter to his parents, undated [21 February 1941]

A "charwoman" or "char" was the term used in England for a household cleaner who was paid by the hour.

"Mr Bradley" is unidentified but, since Penelope was assumed to know him, he may have taught Latin at Edith Spencer's school.

"Lancelot Hog." refers to Lancelot Hogben who, as noted earlier, had stayed with Penroses in August 1940 with his wife and two younger children. Although very able, eventually becoming a Fellow of the Royal Society, he was prickly in character and quick to embark on quarrels. Margaret was clearly responding to a remark made by Penelope in her most recent letter.

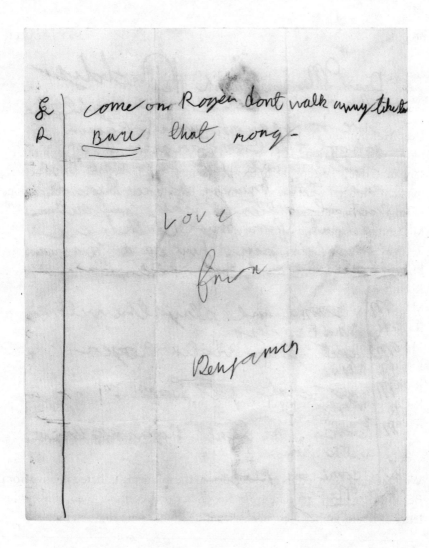

"En route for Britain" refers to Hogben's return to his chair at the University of Aberdeen. He reached Great Britain safely and lived until 1975.

"B's letter" refers to his letter of 26 December 1940.

The envelope, postmarked "London Feb. 22 2.00PM 1941 Ont," has, written on the front by Penelope Barman, "Plus letter about Ryerson and violin." That letter (reproduced below and shown in Fig 3.8) gives, in a humorous fashion not previously employed, Ben's insight into the relationship then existing between child and parent in the Penrose household.

Ben to His Parents

Undated [21 February 1941]

Dear Mummy and Daddy,

I hope you are all right, I am we had a show at Ryeson school + a conjuror. I sang in it. thank you for the book and the muney. I like Ryeson school better than any outher. I want for my Birthday a Fountain pen. here is a description of Roger playin vilin.

M "Come and play the vilon Roger"

R Aww. "Fooey"

M get your violin Roger

R Nnn

M   go and get Lionel.

R   Nets

M   Come on Lionel Roger wants to practice with you.

L   Come on Roger

R   Nets

L   Come on Roger don't walk away like that

R   Bare that mony.

Love from Benjamin

With the above two letters has been placed the following undated missive from Ben, but it may in fact date from November or December 1940, since in his letter of 10 November 1940, Ben asked if he should send some stamps.

Ben to His Parents

Undated [end of 1940?]

Dare Mummy and Daddy,

I hope you are all right, I am. here is some stamps their are 101 stamps. I hope John has not got them. I like school very much.

Love from Benjamin

The 1908 issue of Quebec Tricentenary postage stamps bear the number 101 in the Scott classification. I recall seeing these stamps in my brother Jonathan's collection.
 By "John," Ben meant his brother Jonathan.

No correspondence survives from the month of March 1941, but the gap can be filled by a passage from Margaret Penrose's reminiscences about life in London, Ontario:

"I noted down a teatime family conversation as well as I could, just to show you what our variety of 'Bedlam' was like:
 "<u>Teatime – 1000 Wellington Street, 1941</u>
 MARGARET: Now hurry up Roger. Benny has nearly finished his third helping and you haven't begun yet.
 ROGER: Oh, but I haven't said grace yet: I can't in this noise.
 OLIVER: Margaret, shall I tell you some more about integral calculus? I have just worked out a new equation: dy by dx …
 CLARE: You know us girls in our class were passing round a hoojumaflip paper with personal about everyone on it. I nearly died when I saw mine. It said, 'She's a swell kid but boy, what ghastly nail polish.'
 JONATHAN: I said knight to queen bishop four, what would black do then?
 LIONEL: Bishop to king's three.
 JONATHAN: You can't, there a pawn in the way.
 LIONEL: True, I wondered whether you'd remember it. Queen takes pawn.
 BENNY: I say, Lionel, I've got a good idea.
 ROGER: Do seventeens go into 571? I can't decide whether it is a prime number or not.
 MARGARET: Jonathan, don't pick your nose. Benny, don't use your glass as though it were a telescope. Roger, you've only had one mouthful, take another.
 ROGER: There's bits in it.
 BENNY: I say, Lionel, I've got a <u>good</u> idea. Why don't we send over a big aeroplane and bump off Hitler with a big bomb. Boom bang bang!
 LIONEL: Oh shut up everyone.
 OLIVER: There seems to be a snag in my equation, shall I tell you what it is? You see …
 BENNY: Can I have another piece of currant bread?

MARGARET: I set the limit at <u>seven</u> slices.

BENNY: Well, can I have some more cake then?

ROGER: Benny I don't believe you ever said grace.

CLARE : Of course there's a rule that boys and girls can't walk down the darned corridor together, but I've walked down with dozens of boys.

OLIVER: What, all at once?

CLARE : No one at a time, silly, and no one has ever said anythink – maybe that's 'cos I'm English.

ROGER: But if you took a dodecahedron with the corners partly cut off and you …

MARGARET : Roger take another mouthful for God's sake.

ROGER: There's bits in it.

BENNY: Please can I have some more honey, this pot is empty.

JONATHAN: What would Black do then?

MARGARET: He wouldn't pick his nose I'm sure.

BENNY: I say, Lionel, I've got a good idea.

JONATHAN: Margaret, will you buy us Jumbo comics?

BENNY: And buy me Fantastic comics?

ROGER: And buy me Weird comics? But I must pay for it out of my own pocket money, I won't take if you <u>give</u> it me.

OLIVER: And buy me <u>Analytical Geometry</u>.

LIONEL: Shut up everyone.

JONATHAN: Do you remember a long time ago in the Ark, God said 'rain' and it did. If God broke his promise he would be like Hitler I suppose …"

"Anythink" is how some English accents pronounce the word "anything."

The above dialogue gives a humorous but nonetheless telling insight into a family and household that was in no way staid or conventional. As Benjamin later told me, "In matters of the mind, the Penroses were brilliant. As to handling practical affairs of ordinary life, such as ordering sufficient food for a party, they were hopeless." It was in the latter sphere that Ben excelled; moreover, in contrast to the three Penrose boys, he was cooperative and considerate, spontaneously helping Margaret with the housework and giving her support and understanding. A close bond developed between the two of them.

As the end of the school year approached, Ben found himself involved in planning for what had long been a standard feature of life for many children and adolescents in North America – summer camp. Several weeks of outdoor existence combined with activities specifically catering to the young formed, and still form, an intrinsic part of the process of growing up. Tony Bailey, an evacuee who had travelled on the *Antonia* in September 1940, commented: "The long summer vacation – nearly twice the length of the summer holidays in England – presumably had a practical agricultural purpose in the past, but in the industrial, metropolitan present it has made necessary an alternative occupation so that parents don't go crazy with children running in and out of the house all summer saying 'What shall I do?' and 'I'm bored.'"[12] The question in April 1941 was where and how Ben was going to participate in what was for him a new experience.

UK Post Office Telegram
Ben to His Parents

Barman, Cholesbury 287 Tring   14th of April 1941
Prefer to accept Uncle Ross kind invitation July Massey Beresford's are worse hope you are all right I am – Benjamin Barman

"Cholesbury 287" was the Barmans' telephone number at Twin Oaks.
As noted above, Mrs Helen Massy Beresford lived with her three children in Quebec. Later in life, Ben could not recall why her offer was less desirable than that of Uncle Ross.

The school term was drawing to a close. As the following letter shows, the main impact of the war on school life was the continued raising of funds.

12 Bailey, *America Lost and Found*, 107.

Postcard from Ben to His Parents

Undated [Postmark "London May 2 11pm Ont 1941"]

Dear Mummy and Daddy,

I hope you are all right, I am. Ryerson School has given a $100⁰⁰ to the red cross every month.

Love from Benjamin

Ben celebrated his tenth birthday on 22 May 1941, but the only memento relating to that occasion is possibly a photograph of him, annotated on the back by his mother Penelope "A B Barman Canada May 1941" (Fig. 2.1).

To escape the summer humidity in London, the Penroses travelled eighty-five kilometres to a cabin at Bayfield, a town south of Goderich, on the shores of Lake Huron. It is clear that Ben was with the family until he went, about the middle of June, to Quebec to stay with the Ross Barmans. As the following letter notes, he moved on in mid-July to stay with the Flanagan family at their summer residence in Quebec, a stay probably arranged through the Ross Barmans.

Figure 3.9 Postcard view of Bayfield, Bluewater, Lake Huron, Ontario

Figure 3.10 Flanagan summer cottage, Lake Beavan, Arundel, Quebec

Margaret Penrose to Penelope Barman

30th July 1941, Bayfield, Ont, Can

I have had at least 2 long letters thanking for parcels etc from you & one from your mother [Edith Spencer]. I can't somehow settle down to write letters on a holiday in a cramped cabin. Benny has written 3 times! & I am delighted with him. No word from Ross or Orion – but who cares? B. went to the Flanagans 18th July & I forwarded your letter there. He will return to London at end of Augt & doubtless come out here with us for weekends in Sept. I return to London 16th Aug for two weeks before schools begin – 2nd Sept. It has been terribly hot – 98°F in London & 110°F in Hamilton (not far away). But we have the lake. Love MP

The "parcels etc." most likely contained food of various types.

"Bayfield" is now part of the town of Bluewater. The Penroses became extremely attached to it.

Ben has very happy memories of the weeks he spent at Lake Beaven, Arundel, northeast of Montreal. The summer cottage, expanded into a house, which is still in active use, had been built by Rev. James Flanagan. His son, James Cyril Flanagan, known both as "Flin" and "Doc," was a leading dentist in Montreal, notable for his physical prowess, ebullient character, and social conscience expressed in philanthropic activities and political radicalism. He married Elizabeth Randall Baile, the daughter of a leading Montreal coal merchant. The Flanagans were, accordingly, very much part of anglophone Quebec. The following letter gives a clear picture of life at the Beaven Lake house. The envelope is postmarked "Arundel Aug 28 1941."

Mrs. Elizabeth Randall Flanagan to Penelope Barman

Undated [28 August 1941]

My dear Mrs Barman,

We have enjoyed having Benjamin with us so much that I feel I must let you know how much we all love him – He provides us with many a laugh with his unending questions. He has done well to adapt himself so well to our family for we have been large and varied this summer. I have three of my own, Peter age 14, David age 12 and Patsy age 7.

Our farm is three miles away from the lake house and, as labour is very scarce these days, I harboured four extra boys to work on the farm. These are sons of some of my friends in town. I also had Judith a small English girl – I have loved having them all.

I am enclosing a few snaps which I thought might interest you and will write on the back of each who is who.

Benjamin's chief delights have been swimming and the combine – we fortunately have a nice sandy beach and the weather has been simply divine all summer for swimming – the children have all been so well.

Unhappily the summer is nearly at an end. We have our big bonfire on the Saturday of Labor Day weekend and the following Tuesday the whole family must disburse for the winter's work.

Your son looks splendidly and he seems genuinely happy. We hope to have him again some day.

Yours most sincerely.
Gabeth Flanagan

Figure 3.11 Ben with the Flanagans, friends, and farm workers

"Our farm" was purchased by the Flanagans in 1938 and named by Elizabeth Flanagan Cool Greeny Farm. Doc Flanagan moved to the farm in 1978, living there until his death in 1994. The farm is still the property of the family.

"Labour is very scarce these days": voluntary enlistments in the armed forces and the availability of well-paying factory jobs were causing, as this letter shows, an acute labour shortage in the agricultural sector by the summer of 1941. That spring, the Canadian government established the "Children's Brigade," enrolling boys aged 12 to 14 and girls aged 14 to 16 to do light work on farms near their homes. The Farm Cadet Brigade enrolled boys aged 15 to 18 for work on farms for three and a half months in the summer, and the Farmette Brigade did the same for girls in school who were over 16.

"The sons of some of my friends in town" were, as the photograph shows, in their early teens. The boys are the first and fourth from the left in the top row and the second and third from the right in the bottom row. Among them may have been

the "Soapy, Dugan, Gavin" mentioned in Pat Flanagan Thomas' memoir of Cool Greeny Farm.[13]

The "town" was Montreal, a ninety-minute journey by automobile to the south east of the lake house. The Flanagans lived on Grosvenor Avenue in the heart of Westmount.

"Judy," Judith Gaussen, aged eight, came to Canada in June 1940 with her mother and younger brother on the Duchess of Richmond.

The information on Ben's life with the Flanagans can be supplemented by Pat Flanagan Thomass' memoir of her early years at the family lake house. "The Lakehouse was a more complicated place to live in than today. For me, it was also filled with my mother's warmth and creativity." She provides a detailed account of the "family routine": "We ate breakfast around eight o'clock. I would go out to meet the mailman at the mailbox every morning before breakfast ... I swam every morning for a couple of hours. We had a two-story diving board that was wired to permanent poles every late spring and detached and hauled in each fall." The morning swim was followed by "lunch, which we ate either in the dining room or on trays on the lawn." The children had to wait an hour or two in order to digest their food. "Then swimming again for another couple of hours and supper and card games, singing, reading or board games. Mother always had some project in progress ... sewing, painting, cooking, writing ... On Labour Day weekend, we hosted a big bonfire on the beach for local residents. Mother composed verses for each family attending and put them to a popular tune ... The piano was hauled down to just above the beach to supply the music."[14]

There was, unhappily, one flaw in this idyllic life. As Ben remembers, "Mrs Flanagan was severely diabetic and had to have daily injections of insulin." The malady, diagnosed in the winter of 1940–41, took an increasingly severe toll on Elizabeth Flanagan's health. She eventually had to have a companion to handle her diabetic seizures. Although her condition was finally stabilized, she did not survive a heart attack and died in 1952.

13 See Thomas, "Saturday 14 April 2014 Notes." "David and Peter worked on the farm in summer from early teens through university. Various other friends (Soapy, Dugan, Gavin) worked with them," n.p.

14 Pat Thomas, "Memories of My Childhood," n.p.

Figure 3.12 Ben having his hair cut by "Doc" Flanagan

Following his time with the Flanagans, Ben stayed for August and the first week of September with his aunt and uncle outside of Montreal.

Ben to His Parents

6th Sep [1941]

Dear Mummy and daddy,

I hope you are all right I am. I went to town and I got new sohes [shoes]. I have grone 2 inchs since I came to Canada. The leafs are falling of the treas all reddy. I am goind to Miss penrose already and will be starting school soon.

Love from Benjamin Love from Benjamin Love from Benjamin Love from
Love to ED to Benjamin

Love from Adrian Benjamin Barman ABB

"ED" was Ben's grandmother Edith Spencer.

Figure 3.13
Ben with his uncle
Ross Barman and
his cousin Chris,
St Bruno, Quebec,
undated [August–
September 1941]

In 1941, Labour Day fell on 1 September and school started the next day (usually a half day). Ben's report card for 1941–42 records that he missed 4½ school days in September 1941, which suggests that he returned to London only by September 8, thus missing the first week of school. Some days later, his Aunt Orion wrote the following letter, which provides a good insight into the impact of the war on the life style of well-to-do anglophones in Quebec, particularly with respect to the lack of domestic servants, who had been attracted to industry by the relatively high pay.

Orion Barman to Penelope Barman

Nazeing Lodge, St. Bruno. P. Q. Sept. 13/41.

Dear Penelope,

Benny has returned to Mrs Penrose for school. How the summer has flown by! He was with Dr. & Mrs Flanagan for 6 weeks & with us for about the same length of time. He raved about his visit with the F's, who have a big farm and lots of swimming. We got him some summer togs before he went to Arundel, & shoes. He seldom wore the play shoes, which the others all wear & also got him some, but wore the strong oxfords, so we took him in to town & got him more before going to London. He now takes a man's shoe! Size 6. Equivalent to 6 ½ in a child's shoe, but he finds them very comfortable.

Am glad the movies arrived safely. I thought they were rather good.

Benny was very good. He loves travelling on a sleeper & the black porters are extremely good with children.

Ross is very busy. Business in that line is coming along very fast now.

We are moving to Montreal this winter. The school question has to be faced & as there is only a small French Catholic school in the village, we feel it is not up to date & too many prayers, so we must move in. The address after October 1st will be 14 Hudson Ave., Westmount, P 2.

Is Lowis away as much as he used to be and do you have any help? All the girls here are going into factories & a great many people are maid less, I've been lucky so far.

Love to all Orion.

Ben's father showed "the movies" on the family's film projector (without sound, of course). Included was a scene of Ben, in swimming trunks, first sitting on and then diving off a platform in the middle of a lake surrounded by trees. He looked plump and happy, with bangs and a big smile. Over seventy years later, that sequence remains a vivid memory for me.

"Away as much as he used to be" refers to Ben's father's employment. He was in charge of supply for BOAC, which had been formed in November 1939 by merging Imperial Airlines and British Airways Ltd. His duties took him overseas from time to time.

No letters or photographs survive from the first weeks following Ben's return to London. A Christmas card he sent to his parents, signed "Love from Benjamin," is significant not for his greeting but for the text printed on the card. The month of December 1941 – in the aftermath of the Japanese attack on Pearl Harbor, Japan's conquest of Hong Kong, Malaysia, and the Dutch East Indies, and the Nazi advance to the outskirts of Moscow – can be seen, at least in retrospect, as the nadir of the war. The future looked very bleak and optimism was difficult to maintain.

The following letters, one from Ben and one from Margaret, reveal their respective states of mind.

Ben to His Parents

Undated [1 December 1941]

Dear Mummy and Daddy,

Here are some leaflets that were dropt over here. pretend that you are in canada and a leaflet drops in front of you. Margaret says that "time exposure" has just arrived. Thank you. Marry Christmas and a happy new year.

Love from Benjamin

"Time exposure" was probably a mishearing by Ben of Margaret announcing "Time expired," meaning that he had to stop writing the letter.

Included in the letter were three coloured (green, orange, and yellow) leaflets (Fig. 3.14), which were dropped from airplanes as part of a publicity campaigns to stimulate the buying of new issues of War Savings Certificates. Each individual could purchase up to $600 of these certificates. The money their sale raised was quite small. Their significance lay in the way they mobilized support for the war effort and encouraged a decrease in personal expenditure. Victory Bonds, which could be purchased without limit, provided the bulk of the moneys raised from the public by the Canadian government for the war.

At around this time, the dismal state of Ben's writing and spelling – virtually unchanged since he had come under her care some fourteen months previously – became a major issue in Margaret's mind. It is not clear from the surviving correspondence who suggested that Ben try writing with his left hand. Given

Figure 3.14
Leaflet dropped from the air, promoting the purchase of War Saving Certificates, enclosed in Ben's letter to his parents, 1 December 1941

the assumptions of the time that it was unnatural to use the left hand for writing, the suggestion that Ben's problems could be solved by switching to his left was unorthodox, even radical. The experiment did not bring, as Margaret's subsequent letters show, the improvement hoped for.

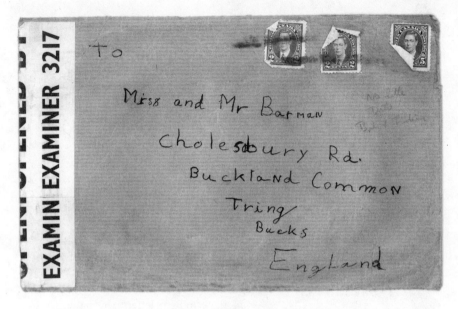

Figure 3.15 Envelope resealed with a sticker reading
"OPENED EXAMINER 3217."

Margaret Penrose to Penelope Barman

1st Dec 1941

The result of <u>4 hours</u> Blood Sweat & Toil (not <u>tears</u>) with the left-hand.
(4–8 PM exactly with intervals for food.) Is it my imagination that though he
writes worse he does <u>spell better</u>? In case you don't get my long one written
earlier this afternoon – <u>many</u> thanks for Xmas books for R & J & <u>me</u>! & for
lovely New Statesman & for excellent sweater & slippers. All came safe & fit
etc. excellently.

M. P.

*"Blood sweat and toil (not tears)" referred to a well-known phrase in Winston
Churchill's first speech as prime minister on 13 May 1940: "I have nothing to offer
but blood, toil, tears and sweat."*

The New Statesman *was founded in 1913 by Sidney and Beatrice Webb. This
left-wing weekly was edited between 1930 and 1960 by Kingsley Martin, who made
the journal very successful.*

The year 1941 closed with Ben sending his parents a Christmas present. He addressed the envelope himself. The postage was 9¢ and there was no cancellation stamp, but the envelope had been opened and then was resealed with a white sticker reading "OPENED EXAMINER 3217" (Fig. 3.15). The envelope held wrapping paper and a book, Lillian Davids Fazzini, *Indians of America* (1935). The cover reads "94 pictures with a foreword by Dan Beard." The subject of the book chosen by Ben showed that he had adjusted to the North American environment and was engaged in life there.

4

Tensions and Anxieties,
January–February 1942

In fact he displays the normal reactions of a displanted child – trying to get the
maximum attention – he'd rather be nagged than neglected.
~Margaret Penrose to Penelope Barman, 27 January 1942

By the end of 1941, Ben had long since moved beyond reception and had
become fully engaged in the fourth phase of the war guest experience, life in
Canada as a child evacuee. Reception had involved many and diverse challenges, none of them easy for either the war guest or the host family to face
and to resolve. Life as a child evacuee, which might appear to be less difficult
and demanding than the challenges associated with reception, presented its
own problems. The caution, forbearance, and good will usually displayed during the reception phase wore thin as time passed. Familiarity with the other's
character and behaviour did not necessarily translate into harmonious and
easy relationships.

In Ben's case, he was facing increasing demands and tensions at the start of
1942. As he approached his eleventh birthday, he was expected to match the
achievements of boys of his age, which included good handwriting and accurate
spelling. Neither of the two was Ben even close to achieving. Another concern,
over which he had no control, was his physical development. In boys of his age,
the genitals began to expand, prior to the descent of the testes, indicating the
approach of puberty. Yet Ben's genitals continued unchanged.

Other, less personal, causes for uncertainty were also present. In Ben and
Margaret's letters of January 1942, the question of money surfaced for the first
time, a topic for discussion and, by extension, a matter of concern. Probably,
Ben's activities, such as his lessons on the oboe, had become a more noticeable
cost to his host family. The war's demands were by then constricting the supply

of all types of goods and driving up prices, which stood in Canada by the end of 1941 nearly 18 per cent higher than they had been in September 1939. The appointment in November 1941 of a new head of the Wartime Prices and Trade Board signalled the imposition of tight controls over prices and the production of goods. The impact of the war could not be disregarded, even in Canada.

By the start of 1942, Margaret Penrose became increasingly concerned – "impatient" would not be too strong a word – with respect to the utter failure of her (and others') constant efforts to make Ben improve his handwriting and his spelling including a scheme that he write with his left hand. Ben's response to these efforts appeared evasive and at times uncooperative. Margaret's training as a medical doctor caused her to be concerned about Ben's physical condition – above all, his huge appetite and resulting gain in weight, although that concern figures only in passing in her letters. In retrospect, it is difficult not to surmise that Ben's compulsive eating, occasional stammering, and the intensity of his ineptitude with writing and spelling were a psychological "misplacement" or outlet for other trauma, such as prolonged separation from his family.

The following two letters reveal the tensions and anxieties that Ben faced.

Ben to His Parents

Undated [11 January 1942]

Dear Mummy and Daddy

Thank you for the last letter. I went to see Dumbo the flying elephant. We have <u>lots</u> and <u>lots</u> of skating 2 or 3 times a day. We are nearly thught ["through" added by Margaret] with the rink. Thank you <u>very</u> much for the money that you gave me, it is very nice. Mr ["Laidlaw" added by Margaret] does not know that I am writing with my left hand. Here is R[oger's] tooth. It is very small.

Love from Benjamin

[Note added by Margaret:]

Despite results during the holidays B practised at least 2 hrs daily at writing with left. It was entirely his own idea.

"Dumbo the flying elephant" refers to Walt Disney's Dumbo, *an animated film released in October 1941, which was a major financial and critical success.*

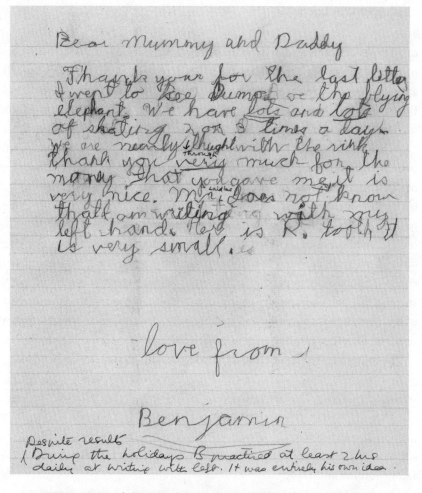

Dear Mummy and Daddy

Thank your for the last letter
I went to see Dumpo or the flying
elephant. We have lots and lots
of skating now 3 times a day.
We are nearly [through] with the rink
thank you very much for the
money that you gave me it is
very nice. M[iss Laidlaw] does not know
that I am writing with my
left hand. Here is R. tooth it
is very small.

love from

Benjamin

Despite results
(During the holidays B practised at least 2 hrs
daily at writing with left. It was entirely his own idea.

Figure 4.1 Ben's letter to his parents, written with his left hand,
undated [11 January 1942]

That Ben's "writing with the left" was concealed from his teacher may have been due to prevailing insistence on writing with the right hand only.

"Mr Laidlaw" was John Laidlaw, Ben's Grade 5 teacher, who taught until he enlisted in the air force in April 1943.

The next and very long letter from Margaret reports the moment when the resources of the Ontario Ministry of Education were, thanks to Lionel Penrose's influence, mobilized to assist Ben with his problems in writing and spelling. It

is obvious from the information given by Margaret in this and succeeding letters that since the nature of dyslexia was not understood by the experts, and
so, not surprisingly, the various forms of remedial treatment they suggested
were not effective. It was, paradoxically, Ben's Grade 5 teacher, John Laidlaw,
who would find a way for Ben to improve his spelling and to begin to write
quite elegantly.

Margaret Penrose to Penelope Barman

Sun. 11th Jan 1942

My dear Penelope,

Lots and lots of letters have arrived from you of late. Some took only
about 2 weeks to come. Perhaps they came over with Winston. I hope he
gives back safely. No – I won't write about the war. It dates much more
rapidly than B's news.

I have come to the conclusion that if I can do so tactfully it would be best
for me to write out B's letters (at his dictation) for him to copy. He makes
such lamentably unexpressive efforts & it takes up SO MUCH of his time. This
misery – written with his left hand (!) took 2 or 3 hrs yesterday & ½ hr today.
And the spelling was at its worst. He tries to put "wrighting" <u>every</u> time he
writes. When I asked him if he really thinks it to be correct he replies "well it
begins with a 'W'!" Of course the 3 meanings of the word confuse him.He
spelt money "muny" & when I asked if it was right – he said "oh no – <u>two</u>
Ns." We were playing "coffee pot" at lunch. The word was "ball." B. got v.
excited. "I know <u>another</u> meaning – ball head" (in the same way "car-board")
& other <u>speech</u> failings.

I'm afraid he's got his spelling defects on his nerves & writing home makes
it <u>worse</u>, just like his stammering suddenly appearing on the record.
("Dumbo the Flying Elephant" is a Walt Disney film – have you seen it? It is
fascinating. B R & J went twice).

We've started on the thyroid. (Do let me know about the balls' descent
when you remember). B is <u>full</u> of beans – but he was before. He is still too
lazy to walk far or run at all or lift his feet off the ground – shuffles <u>always</u>.
When I send them out to play he comes back after a second or two to say

"May I come in it's so cold <u>standing about</u>!" The others charge around &
keep warm. But I must admit it <u>has</u> been cold. 10° <u>below</u> zero for 3 days and
around zero for a week. The gas supply is getting weak & beginning to fail to
keep our thermostaticly controlled temperature up to its regular 70° (in this
house – 80° in most peoples). I hope the furnace doesn't go out altogether &
gas us all in our beds. If I stop writing you will know why.

Here is a copy of his Jan[uary] report. "Ben is doing good work in arithmetic. Spelling is still the problem. He is writing with his right hand. On account of the size of the class it is impossible for me to devote enough time to
Benjamin during school hours to teach him to write with his left hand. I
would be willing to give him extra time out of school hours & would welcome any suggestions. In our oral classwork in spelling B seems to be getting
the spelling idea, & at times surprises me. Benjamin could work harder in
school. J Laidlaw."

My theory about B.'s spelling is that he is terrified about it & has given
himself up as a bad job. When he first tried writing (at home) with his left
hand he was so full of confidence that he forgot himself & spelt better. Now
he seems to be relapsing. The original effect was deceptive.

I shall really have to keep him back from Montreal &/or the Flanagans this
summer, till Dr Secord has seen him here. He is the Ann Arbor speech specialist – the heartiest of fellows & so encouraging (wonderful results). Dr S.
comes for the Univ. summer school (to teach). I hope he comes again.

The present from the Lt. Col. whatnot of Toronto was most welcome. B
has agreed to transfer his oboe expenses to this account. He will get roller-
skates & any further requirements (I can't think <u>what</u> at the moment).

I hear that money is now permissible for evacuees – up to $12^{00} monthly
(newest regulation). It was announced on the radio. But when Lionel was up
in Toronto – (he goes & helps the deputy minister of health there every Friday), they were discussing the problem of having a general pool at Ottawa so
that parents who could afford more (it amounts to abt. £40 a year I reckon)
could send more & help contribute to the upkeep of evacuees whose parents
could not afford so much. I don't know what has come of that scheme so far.
Nor does anyone else to date. Will keep you posted.

The deputy minister also had a letter from Mr McFee (who used to be
mixed up in Lionel's racket here) asking for B's I.Q. scorings etc.& suggesting

that B see a Miss Lewis (who we also know) & be investigated by <u>her</u> (or words to that effect). Next time she is in London that can be done. She stays with a friend of mine, when here. Used to work here herself. Anything you want to know further we can supply. Being in that particular racket makes it as easy as pie. But the deputy minister is an angel. He & Lionel are as thick as thieves. And neither minds being bothered in the least. So Mr McFee can go straight ahead with his queries. It would be nice if all these great heads rubbing together produced the goods in spelling. Maybe they will. Everyone here thought McF[ee] was in Dents gloves not Lewis' line of business at all. You see what delusions we labour under.

No exaggeration about O[liver]'s I.Q. by the way. Whenever I go anywhere e.g. in Toronto I'm met by people who hail me as the mother of the highest I.Q. in Ontario. What gossips these psychologists are (not L[ionel] or me). O was demonstrated at the Univ[versity] as a kind of pet monkey with a prodigious IQ when we first came here. In Philadelphia they made the same astonishing discovery all on their own too. I forgot I'd told you – I thought it was E.D. only. Never meant to bother you on the subject let alone the incredible McFee. Did you get the record?

Love M

PS Of course we don't have blackouts. I suppose we're further from the Pacific than we are from you! It would be the hell of a nuisance if we had to. I have no curtains in the making.

I don't know <u>why</u> B wants to return the tooth. His must have bust en route. His teeth are passed okay but I may spend some of the £10 on further private investigation later on.

The comment "came over with Winston" referred to Winston Churchill's participation in the Arcadia (First Washington) Conference on war planning in Washington, DC, from 24 December 1941 to 14 January 1942.

"Coffee pot" is a child's game for several people in which one player must find the word chosen by the others and does so by asking questions such as "Is the coffee pot larger than a bread basket?"

"Ball head" and "car-board": By "ball head" Ben may have meant "bullet" and certainly he meant "cupboard" for "car-board," which approximates to how cupboard is often pronounced in England.

As to "started on the thyroid," Ben would be eleven on 22 May 1942, and the advent of puberty could be expected. The thyroid (iodine) pills he took were believed to promote the onset of puberty.

"The present from the Lt. Col. whatnot, amounting to £10 ($48), as a later passage in the letter shows, was patently an illicit transfer of funds from Lowis Barman to the Penroses, delivered by an unidentified military officer.

"Montreal and the Flanagans" refers to Ben's experiences in the summer of 1941, discussed in the previous chapter.

Dr Secord, who is otherwise unidentified, was most likely a faculty member at the University of Michigan, in Ann Arbor.

The "oboe account" is the first mention of Ben's oboe, an instrument he played into late adolescence.

As to "$12 a month," which amounted, with the pound sterling worth $4.38, to about £3 a month, the British chancellor of the Exchequer, Sir Kingsley Wood, announced in the House of Commons on 8 January 1942 that from 1 January, sums not exceeding £3 a month could be remitted for the support of a child evacuee under the age of sixteen at the time of evacuation. The remittances were be handled by the CORB, which would make a register of all children involved.[1]

The "Deputy Minister of Health" was Bernard Thomas McGhie (1889–1945), a medical doctor who spent most of his career in the health services of Ontario, rising to be deputy minister of health and hospitals in 1935.

Mr McFee's identity is unclear beyond his expertise in speech and writing problems.

By "Lionel's racket here," Margaret Penrose meant, using a British slang term, his business or occupation.

The identity of "Miss Lewis" is unclear beyond what this letter states.

"Dents" are a firm of British glove makers, established in 1777, suppliers to the royal family and the upper classes.

The "astonishing discovery" in Philadelphia regarding Oliver's IQ was during the three months that the Penrose family spent in that city in 1939, prior to the move to London.

"E.D." was a variant name for Edith Spencer, Ben's grandmother.

---

1 Overseas Evacuation Remittances website, and see the article "British Board Keeps Watch Over Children Sent to Canada," *Windsor Daily Star*, 28 January 1942, reporting on the British government's authorization of the monthly payments.

*"Blackout," the covering of all windows and other sources of light, was not gen-
erally imposed on Canadians, but there were some practice blackout nights.*
By "the Pacific" Margaret Penrose was referencing the war with Japan.

Margaret's long letter contains much that merits comment. The sense of frus-
tration evident in her writing may have been intensified, if not caused, by the
severe and prolonged winter weather. Denied most outdoor activities, the residents in what was, given their number, quite a small house must have felt claus-
trophobic and on edge. The house's furnace, probably ancient and not well
maintained, would have had difficulty in keeping the rooms heated to the accustomed 70° temperature. Margaret's attributing this problem to the fact that
"the gas supply is getting weak" is typical of her quixotic response to the challenges intrinsic to housekeeping, as the following passage describing an encounter with the Penroses in 1968, in Renata Laxova's 1998 appreciation of
Lionel Penrose, shows: "They met us at the door [of their house in England]
and, to our amazement, instead of a handshake they handed us their house
keys, their only set; characteristically, the spare keys were nowhere to be found.
Before they drove off waving breezily, and before we realized what was hap-
pening, Margaret managed to show me how to prevent the hot water system
from exploding and the contents of the linen closet from toppling over and to
give me instructions for Mrs. Lee, the cleaning lady, who was apparently expected to arrive at the house at the beginning of the week."[2]

Margaret's letter refers only briefly on Ben's weight, but a passage in her reminiscences that would seem to relate to this period in Ben's time with the Penroses is much more explicit on the subject: "He exhibited but one feature of
concealed home-sickness" in that "he had a pathologically enormous appetite.
It had to be seen to be believed. He sometimes cried if I was too late with his
second helping before I'd finished serving the others' first helpings." Margaret
tended in her old age to embroider her memories, but the photos of Ben taken
at this time do show him to have been large.

Also writing in January (misdated 1941), Ben recounted the news about the
proposed treatment for his dyslexia in a far more measured fashion and with

2 Renata Laxova, "Lionel Sharples Penrose," n.p. The Soviet invasion of Czechoslovakia in
1968 forced Laxova and her family to seek refuge in Great Britain. Their only previous encounter with Lionel and Margaret had been at a scientific conference.

Figure 4.2 Ben with Roger and Jonathan in the snow, February 1942

far clearer writing than was previously the case. As Margaret noted in her accompanying letter, the improvement was due to Ben's copying, with omissions, the text that she had typed from his dictation.

Ben to His Parents

18th Jan 41 [sic]

Dear Mummy and Daddy,

I hope you are all right. The Deputy Minister of Health have appointed a special lady to come and teach me to spell. She will help me to write with my left hand. I don't know what her name is but Mr Laidlaw has got your letter and he says he is very pleased with it. School has been going fine lately.

Tonight there is to be a concert of Russian music for Russian medical aid. I think we are all going to it. I bought a new hockey stick it is very nice one. On Friday I went to see the "tin soldiers", it was a play put on at Ryerson. It was a good play. I sold some tickets.

Roger is in bed, not very ill but they sent him home from school as he had a temperature and they have scarlet fever in his class. I hope he will be up soon. Last week it was 10 below 0 zero. Pussy is always meowing to go out but it is too cold for her. We got Jonathan's card it was very nice. Aunt Orion sent me a toy cannon for the New Year. The oboe has been coming on very VERY well lately. I sell a ticket for the tin soldiers.

Love from Benjamin

"Russian medical aid" was one of the fund-raising events on behalf of the Russians that were frequently held in Great Britain and Canada following the German invasion of the Soviet Union in June 1941.

The play "tin soldiers" was possibly based on one of the several show pieces inspired by Leon Jessel's 1897 composition "The March of the Tin Soldiers."

Margaret Penrose to Penelope Barman

19th Jan 1941 [sic]

Dear Penelope

Thanks the cable – it was sent to <u>Ottawa</u>! by mistake for some reason, so we had to have it forwarded. Glad you got the record. (I suggest you using telegraph address Penrose 1000 Wellington, London Ont just as short as phone & clearer – yours is more cumbersome) I shall be interested to hear your comments.

As B. tells you a Special Lady has been appointed to coach B in spelling by the D[eputy] Minister of Health – due to Mr McFee's letter & Lionel's pressure at the time. The letter from McF arrived. B is <u>very</u> excited at the prospect. She will have time to give to the subject. Apparently the powers that be think it's a good idea to go on trying L. hand. Personally I think that the stimulus of trying something new was what bucked him up at first to make an extra effort – now he is lapsing again. However, nothing will induce him to use his R. hand at home so lets hope the word blindness <u>is</u> unilateral. This letter of his is extracts from a <u>long</u> one I typed to his dictation – but he got bored with copying it out & missed out all the bits I thought you would like best! Still – it's <u>his</u> letter and he will do it laboriously with his left.

Much love BM

The reference "got the record" must be to the phonograph record, which I remember arriving one morning after my father had left for work, which he did very early to get to his office in London. My brother Jonathan and I lay on our parents' bed while our mother played the record. It boomed out "Hallo Pa! Hallo Ma!" and went on with words no longer remembered. Penelope, although she knew it was only a wax recording, could not resist playing it two more times, with the result that Lowis, on his return, listened to a very faint and faulty version.

"Bor" may have been a childhood nickname.

The following lengthy letter shows Margaret Penrose at her most insightful, and it attests to her care and affection for Ben. It marks the moment when she seems to have accepted that Ben's dyslexia was not susceptible to easy correction and that she had neither the ability nor the patience to undertake the task. Clearly, this distancing had its effect on Ben, who sought, as the postscript to the letter shows, reassurance as to Margaret's concern for him.

Margaret Penrose to Penelope Barman
I

1000 Wellington
London Ont   27th Jan 1942

My dear Penelope
    This letter is in response to your no I – it may be about my 3rd or 4th this year. I can't just recollect. Anyway it will be the first that I post after I reached the momentous age of 41! I never congratulated you on reaching your 4th decade did I? But for all I know you may be coyer about your middle age than I am – I'm still at the stage of always wanting to know how old everyone is & being the first to impart the proud information about my own years. Maybe that's because I fondly imagine I look less. But by now I probably no

longer do. Anyway – cheer up – you'll never catch me up even after I've pre-deceased you. Now let us leave the peroration.

Lionel has written out the Water Music (Handel's) from memory (as we can't get the score) & Oliver, Roger & Jonathan are playing it & going to make a record to send to the grandparents. Lionel has had all the hard work as there are many things J can't play as 2ⁿᵈ fiddle. Benny is the <u>conductor</u> – takes after Uncle Adrian Boult. B fancies himself enormously as conductor & says he'd prefer to be like <u>Sir</u> Adrian than Mr Metropoulis (conductor of American radio orchestra) because it is grander. His Boult blood coming out I suppose. Lionel tried very hard to embody Benny's oboe into the program but I regretfully have to inform you, that although B says he is "getting on <u>very</u> well" (etc etc) & although there is a note on it somewhere that he <u>says</u> he can play – none of us have so far been able to detect which it is! It is true that he can make a double bray – with the "ee" & the "aw" at different pitches – but these are utterly inconsistent & therefore would almost certainly ruin the recording of this masterpiece. Mr Palmer (the teacher) when telephoned to is quite unhelpful although he generally marks B "excellent" each lesson & therefore can hardly be disappointed with his progress. B is completely satis-fied himself & very happy about it (except on the days when he asks whether he "may change to the 'cello"!) But as he almost never practices he has hardly given himself a chance at the oboe yet. I hope it won't prove too difficult for him & that his enthusiasm will persist. Incidentally I rather fear the "word blindness" applies also to naming the notes in music. I taught them to him before he began learning the instrument but they get wiped off the slate completely like the spelling (overnight) & he now has the cheek to tell me that they are <u>different</u> for the oboe! As I can't play that instrument he won't take my word for the names of the notes on the page. However, when possi-ble I leave him severely alone in this matter as I do in the spelling (since September). Miss Dunstan (local speech specialist) came to see me & B the other day at the request of the D[eputy] Minister of Health (result of McFee's letter). Of course I knew her before and she kept apologising to me for mak-ing suggestions – as she knew less about it all than I did etc etc. But I <u>did</u> hope that she would be helpful though I really <u>hadn't</u> been worrying). I think she may find someone to help B. write his letters to you. I would rather they were <u>not</u> done through me as at present – he very likely spells so queerly as reaction to the home situation via my humble self (see how he stammered on your record!) And I have bullied him a lot in the <u>past</u> to try & get through to him on the spelling subject. Miss Dunstan (a very busy school teacher with <u>no</u> free time) said I was never to mention the subject of spelling to him again which oddly enough was a very course I had adopted since he came back from Montreal. (I hope you have noticed the resulting improvement in his letters. She <u>likes</u> the left-handed notion, so does Benny. I'm no longer so sure myself. I think it possible B may be better at school than he is in his letters (though his report would hardly imply this!) Anyway, I hope she will find someone – (she had a woman in mind) – to help with the <u>letters</u>. Then I shan't feel in any way responsible. I am <u>well</u> aware of the fact that he uses his deficiency in this respect to draw my (for good or for bad) attention to himself. For example, he always gets between me & the stove when I am cook & into the essential doorway when I am parlour maid (with 2 red hot dishes) for the same reason. That's why I feel the spelling subject should be tackled by <u>outsiders</u>. Don't you agree?

Much love Margaret

PS If I get interested in a conversation with Lionel, B shakes me by the shoulder to ask if I want him to cut me bread etc. which he would never <u>think</u> of otherwise. In fact he displays the normal reactions of a displanted child – trying to get the maximum attention – he'd rather be nagged than neglected. You know it all as well as I do. But thus he keeps perfectly <u>happy</u>.

In reference to her "age of 41," Margaret was almost exactly eleven months older than Ben's mother, who was born on 30 December 1901.

The "Water Music" was composed by Georg Friedrich Handel in 1715. Containing three suites, it remains a central component of British cultural identity.

"Sir Adrian Boult," Ben's first cousin, not his uncle, had received his knighthood in 1937.

"Mr Metropoulis" refers to Dimitri Metropoulus (1896–1960), the principal conductor from 1937 to 1949 of the Minneapolis Symphony Orchestra, which may have given broadcast concerts on the radio.

"Back from Montreal" in September 1941.

By "displanted child" Margaret Penrose probably meant "uprooted child."

The briefness of and discontinuity in Ben's ensuing letters indicate the tensions and anxieties that he was experiencing. From January 1942, he began to number his letters, copying Margaret's system.

Ben to His Parents
I

[27 January 1942]

Dear Mummy and Daddy,

Hope you are all right. In the next room the children are playing the water muice ["music" added by Margaret]. I have to go to the dentist on the 30th. In the music I conducted it. I am going to number my letters too. I like bening ast [asked] questions.

Love from Benjamin

[Added by Margaret:]

"But can't be persuaded to answer them! MP"

The following letter reveals, with much honesty on Margaret Penrose's part, the tensions and complexities in the relationship between her and Ben. The letter also notes the entry into Ben's life of Mrs Elsie Hart, who would be a calming and reassuring influence.

Margaret Penrose to Penelope Barman

1000 Wellington
London Ont

This is My letter II, your number II hasn't come yet.

Sat. 7th Feb. 1942

My dear Penelope,

Benjamin is away for the day with his new – shall I call her "patron"? Her name is Mrs Hart & she lives at 68 Byron Ave. She was recommended to me by Miss Dunstan the local psychologist & speech specialist. Miss D says she

(Mrs H.) is one of her <u>best mothers</u>. Miss D has taught 3 of her sons being a schoolteacher at Victoria School. [Psychology is Miss D's sideline.] Mrs Hart has 2 big boys in the army and R.A.F. – overseas I think. She is left with a boy of nine in grade V at Victoria School. (B is in grade V too.). So it was thought that they might spell etc together. My Roger is in grade VI & Jonathan in IV so I have no means of combining them. Also I think she may be able to give B. that little bit of extra petting & attendance that he lacks from me as I have 4 boys all about his age, & I just <u>have</u> to divide my attention between them – which B not unnaturally resents (being so far from his own home) so we are trying this experiment.

Miss D thinks B. may very well do some of his most atrocious spelling howlers (in his letters home etc) just to attract my attention to himself! Maybe if she is write (see – it's getting me too!!) So <u>you</u> will probably be the first to discover. I sent him off this morning with 2 stamped and addressed envelopes – one to you & one to Lowis' friend Mr Blackmorestone/burn at Detroit. [Added in the margin: Mr Blackmore/stone/burn enclosed 3 lovely photos of you & Jon & Rod. You look exactly like your mamma did 30 yrs ago. Ben was sure it was a photo of <u>himself</u> and Rod (years ago) and said he remembered it being taken!! Finally he agreed it must be Jon & not his former self.] I don't want to see the contents of either & hope he will post them on the way home. B came back 7 pm from the Harts – pleased as punch (as usual) & full of complimentary remarks about Hart <u>food</u>. The letters were written & posted. Next time I will address a letter to his girlfriend Shirley whatever-she-was-called (Bowman) that you've told me he was to write to. I just can't get him to write to anyone besides you. His mouldy little scrawls take hours & hours of nagging to produce. He just <u>loves</u> being nagged (did you know that?). I discovered it years ago but I can't find any other method of getting him to do anything. Can you? I'm sure he'll be a henpecked husband some day. Probably Mrs Hart will. She is full of promise at the moment & invited B for the whole of today & tomorrow too. My Roger will go on strike as they (B & R) are thick as thieves – possibly (???) too thick to be healthy –. One can hardly separate them with a saw! Then Mrs Hart says when it is warmer she will take B out for weekends at their farm if he hits it off with her little boy. I suppose that remains to be seen. Anyway if she is any good I propose to remunerate her from the allowance that the authorities now permit you to send him. I think you would wish this to be done would you? If I can find it I will enclose a newspaper cutting on this subject in case it is new to you. Lionel says there is some question being raised about richer parents sending more (to Ottawa) so as to help out the poorer parents of evacuees. But I've heard no more of that. Alfred Braithwaite wrote to L and asked if we wished any steps to be taken about it by him, but L said to wait until you got in touch with him (or us) yourselves.

The money that came from Toronto has proved most useful & has brought the right kind of winter trousers, windbreaker jacket (zippered front) ice hockey stick & "puck," several oboe reeds, more roller skates, & many items such as galoshes that are essential. About ½ is still left over for future requirements. It certainly came in handy.

I sent B out with $5 (over £1) yesterday to get the oboe reeds, roller skates & galoshes. He came back glowing with excitement – "Oh Margaret, good news, good news, for forty cents I can order a song called 'but I've never seen an elephant fly'" – M. "how lovely – did you get it?" B "no" M "what did you get?" B "I got the galoshes (rubbers)" M "what about the roller skates?" B "Oh I forgot" (his favourite phrase) B "Oh I think I left my arithmetic book in the shoe shop" So I went round this afternoon (in a snowstorm) picking up the bits – i.e. arithmetic book & oboe & buying roller skates for him (before steel is forbidden to be sold by the govt in March)

Note on the side: On returning from the Harts B settled down with a <u>book</u> – "Huckleberry Finn" & began to read it. He is still at it this morning (Sun) & must have read nearly half of it. It is the first prose book he has read since he has been here. I am very pleased. Can it be Hart influence? On examination he has read it to p. 48. But – he is really engrossed.

Last Sat. B went down town with me and J to go to the movies. While J & I were looking at the queue speculating B ran off saying "it's not a good movie so I won't go – I'm shopping!" Later J & I met him accidentally in a large departmental store (like a small Harrods) raptly gazing at the ladies underwear & haberdashery! (B is an ardent "window shopper") He said he was going home. So J & I went to the movie, the crowd having cleared off & saw Laurel & Hardy. We went home – B wasn't back! An hour later L & I had to go out to dinner, so I felt bound to telephone the police — just to enquire if he'd been found wandering. The policeman said "Oh don't worry, lady. I know them kids – they go into the movie & see the programme over 3 times." So L and I went out. Later O telephoned & said B was back – about 8 pm. When I asked him next morning what movie he had been to he said "Oh you know, that fat man & that thin man, I didn't know their names." And sure enough he'd been in the same cinema as us – only stayed there much longer. But he likes to feel independent. I quite understand. But it would be a great blessing if he & J would take <u>each other</u> – as they're both movie fans – R & O don't like the pictures much. That would save my wasting so much time!

I was quite overcome on my birthday last week. Apart from having made me (with Roger's help) a wonderful painted macaroni-shell necklace (of <u>vast</u> dimensions) B rushed out in the evening & spent <u>two dollars</u> on me (nearly 10/–). He bought two enormous boxes of chocolate creams & a very expensive box of Parisian powder! I was extremely touched by his generosity. He spent all the Xmas money Mrs Massy Beresford gave him on <u>me</u>! I'm sure I didn't deserve it but it certainly was <u>very</u> sweet of him. Shall I send you the powder? Is it one of the things you are out of?

L has just returned from Toronto (this minute) & says as his first word "how lucky we are to have Benny for our evacuee – the people in Toronto are all having such a <u>terrible</u> time with theirs." & he enumerates a lot of the stories of their youthful atrocities towards their benevolent hosts.

We certainly <u>are</u> lucky. Thank you very much for having sent out such a nice boy. I hope you won't want to disown him when he returns on account of his bad Penrose manners.

Love from M.

I'm trying to borrow a movie camera to make you a film.

The snow is dazzlingly beautiful

We've made a record of the "Water Music" (Handel) & a carol under the baton of (Sir) Adrian B. Barman. I am trying to get 3 copies – (A) goes to my parents, would you like to borrow (B) and send it on to someone else when you've heard it? I will enclose other addresses. If you <u>want</u> you could get it copied to keep for a few shillings but I don't know how good the copies are. For home consumption records need not be unbreakable. More music to follow. (C) we shall keep ourselves.

"Mrs Hart" was Mrs Elsie Alice Hart who, with her husband, Russell John Hart, resided at 68 Byron Street, lying on the west side of the Thames River and so away from the Penroses at Wellington Street. Her three sons were Beverley, Kenneth, and Donald.

"*Victoria School*," *a public school, is situated at 130 Warncliffe Street South, London, virtually next door to Mrs Hart's residence.*

"*Mr Blackmore*" *cannot be identified beyond the information in this letter.*

"*Jon*" *refers to Jonathan, Ben's younger brother.*

As to "*Shirley Bowman*," *Ben had no recollection of her and she cannot be identified.*

"*Too thick to be healthy*" *is a comment typical of the period in its oblique suggestion of possible same sex attraction, a subject that could not be publically discussed and that, not being "normal," was regarded as unhealthy, even among those of "progressive" views.*

"*Alfred Braithwaite*" *was the lawyer to the Penrose family, handling their business affairs.*

"*The money that came from Toronto*" *was most probably the "present" brought by the unidentified lieutenant colonel.*

"*But I've never seen an elephant fly*" *The correct title is "When I See an Elephant Fly," a song from the film* Dumbo.

"*Before steel is forbidden to be sold by the government in March*" *refers to the ban imposed by the Canadian government on the manufacture of all consumer goods requiring the use of steel, which was reserved exclusively for war production.*

Great Guns, *starring Stan Laurel and Oliver Hardy, was released by 20th Century Fox in October 1941.*

"*(nearly 10/-)*" *The English pound was until 1971 divided in twenty shillings, each divided into twelve pence. Ben was therefore spending ten shillings (the symbol for shillings being /-), or half a pound.*

Mrs "*Massy Beresford*" *lived with her three children in Quebec.*

As to Lionel's comment, "*how lucky we are to have Benny for our evacuee – the people in Toronto are all having such a* _terrible_ *time with theirs," a leading study of Canada in the Second World War noted that, "to their credit many Canadians stuck it out with very difficult children. But the public rarely heard the less pleasant stories.*"[3]

The passage in the letter describing Ben's behaviour during the visit to the cinema with Margaret and Jonathan suggests a high degree of tension. Ben's running off and his subsequent wanderings, including seeing the film more than

3 Keshen, *Saints*, 199.

once by himself, suggests that he wished to assert his separate identity and his capacity for independent action. His behaviour also indicates that he was comfortable being by himself in downtown London. What is perhaps surprising is the way in which Margaret reacted to Ben's disappearance. She did no more than telephone the police, whose soothing response apparently satisfied her. She and Lionel had no qualms about keeping their dinner invitation. Margaret was honest in reporting the episode to Penelope but was careful to downplay its significance. The trouble that Ben went to in order to construct a necklace and to buy her two birthday presents suggests that the episode did not spring from any dislike for Margaret.

Enclosed with the above letter was a clipping from the *Windsor Daily Star*, 28 January 1942, entitled "British Board Keeps an Eye on Children in Canada." The article mentions a statement, made on 8 January 1942 in the British House of Commons, regarding the £3 a month remittance discussed above.

If the neater writing in the following letter is any guide, Ben was clearly enjoying and benefiting from the hours he spent each Saturday at Mrs Hart's home.

Ben to His Parents

                              II   February 7 1942

Dear Mummy and Daddy,

I hope you are all right. To day I am over visiting the Harts, they have a little boy Donald and another boy is over here too. It is snowing now, I bought my skates over but it [is] not good. "I mean the ice!" I came over in a bus. I got the snaps from Mr Blackstone and sent him a letter.

                              Love from Benjamin

"Another boy" may have been Jim Collier, mentioned in Bev Hart's letter to Lowis and Penelope Barman of 18 October 1942.

"Mr Blackstone," who is also mentioned in Margaret Penrose's letter of 7 February 1942, had, on a recent visit to England, taken photographs of Ben's mother and his younger brothers.

In the next letter (annotated by Penelope Barman "undated but got Feb. 14 42"), Ben used a hand-drawn image of an eye for *I*, of a letter for *letter*, of a house for *house*, and of a heart to refer to members of the Hart family. Elsie Hart's note at the end of the letter gave the explanation: "I trust you will be able to decipher the above. He has sent me a valentine along the same line thus the idea. He thinks of things to tell you but feels that he is repeating the same, but I told him Mummie loves to hear things repeated. I trust Benjamin has had a happy day with us and hope to see him again soon."

Ben to His Parents

2   Undated [February 1942]

Mummy and Daddy

[eye] got your [letter] it was very nice and Jonathan's [letter] too. [eye] came on the bus this morning to [heart]'s and skated and had lunch at a friends [house]. Donald [heart] and [eye] went to a show the Shadow and we liked it and walked [house]. [eye] hope [eye] will see you soon.

Love from Benjamin

"The Shadow" refers to the fifteen-part series of films with that title, produced by Columbia Pictures in 1940, and based on the pulp novels of the same name.

The following letter, which illustrates Margaret's Penrose's character, her handling of Ben, his attitude to her, and her running of the Penrose household is unusual in that it contains a direct reference to the course of the war – the loss of Singapore to the Japanese in February 1942. The letter also mentions that Margaret was providing "safe keeping" for Penelope's eldest son, a topic not otherwise alluded to in her correspondence.

Margaret Penrose to Penelope Barman

No III   1000 Wellington, London, Ont, Can
18th Feb. 1942

My dear Penelope,

This numbering business is going to show up one or other of us as less energetic than the other! Here is my letter III in answer to your (2) of Jan 14.

I began numbering on my birthday – 28th Jan at about which time your (I) arrived.

On the side of the page: B sent a valentine to Shirley [Bowman]. Will that do? He received dozens himself & said – "do you know I think some of the girls are beginning to love me – they stare at me so much."

As a matter of fact I've been meaning to send you the results of B's snap shooting during the past 12 months or so! Here it is. I had to take the last 3 myself (on the skating rink that we've made) and take them to be developed (he couldn't be bothered) & for a week I reminded him to fetch them back from the chemist – but he always had some more interesting occupation so in the end I trudged out in the slush & got them myself. They're not much to write home about, but still.

I'm trying to get a movie of them all (particularly B), but the movie camera I borrowed has refused to work each time it's been sunny. (& I've collected all the right people together). At other times it works like a dream of course! The Water Music record (B conducting) is lovely but the copies I got made are awful. Lionel is trying out another copy and found it was better with a fibre needle & not the kind I sent. I've sent one to my parents & will send them the original by the next mail. I wish you'd tell them if you're writing. Posts are so uncertain. Before that I will try to get better copies. If this proves impossible they (my parents) will have to keep the original. I don't think the copies are worth sending to you. I wanted to have several in case the original got sunk as it well may with this Scharnhorst & Gneisenau at large in the Atlantic. But the records are not easy to reproduce it seems.

The electrical set & the penknife arrived at Xmas & were enormously appreciated. The Williams-Ellis book was read from cover to cover by Roger & adored. The jun. weekend book they already had so I gave it to someone else.

Don't worry about B's letter writing. I don't supervise it any more but am leaving it entirely to Mrs Hart – who has him over on Saturdays. I understand she wrote to you. The idea is that he's spelling badly just to get my attention! (Psychological-view-set-in-motion – by Mr McFee – via – Minister of Health – & – his retinue!) Between you & me & the gatepost I think that theory is all "my eye" but still. I picked up one of B's school books yesterday – not meant for my inspection – & saw a short sentence (the only one in it) just stinking with spelling howlers as for example "perpers" (for purpose) &

"acidetat" (for accidental) and ending triumphantly with – "the boy was maid to pay a fin" – the latter subsequently corrected to – "a find". Personally I accept no responsibility moral, psychological or otherwise for it but I say nothing whatever to him about spelling. So they can let their theory have its way for the time being. When he does sums – copied out of his arithmetic book it is like this; –

Q. "How much of the money would he need?"

A. "He wood need all the munny"

Q. "How many dollars?"

A. "100 dolers" etc. etc. etc. No exaggeration! And really I never have anything to do with any of his schoolwork on principle.

But I admit that he does spend a large part of his time at home trying to attract my attention in case I should take any interest in one of the other boys for a moment. The spelling was all in with his scheme of attention-fishing when I was helping him with it but now I'm not – so the spelling is off that programme. The other day he had quite a tantrum when I refused to hear his spelling & suggested that Roger should. "It's no use, it's all no use" he repeated over and over again amid floods of tears until eventually I inevitably gave way & heard him, whereupon he became as cheerful as a lark. Funny thing little boys. Yours is a perfectly nice one so don't worry.

I hope Singapore doesn't postpone your reunion ad infinitum. It can hardly have speeded things up. Maybe there's going to be more trouble in western Europe soon too. You will be glad to have one of your brood in comparatively safe keeping though I would wager no one would send out a second child with the end so far beyond the horizon. Ah me! But I don't talk war to you.

Your Jonathan's letter was lovely. Mine write quite fluently too once they've been stimulated to start. Luckily I rarely have to. Yes – I've got the complete works of Proust too (came at Christmas) but I never had time to settle down to them so far. Always seem to find something more active to do. For instance now I must go and cook supper & stop drivelling.

Sorry not to be able to comply with your suggestion to send B "up to his room to be alone for a time" – he & Roger sleep downstairs in the sunroom which is also the playroom & opens out of the dining room. The noise & the mess in there has to be heard to be seen to be believed! Only a glass door

separates that room from everyone else & the intercommunication is unsev-
erable. I'm the one that retires to the upstairs bedroom for peace & solitude –
as now! But we rub along happily enough. We enjoy it all.

Love – M

*"Snap-shooting" refers to the taking of photographs, which were often during this
period termed "snaps." Six photographs, all stamped "30," have survived. The proposed film was obviously quite separate from Ben's photographs.*

*Mary Annabel Nassau Williams-Ellis (1894–1984), pen name "Amabel Williams-
Ellis," was born Mary Annabel Strachey and married the architect Clough
Williams-Ellis. I have not been able to identify the book sent.*

The "weekend book" probably refers to Francis Meynell, The Weekend Book
*(1922), which was a compilation of stories, poems, games, and drink and food
recipes designed for those from the middle class who spent weekends in a countryside cottage.*

*"Scharnhorst and Gneisenau" refers to two German battle cruisers, launched in
1936 and engaged in commerce raiding early in 1941 before withdrawing to Brest
harbour in northwestern France. Exposed to constant British air attack, the two
ships left Brest on 11 February 1942 and made a dash through the English Channel
and North Sea to Kiel, Germany, successfully evading the British Navy.*

*"Singapore" referred to what Winston Churchill termed "the worst disaster" of
the Second World War. On 8 December 1941, conterminous with their attack on
Pearl Harbor in the Hawaiian Islands, the Japanese invaded Malaya and advanced
rapidly on Singapore, then a British possession, which surrendered on 15 February
1942.*

There is no information on what was "the reunion" attended by Penelope.

*"The complete works of Proust" refer almost certainly to the seven-volume trans-
lation by Charles K. Scott Moncrieff (1891–1930) of Marcel Proust,* À la recherche
du temps perdu. *Penelope Barman possessed this translation, bound in light blue.*

Included in the envelope containing the above letter are seven photographs,
four taken by Ben during his time with the Flanagans (two of a combine har-
vester and two of a picnic), and three of Ben and the Penrose sons in the snow.

The following letters attest to Ben's continued difficulty in writing and the
undiminished admiration felt by ordinary Canadians for the British people in
the fight against Germany.

Ben to His Parents, and Mrs Elsie Hart to Penelope Barman

3

Feb 21 [1942]

Dear mummie and Daddy

I am having a nice time to day at the Harts. I am now playing "cow-boys." Oliver and I were tobagong it was great fun rushing down the hill. We did it in the morning.

Love from Benjamin

(over)

Dear Mrs Barman; –

Saturday early evening and a beautiful winter's night. Benjamin had tea with us and now in living room playing before leaving for home. I said "Benjamin your letter is rather short," but he says it is the same old thing to tell.

We think you a brave people and our hardships are very few – but we are willing to sacrifice. Pardon rush – and your son is certainly a nice little fellow. Asks me if he can help – sometime I'll let him.

Yours sincerely E. Hart

The progress finally being made in Ben's writing and his increasing command of language is patent in his next letter.

Ben to His Parents

4

1,000 Wellington Wed. Feb. 26\¹⁹42

Dear Mummy and Daddy

I am, haveing a very nice time here. I am writing in the dark. may I please have a watch for my birthday. Last Monday at school we had a sleigh ride. A sleigh is a big sleigh with to horses to pul it along the rode.

Love from Benjamin

That Margaret Penrose led a busy life outside the home is apparent from the following letter, written on the back of a used chess scoring sheet headed "Warner Hall Chess Club London Ont." The hall was part of the Bishop Cronyn Memorial Church in London.

The following letter contains a final reference to Ben using his left hand to write.

Figure 4.3 Margaret, her sons, and Ben with a snowman, late winter 1941–42

Margaret Penrose to Penelope Barman

IV   1000 Wellington
                                      26th Feb [1942]

My dear Penelope

I'm a wallflower tonight at the chess club – odd man out. So I write. Your III arrived the day after I sent my III. I was much amused on the subject of Canadian accents! <u>Can</u> my speech have altered so greatly that you take it for granted that I am "a lady" tipped off with questions to ask B? Do you imagine that I could possibly have found someone to take over that task? It was most difficult to know when to chip in & when to let him amble on but I don't see how anyone but me could have done it. Anyhow <u>me</u> it was! I had a chat with Malcolm MacDonald today while he received the "freedom of the city." He hailed me by my Xtian name. So I can't have changed all that.

Now I've my games of chess & so have Oliver & Lionel. A night & a morning have again slipped by with sleep & charring. Once more I am over the chessboard for the afternoon. What a lazy life I lead! And you pity me for overwork!! Benny has been having quite a pleasant life. His class was taken for a sleigh ride – horses & big sleigh the other day & came back glowing & full of hot tomato soup. We took him & J. & R. to an evening chamber music concert – on Saturday. He seemed to enjoy it particularly the clarinet. B forgot his oboe at yesterday's lesson & on his report card was caustically written "remember instrument next time." He seems to be having fun at the Harts, but they tell me his letter writing is a great trouble to him. He has gone back to his R. hand but they may be going to try him with his L. again at the Harts. He <u>was</u> so keen but forgot when he first went to the Harts. This one he wrote on his own entirely when I was out (& I think in bed in the dark!).

Do what you think best of course. But I'm not <u>madly</u> enthusiastic about you sending on my recent letters to you. She gets as many as you do & often very much the same (with certain intentional differences!)

Love from Margaret   P.T.O.

Benny's marks in an arithmetic test that he has just brought home appear to be <u>92</u>.

Class average 80%.

Junior "averag" 74

"Natness" = Neat (I copy what he wrote) It means little to me.

If my parents do send you one of the <u>copies</u> of the "orchestra" record, play very <u>slowly</u> (if your machine will) with a <u>fibre</u> needle. The original is okay but the copies were made on a gramophone that revolves too fast so played at ordinary speed they squeak like mice. The original is just lovely, I think, I sent that off yesterday. But the copies are sure to arrive and the original I sent 10 days ago.

As to the "chess club," all the Penroses save Roger were chess fanatics, Lionel being an expert on the "end game." Jonathan, the youngest son, learned chess at the age of four, was British youth champion at the age of fourteen, and won the British chess championship ten times.

"Can my speech have altered so greatly" indicates that Margaret and Ben had taken part in a radio broadcast, either live or recorded, for transmission to England. Some of these broadcasts involved live exchanges between individual children and their parents or guardians. Ben cannot recall any specifics about the broadcast. Obviously Penelope had not recognized Margaret's voice.

"Malcolm MacDonald" (1901–81) was the son of Ramsay MacDonald, who had been prime minister of Great Britain in the 1920s and 1930s. He served as an MP and as a minister, holding three different portfolios, before serving from 1940 to 1946 as British high commissioner in Ottawa.

"You sending on my letters" indicates that, in a recent letter, Penelope had suggested that she send on Margaret's letters to her to Sonia Leathes, Margaret's mother.

The anxieties and tensions felt by both Margaret and Ben, evident from her letters at the start of 1942, had considerably diminished, as the remark in her missive of 18 February shows "we rub along happily enough." The severe weather in southwestern Ontario that during the winter of 1941–42 limited indoor activity probably exacerbated, even if it did not create, the tautness evident in the atmosphere at 1000 Wellington Street. Perhaps the root cause for the tensions between war guest and "foster mother" lay in Ben's entering a new stage in the life cycle, one that required both assertion of a separate identity and rejection of dependence. The days that Ben spent at the Harts provided him with both separate space and a life on his own, and Margaret's disquiet about his writing and spelling, even if not openly expressed, was not a positive factor in their relationship.

5

Beginning to Become a Good Canadian, March 1942

Daddy I do say gas and street-car, I suppose I'm beginning to become
a good Canadian.
~Ben Barman to his parents, March 1942

Milder weather, as the end of winter approached, made outdoor activities possible and helped diminish the anxieties and tensions at 1000 Wellington Street. A set of photographs taken at this time, showing Ben and the Penroses next to a snowman, attests to the improving weather. What also helped was the beneficial influence of Ben's Grade 5 teacher. All his teachers at Ryerson School were kind and patient, Ben recalls, but it was John Laidlaw (Fig. 6.2) who, through his deft handling of Ben and his willingness to coach him outside of school hours, was responsible for a dramatic improvement in his writing and spelling. Ben mentions his help in his letter to his parents from March 1942.

Ben to His Parents

5   1,000 Wellington Mar. 2/42

Dear Mummy and Daddy,
  I got your letter to-day. I went to a concert at Central School Friday night. I'm visiting Mr. Laidlaw to-night at Huron College. I'm going to the college every Monday night to write my letter.

Love to all,
Benjamin

The following very long letter from Margaret Penrose provides a spontaneous description of and extremely revealing insight into the different personalities of the Penrose family and their style of life.

Margaret Penrose to Penelope Barman

5·   1,000 Wellington St
                                          London. Ont
                                          3rd March 1942

My dear Penelope,

A thousand thanks for "Cambridge Evacuation Survey." Afraid you had the hell of a time getting hold of a copy. I find it most interesting. Do tell my mamma are how easy it is to send parcels that one packs & posts <u>oneself</u>. No questions asked either end are they? If parcel comes from a shop fusses are made & even I have to go to the Customs House. <u>Bridge Book</u> just arrived too. From ma? Many thanks for posting.

Your letter number IV (Jan 28) arrived as I returned from posting mine. This seems to be the inevitable rule – a sure way of getting a letter from you is to post one to you. My 4 enclosed B's <u>first unsolicited</u> letter to you!!! Mine was written on a chess scoring sheet that should place them – 26th B has had airmail letter dated Feb 10 ard yesterday with ordinary Eng. mail of the same date.

Yesterday I had B's Mrs Hart to tea. She is very nice. But she is (not unnaturally) so wrapped up in her overseas boys that I found it hard to get her to concentrate her attention on B – the matter in hand! Mr Laidlaw came in to tea too later & that was fine. He said he had been in touch with Miss Dunston the psychologist about B's spelling and it was decided that they should let the matter drop altogether because drilling & nagging & low marking are obviously useless & it was clearly a psychological block of some sort which might clear up as a result of neglect. Anyway, as Mr L aptly put it, that was "much the <u>easiest</u> treatment" for him to administer. But I raised the question of letter writing & Mr L <u>offered</u> to take B every Monday evening & help him with that & give him some individual attention. This seems to be in direct contradiction to what he had decided with Miss Dunston, but I thought it an opportunity to be seized upon nevertheless! It needn't be all (or any of it) letter-writing but it might well stimulate B. to take an <u>interest</u> in spelling & writing the lack of which (as Mr L admits) is obviously one of the reasons for B's failures in this respect. So last night at 6.30 B went off to Huron (theological) college where Mr L resides, and had a hell of a good time with "the boys" there. He came home glowing with pride & glory at about 9 PM. This episode is to be repeated of a Monday till one or other of the parties concerned gets bored. I believe a letter was dispatched yesterday. You will know more of the result on B's calligraphy than I shall. Do let me know which scheme produces the best results. I must say I think Mr L has turned out trumps. Can you imagine an English elementary school teacher taking so much trouble? I didn't even offer him a sou for the v. simple reason that our banking account has just gone below the zero mark. (L[ionel]. Bought 6 Victory Bonds the other day when I wasn't looking) and unless and until some more cash wafts our way I can't even pay the dentist's bill or the music teachers'. I've never been in such a state before. It is most mortifying. But I suppose it's all in a good cause – Victory Bonds bought on an overdraft at least blow good to the <u>bank</u> in the way of interest I presume. [I've never had an overdraft before] So far it is only £2 & I'm paying household expenses out of Lionel's last month's refunded railway fares. So I may be able to last out a few more days by which time L. may have remembered to pay in his monthly salary cheque which should nearly keep us for the rest of the month if there are no more extras.

For goodness sake don't send this letter on to mamma or she'd have 50 fits. She is so used to our being bloated millionaires. And so, alas, are we (or at least is Lionel – or he wouldn't be so lavish with his V. Bonds). It is no use my earning or even stinting & saving, if every time there is a tiny surplus L goes & buys a bond (repayable in 1952). Forgive this waffling – as you say you do – I just babble whenever is passing through my mind. It is not really of the slightest consequence. Probably by tomorrow L. will have sold a railway share (we have some) & we shall all be on top of our form till we've used it up. It's a funny life.

Anyway Mrs Hart is a dear & is having B. round regularly to spend Saturdays with her Don (age 9) but in future won't bother with <u>letters.</u> So I don't think one need feel that one is presuming on her kindness in any way. B quite

likes going & I quite like having our boys to ourselves for one day in the
week. It seems to brighten one up in the way. The only trouble is that B. is so
terrified of missing anything that's likely to be going on here that it's quite
pathetic. Once L. took O R and J to a biological exhibition at the University –
(that happened to be on a Sat afternoon) –& B was quite green with jealousy
though he & Don had been to a movie (so Jonathan was jealous of <u>them</u>!).
B even goes the length of asking what we have for Sat. midday dinner & since
(2 weeks ago) it was chicken that he missed, thus he was so envious that I
had this week to cook a special chicken for him on <u>Monday</u> (washing day!)
& (particular request) make BREAD SAUCE. No – I'm not spoiling B. It happened that the farmer left a chicken here that I had not ordered & since
I don't see Farmer "George" again for a week & don't know where he lives
I had no means of discovering who really had ordered the bird. I thought it
wisest to cook same, please B & kill two chickies with one stone.

Lionel has just been urgently re-invited to Ann Arbor. The substitute was
a failure (since the job was made for L.) and the substitute has already done a
bunk. But I imagine the offer will have to be refused once more. I think one
would feel even less financially secure in the U.S.A. then here – even on a
larger salary. We settled into our own niche here & L seems to like his work &
I enjoy my chess – (although I am suffering from a surfeit of it at the moment & am quite off my game.) This seems to be such a wonderful place for
children & we have all got a selection of friends that we like. I don't know I'm
sure. It is really quite easy to settle into a new place isn't it? – until one has
grown quite old. We always seem to make more friends than we have time for
& lead a round of social life of an evening what with politics & bridge &
chatter & chess. I am happy almost anywhere. But this city is quite a satisfactory place to live in. And surely I don't complain.

As regards B's balls I shan't bother with the clinic for the present. Operations are not advisable & there could be no possible object in <u>our</u> embarking
on such a drastic line of action with <u>your</u> child. Endocrines of that nature are
not very effective as far as I can make out. If you take them by the mouth
they are not absorbed. Thyroid is the only endocrine that functions well if
swallowed & it may help. He takes ¼ grain daily not enough? But I do think
that probably the trouble is basically lack of proper development in the "private" part of his anatomy. He is getting to look quite like a textbook picture

of a case of that sort. How does it come about I wonder? – No one knows. So strange that he & Jonathan (excuse me 4 ½ stone = 63 lbs!) should both show signs of the same sort of condition and no one else in the family. Of course I believe it often clears up at puberty. (a stage that Oliver reached at eleven – Did I tell you O now has a girlfriend & dates her for dancing – and so this stage may come early with B too if the climate makes kids develop earlier over here). I shall really have to read the subject up – if I ever have time. Time never seems to crop up these days. Gosh – I have let myself in for slopping out tea to soldiers on a Friday. It is supposed to be so unpatriotic <u>not</u> to. So I have to hire a woman to slop out tea to my family (L. is in Toronto of a Friday). I'd much rather hire the woman to slop out the tea for the soldiers. But that of course would be unpatriotic & incidentally more expensive as the soldiers take 3 hours.

Love M.

[Written on the side of the page:] If the subject of sex ever arises I will of course try to do my duty in instructing B (as you say I must). It is <u>so</u> much easier to do it when (at a much earlier age) they ask questions. <u>Do</u> take my advice and instruct the others good & young. 10+ is such a silly giggly school <u>girly</u> stage. It's so much harder. But probably Roger will tell him all he wants to know. My 3 know all the facts of life thank God, and they seem sensible about it.

The Cambridge Evacuation Survey *(1941) was a wartime study in social welfare and education edited by Susan Sutherland Isaacs (1885–1948), who was a leading social scientist with innovative views about child development.*

"Her boys overseas" were Beverley and Kenneth Hart, both in the military.

"Huron (theological) college" opened in 1863 to train clergy for the Anglican Church. It became a constituent part of the University of Western Ontario, when the latter was created in 1878. The original campus, known as Rough Park, stood quite close to the Penroses' house.

"Victory Bonds" were created, along with War Savings Certificates, by the Canadian government to meet the costs of the war. Bonds were sold in values ranging from $50 to $100,000, with a six- to fourteen-year maturity. The sums raised by nine successive bond campaigns were extremely large.

"Railway share" refers to Lionel Penrose's holding of some Grand Trunk Pacific

shares, according to a financial statement, dating from early 1939, held in the Penrose papers.[1]

"Bread sauce" is made by taking bread and milk, mashing them together, and heating the mixture until it blends. The sauce is poured over chicken or another meat dish.

"Ann Arbor" must refer to an offer to Lionel Penrose of an academic post (presumably permanent) at the University of Michigan, an offer he obviously did not accept.

A "stone" is the equivalent of 14 pounds. The measure was used in Great Britain, until metrification, for human weight.

By "puberty," Margaret clearly meant the onset of the ability to ejaculate sperm.

As to the "subject of sex," sex education for children during the interwar period usually took the form of books given to children by their parents. The subject was not treated in the schools, either public or private (unless the latter were very "progressive").

"Slopping tea" is a reference to the tea parties that were one of the varieties of "wholesome" entertainment that civilians provided during the Second World War for members of the armed services.

If Ben's letter number 5, dated 5 March, had shown a marked improvement, this letter easily surpassed it, being elegantly written – the best so far.

Ben to His Parents

6

1,000 Wellington Street,
London, Ontario,
March 9, 1942.

Dear Mummy and Daddy,

We are having a very bad snowstorm to-night but I managed to come over to Huron to write my letter.

---

1 See the written statement of income not taxed at source for the period 12 April 1938 to 5 January 1939 in the Penrose Papers University College, London, Science Library, Special Collections, 1/15/1.

There was a special movie at the school Friday afternoon but because
I had to take my music lesson Friday afternoon instead of Tuesday I had
to miss it.

On Saturday I wrote a letter to Uncle Ross.

I always look forward to your letters. I hope Jonathan and Roderick
are well.

Love

Benjamin.

In the following long letter, Margaret Penrose provides a vivid portrait of her
personality and her handling of life.

Margaret Penrose to Penelope Barman

6   1000 Wellington Street London Ont Friday 13th March 1942
My dear Penelope,

Your 5 (Savoy hotel airmail) arrived on Tuesday, 10th March, and your
number 4 arrived yesterday by sea mail. Incidentally the books arrived a week
earlier than the letter of the same date – I've often noticed parcels are
quicker. I thanked for those in my last letter. So air is quicker (three weeks) –
(to just over four weeks). I am having a wonderful day to day for a Friday
the 13th.

Lionel and I went to a junk shop to buy an old gramophone turntable to
make a radiogram out of our little radio with – but for a few shillings we
purchased a complete gramophone (clockwork type). It is quite a decorative
piece of furniture with record cabinet etc. Lionel sat up all night with it tin-
kering and oiling and lo and behold to my intense amazement – I now have a
faultless gramophone! One only needs to wind it up 2 or 3 times in an hour
and its tone is as good as an electric one without the "Wurlitzer" effect –
which I never cared for anyway. The Pub[lic] library has a brand new record
collection of 500 records to be hired at a 1d a day and my goodness, I had fun
today. I've forgotten all about the darn war and the very notion of Mozart
and Bach being by birth HUNS seems beyond the bounds of lunacy. I only
have two records today (A) Bach prelude in B Mi (Philadelphia Orchestra)
and the Pastoral Symphony and (B) Mozart andante for flute and ballet

music from "Idomeneo" and I can tell you I had a day – played each side 20 or 30 times and pranced about all over the house waving a dish towel and a potato scraper. It's wonderful to be able to have all the music you want and when you want it – which with me seems to be all the time! I'm just playing a Brandenburg on the radio as I write and it is so maddening to have to keep getting it back into tune and having to put up with its moods and its atmospherics that I look forward to getting back to my gram and my two nice records when this is over. Our radio is a devil. The only thing it can bluster out efficiently is news – and damned bad news at that. I doubt whether I will use it again till the gramophone busts and I've worn out all the library's records and that may not be for ages as I seem to be the only person that patronises this new service and nearly all the records are unplayed so far!

We're having our first dinner party tomorrow and I shall soon have to start preparing for that: I'm going to feed the kids at six and pack them out into the street to roller skate or something (B will be at the Harts don't worry). Then I shall set to work to produce a table worthy of the name for 7.30. I'm glad to say I have someone to wash up. Maybe she'll even take out the dirty plates. You never know. Though that's a thing I've never seen done in this country.

You know I think it's a demoralising thing to be sympathised with. I won't let myself concentrate on the idea of your night at the Savoy. I'm not sure that I'm not better off <u>without</u> someone to take over for me and mercifully mind the kids while I go on the razzle. How awful it must be to come back to the kitchen sink – or isn't it? I'd really far rather have my 10 shilling gramophone and make my own house seem scintillating with music than spend 35/- on a portion of pheasant which is all eaten and over in no time. But then I take it out on the household with bad temper in between whiles which doubtless hurts them more than it does me. Maybe you don't?

I certainly know well what it is like to play snap with a little patient while the dinner burns – I did a lot of that during the measles epidemic 2 yrs ago. That's one of the reasons why I'm all in favour of having a nurse in when they're very ill. You seem to be having a bad time of it this year. Hope you're all better.

Orion <u>wrote</u> (!) to Benjamin a week or so ago! and told him all about the appendices and the measles and the crushed fingers (or was it head?) and what not and all (B answered from the Harts so I can't tell what he said). So she must have thought she had done her bit and could neglect poor Ursula. She certainly has never written to B out of the blue like that before. Said she was about to send his name tapes (left there 2 yrs ago I presume!) or something. This she never did. But they're no use to me unless she's going to sew them on for me. I only meant (when I asked you to mark his things) in the event of your intending to send him to <u>boarding school</u> (you once had that idea). I would never put myself to the trouble of sewing tapes onto vests, pants and sweaters that I know so well individually and have seen in all stages of cleanliness and decay. I could almost introduce you to each garment by its name. And I wash everything myself anyway. People don't seem to use laundries here – they are certainly expensive and washing machines are much more fun though unfortunately mine does not iron (it too came out of a junk shop!)

Emily Penrose of Somerville is only a very distant relation of Lionel's – not even a Quaker I fancy.

L is off to Ann Arbor next weekend. He is the only person who knows the stuff they want. I cannot prophesy the result but I trust it will at least be remunerating. His last visit was. I've bought a second-hand bone rattler of a bike and LOVE it. Petrol is to be rationed on April 1. That cleaned us out pro tem!

Now I must go off and help arrange a big mass meeting tonight – Anna Louise Strong on "Russia at war." She's a good egg. I met her last night. Sorry I've said so little about Bennie. He thrives.

Much love Margaret.

PS What are B's letters like now that he writes them at the Harts or with Mr Laidlaw? It certainly is a great relief to me to have them off my hands. Some of them put me to shame. B's complete time now spent roller skating. The snow has suddenly vanished (this week). I've got a <u>film</u> of B ice skating to send as soon as we've seen this ourselves.

The Savoy Hotel, opened in 1898, was a fashionable luxury hotel in London.

The "complete gramophone," the British term for a phonograph, was necessarily purchased second hand – as was the washing machine referred to later in the letter – because consumer appliances were no longer being manufactured.

"10 shilling" and "35/-" amounted to $2.17 and $7.64 respectively.

The Wurlitzer organs were installed cinemas during the era of silent films and provided music appropriate to the film's plot. They were and are loud and brash.

"Mozart and Bach being by birth HUNS*" refers to the virtual ban, in force in Great Britain during the First World War, when Margaret was an adolescent, on playing music by German composers.*

"Two records" refers to the fact that 78 rpm records had recordings on both sides, hence the four selections reported. Each side only played for about 3 to 3 ½ minutes.

"Ideomeo," refers to Mozart's first mature opera, composed in 1781.

Margaret Penrose wrote "Ursula," who was Ben's paternal aunt, but it seems more likely that she meant to refer to Ursula Dewey's daughter, Rosemary, who had travelled to Canada with Ben, since Ursula was resident in England.

"Name tapes" were long narrow bands of white tape with the individual's initials and surname printed on it at regular intervals. The portion of tape containing the names was cut off and then sewn onto the collar or back of garment. Name tapes were an intrinsic part of private school life at this period in Great Britain.

Dame "Emily Penrose," the former head of Somerville College Oxford, was a pioneer in securing higher education for women in England. Born in 1858, she had died on 26 January 1942.

"Anna Louise Strong" was a leading "progressive" journalist and a passionate supporter of the Soviet Union and later of Communist China, where she settled, dying there in 1970.

The following letter from Ben, if not quite so elegantly written as his previous missive, is certainly more informative about his current activities.

Ben to His Parents

1,000 Wellington Street
London, Ontario
March 15, 1942

Dear Mummy and Daddy,

I have been roller-skating during the last few days. This is one of the first signs of spring. We will all be glad when the warm weather comes.

We are studying about Africa in school and are making a book about it. The teacher has been quite cross lately. Mr. Durant one of the teachers at our school and who rooms with Mr. Laidlaw is sitting beside me marking some Literature papers.

The two teachers are ready to go to a meeting so I will roller skate with them.

Love and kisses
Benjamin

The following letter from Margaret is notable for the very little mention it makes of Ben and his behaviour, instead commenting on recent developments in London. The text reveals the "alertness, humour and subtlety of mind that were uniquely her own," lauded by Margaret's second son, Roger, when he spoke at her funeral.[2]

Margaret Penrose to Penelope Barman

My 7
1000 Wellington
London Ont
20th March 1942

My dear Penelope,

Here at last is your film. Eventually sent separately at same time. I took it so many times with blank results (the camera was wrongly loaded) that I had no idea which setting was going to come out. The one that appears is the one where Benny went to his music lesson halfway through, so you will have to satisfy yourself with Roger & Olive (Clarke) Asheshov in the second half. I am sorry that none of the other children are in this particular edition. They got quite tired of being hounded out onto the rink to be photographed with no result. So they just don't appear this time. But there's quite a lot of Benny & almost too much of Roger. Doesn't Olive skate well? It appears she used to skate with Cecilia College etc. in London Eng. and is quite an expert. The whole scene is on our home-made rink beside the house. I'm sorry I kept

2 "Obituary: Margaret Penrose," 207.

tipping up the camera. It seemed to need winding every 10 seconds & I was never sure when it was taking & when it wasn't. I'd do better another time if I ever worked to get the loan of it again. I hope the film fits your projector.

My parents (now at "<u>The Court</u>," Charmouth, Bridport, Dorset) might like to see it if they can borrow a suitable projector. So will you please ask them first? Then Olive's sister Mrs Willan, "Brachen" Lower Bourne, Farnham, Surrey might like to have a squint to (she owns a projector). But the film is, of course, yours for keeps. Roger is ecstatic about the Bragg book – it was for him wasn't it? It arrived this morning when B was at the Harts. I can't think why my parents are so convinced that they can't send us parcels? I see it only cost you four pence & it came quite snappily no fuss or bother!

I am sending you a photograph of the Harts' son Beverley. He has just arrived in England. It would be wonderful if you could look him up & be nice to him in exchange for some of what they've done for Benny – they really have been magnificent. No one has "Bev"'s address of course but he has a friend Capt. Ernie Grove who belongs to the YMCA London (Eng) & you might be able to get in touch in care of Ernie G. or else – maybe Bev has also joined the London YMCA himself – or maybe you could get him through the Can. Armoured Corps. The Harts don't seem to have a regimental number for Bev. I don't know why. But I know that if you were nice to Bev you'd earn Mrs Hart's undying gratitude. She really can't think of anything else much but her big boys – the next is due to go overseas soon they tell me. And the next knows Benny. I believe Bev left just before Benny's first visit. But he (Bev) has heard all about him (Ben) from his mother in letters.

My gramophone is still a great delight – I've got the Mozart clarinet quintet out of the library. The children are crazy about it. They won't play swing though, I've got some records of that too. Benny likes the clarinet quintet to be played outside the door of the room where he & Roger sleep – after the light is turned off. It makes them so happy.

Lionel tried to go to Ann Arbor today but I have just been phoned by him to say that he was turned back at the frontier – awful red tape! He is perfectly furious. Last time they made the fuss over <u>me</u> & let him through without a murmur. You never know what they will do next, but I shouldn't like the process of <u>immigration</u> into the USA! L was only going over for 24 hours for scientific discussion!

Much love, Margaret

Yes we heard from your Toronto friends & from Mr Blackman at Detroit. Replies were duly dispatched. No letter from you since airmail 20th Feb.

"Olive (Clarke) Asheshov": Rosa Olive Jane Clark (1904–74) married Dr Igor Nicholas Ashehov (1901–61), a leading Russian-born bacteriologist who taught at the University of Western Ontario, 1937–48. The couple had four children.

"Here is your film": I have no memory of having viewed such a film, if it did reach my parents.

"Cecilia Colledge" (1920–2008) was a British figure skater who won a silver medal at the 1936 Olympics and several other medals and championships.

The reference to "the Bragg book" is too brief for it to be identifiable.

The "photograph of the Harts' son Beverley" appears in an article, published in an unidentified newspaper, reporting his arrival in England as part of the tank corps.

"Mozart Clarinet Quintet": The Quintet for Clarinet and Four Strings K581 was composed in 1781 for the clarinettist Anton Stadler.

"Swing" was a style of music popular during the 1930s and early 1940s, derived from jazz, involving big bands and a soloist. The tempo was fast and the beat irregular, with the soloist improvising on the theme.

The "Toronto friends" cannot be identified.

"Mr Blackman," previously mentioned as "Mr. Blackstone," had recently been in England.

Enclosed in this letter was an undated newspaper clipping, captioned as follows: "Overseas [Photograph] Lieut. Bev B. Hart, son of Mr. and Mrs. R. J. Hart, Byron Avenue, has arrived overseas, according to a cable received by his parents. Lieut. Hart went as a reinforcement of the fourteenth draft. He is with the Canadian Armored Corps." On the clipping Penelope Barman wrote, "c/o Cpt. Ernie Grove YMCA."

As the next letter shows, Ben had begun to achieve a certain fluency in writing.

Ben to His Parents

8

1000 Wellington Street
London Ontario
March 23, 1942.

Dear Mummy and Daddy,

To-day I played pin-ball. We had two games one of which was a championship game. The side I was on lost by two points. We call our teams after the great Canadian and American hockey teams.

I received a letter from Nannie Collison yesterday. I was very glad to hear from her.

Mr. Laidlaw and Mr. Durant have joined the Air Force so we will have a new teacher after April seventeenth.

Love,
Benjamin

"Pinball" probably refers to pin bowling, also mentioned his later letter of 16 May 1942.

"Nanny Collinson" was the Barman family nanny until 1940. I recall that, as a teenager, I was summoned to meet a trimly dressed Scots lady who clearly still regarded me as a baby and who must have been Nanny Collinson.

The following letter is typed, save for some handwritten changes and additions, both which are placed in italics. Its contents show that Margaret's anxious concerns about Ben, so evident in her letters at the start of the year, had transmuted in a cheerful tolerance of his activities, even when he, at the age of almost eleven, arrived home very late at night.

Margaret Penrose to Penelope Barman

No. 8   1000 Wellington St
LONDON Ont.   26th March 1942

My dear Penelope,

I am going to take to the typewriter again, after years and years. I have just bought myself a sixpenny book on how to teach oneself touch typing. This should add a new interest to life. I gave up trying to touch type 11 years ago when I had a manuscript sent back by Dr Ernest Jones because it was too badly typed. It was my first blindfold effort. Now of course I am looking at the keys but I shan't next time so my next effort may be quite unrecognisable, who knows?

Thank you very much for Benny's cheque. It was a pleasant surprise. $26 odd. I have not had to go to the bank since it has done my week's shopping for me including a lot of quite playable gramophone records from a junk shop at 2d a piece.

What plans are there in the offing for Benny's summer holidays? Shall I get in touch with the Flanagans again? He was so happy there. Maybe the Harts will invite him for part of the time. They have a country house somewhere not far off I understand. Not that I want to get rid of him but at the moment I am inspecting second-hand tents with the idea that we might camp 3 or 4 miles away by the river and Lionel could bike into work. If this plan works out the fewer the merrier. My chess playing friend has offered me a perfectly divine site. We can spend the dull or rainy weather with every modern convenience in this house, the rent of which we have to pay anyhow. I could bike in and do the family wash and marketing when I felt so disposed. And anyway we shall be allowed at least 3 gallons of petrol a week, probably more, when the rationing comes in on April Fools Day. So the scheme may possibly be a success. The city gets so intolerably hot periodicly during July and August. I can't stand cooking when it is over 95 in the shade anyway.

I think, when Mr Laidlaw leaves – April 17th – to join the air force – I shall let Benny try typing his letters home. Maybe they will come out more interesting as he will surely enjoy doing it. They will hardly be less legible. I saw his last one as it had to be re-enveloped, the original envelope having been chewed up in the rain while he diverted his homeward route in order to buy himself an ice cream at 9:30 p.m.

Do you disapprove of those late hours? I must say I did rather as Roger had to stay awake till he got in and B wasn't in bed till 10 that night. Usually they go at 8 with lights out not later than 9. It is hard to do it earlier as there is so much practising – 4 lots of it – and home work to be got in. I was going to say – I saw Benny's last letter and thought it neat but dull. Perhaps if he types it will be peculiar but interesting. I can't let you have the original of the letter he copied from my typing because he made such a mess of it, crossing everything but the bare bones out, that I threw it away.

Fancy your thinking of munition work rather than minding your own children. Dear, dear, I wonder what anyone would say if I took that idea into my head? You for example? But I shan't yet. In a few years' time the kids will all be in that kind of thing themselves. Time flies. I was told in a letter from England the other day that I was so far away that I couldn't see things in their proper perspective! Quite a "carrot" for the N.S. and S. I thought. Not that I sent it in. In the same breath the writer said that I seemed to think that Europe was indulging in an orgy of self-destruction and also that he and his wife had decided to kill their children if the Germans landed in England. It gave one quite an unpleasant picture of existence over there, but I am not one to judge, being too far away to come to any conclusions.

Did you get the film? And the letter that I sent at the same time? Yours of March 1st (6) and Benny's of March 8th (air mail) arrived together yesterday.

I think the thyroid is doing B. good. He has lost about 2 pounds (which he can well spare) and seems very bright and cheerful. I got his balls inspected and they're O.K. but he does seem to be going through a phase of some sort of glandular deficiency.

Much love.

Margaret

"Dr. Ernest Jones": Alfred Ernest Jones (1879–1958) was a pioneering psychoanalyst in England. In 1920, he founded the International Journal of Psychoanalysis, *which he edited until 1930, and the following year the* International Psychoanalytic Library. *Margaret's manuscript could have been submitted to either of these.*

"A 'carrot' for the N.S. and N." refers to a column entitled "This England" in the weekly New Statesman and Nation, *which reproduced extreme and absurd remarks recently appearing in print.*

"$26 odd" amounted to £6, the monthly remittance allowed to each evacuee child. The pound sterling was then worth about C$4.38.

"The Flanagans" were the family with a lake cottage at Arundel, Quebec, where Ben had spent most of July and August 1941.

Penelope Barman's "thinking of munition work" became a reality. She worked in a local factory. The youngest child, I was sent to preschool in order to make this employment possible, and I recall seeing my mother dressed in overalls and a head scarf. The scarf had the two twisted and protruding ends, the style customarily worn by female factory workers.

The "glandular deficiency" (if it was an inability to ejaculate sperm) was not enduring, since Ben was to father three children.

The following letter (Fig. 5.1) from Ben is notable on two grounds. It is so beautifully written that it is hard to credit that Ben suffered from dyslexia. In addition, its contents mark a new stage in Ben's development. In it Ben both asserts his own views and personality and in effect stands up to his father and the latter's assumptions. The letter is undated, but the envelope is cancelled "London Mar 31 10AM 1942 Ont."

Ben to His Parents

1,000 Wellington Street
London, Ontario

Dear Mummy and Daddy,

I received your letter this week. Yes your letters do come quicker when you send them by air-mail. The last letter was no. 8. We are beginning to have spring weather, the robins are hopping about everywhere.

Roger has a very bad cough so he has to stay in bed. I also have a slight cold.

Daddy I do say gas and street-car, I suppose I'm beginning to become a good Canadian. I came over to the college tonight on my roller-skates. The Easter holiday start on Wednesday and I'll be glad. We have a student teacher her name is Miss Fenton. She will teach one week at school. We still have bananas in our stores.

Love from
Benjamin

"Wednesday" was April 1.

In British usage, "gas and street-car" were, and remain, "petrol" and "tram."

Bananas were unobtainable in England. On one of his trips abroad for BOAC (probably to West Africa), Lowis Barman purchased and brought back to Twin Oaks a small bunch of bananas. My brother and I, already in bed, were awoken to

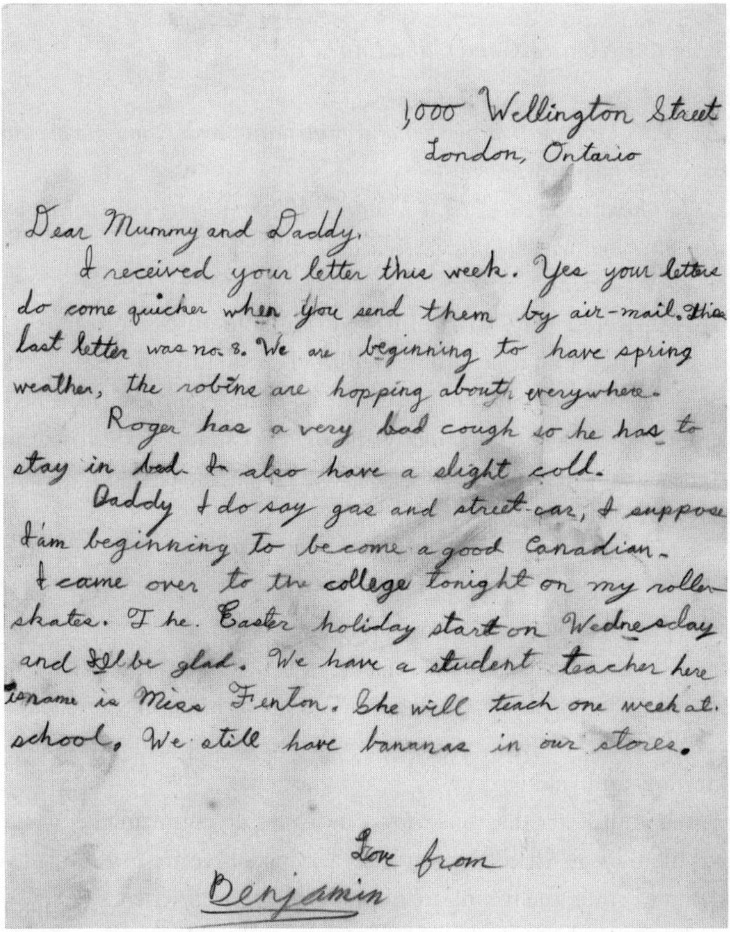

Figure 5.1 Ben's letter to his parents, undated [end of March 1942]

receive the treat. Closely watched by our parents, we ate the bananas. I recall finding the taste so utterly bland as to make me wonder what the fuss was all about.

During the month of March 1942, the relationship between Ben and Margaret moved increasingly into smoother waters. Ben seems to have acquired a greater sense of self and to have become more adept at expressing himself. John Laidlaw's coaching certainly helped to improve Ben's writing and spelling, but that advance also sprang, it may be inferred, from Ben's greater willingness to tackle his dyslexia. Margaret's letters during these same weeks moved from expressing distress about her charge's behaviour to adopting a more hands-off attitude towards his conduct.

6

Finding His Voice,
April–September 1942

This coming Friday I get out of school!
~Ben Barman to his parents, 25 June 1942

Margaret Penrose's letter number nine, presumably dated 6 April 1942, has not survived. Ben's letters, of which number ten is missing, display a growing command of language and a burgeoning interest in and analysis of the world he encountered. The first letter typed by Ben himself establishes this change. The letter's envelope now contains nine photographs of Ben with the Penroses in front of the Wellington Street house. A shot of Ben showing off the salvage materials he had collected attests to his physical growth and his increasing

Figure 6.1
Ben and the items he
collected for the Red Cross

maturity. On the back of that photograph, Ben wrote "Ben and Red Cross," with Margaret adding, "Junk collection. B & R sleep in sun room behind Ben's head."[1]

Ben to His Parents [typed]

NO 9

1000 Wellington St.

London Ont.

April 6 [1942]

Dear Mummy & Daddy,

April the 1 we saw a conjure – he did some good trcks like cutting someons hed off but it dus not come off. School stop on Thursday & on the same day I went to the Harts thir I stady untill until Sunday. Friday I went on a hick [Added by Margaret in handwriting: = hike (= country walk)] to springbank. It is about 3 miles from the Harts & about 4 miles from here. On Easter I was ill so I did not eat any Easter egg. We do not know what I had but it is all over now. Margaret said to me Would you like to typeawrit your letters "instead of writing.""

LOVE FROM BENJAMIN BARMAN

"6ᵗʰ April" was Easter Monday.

"Springbank," about 300 acres in size, is a park that lies on the south bank of the Thames River in London, Ontario.

The next letter contains important insights into the character of both Ben and Margaret. For the first time, Margaret provides information about Ben's attitude towards his relationship with his absent parents. The letters he received from

---

1 The letter's envelope contains nine photographs, all stamped "224" and therefore part of the same roll of film. However, not all of them were sent on 6 April. At least three must have been sent in Ben's letter postmarked 18 April 1942, since in it he mentions the subject of the three. A reason for not sending all nine at once may have been a desire to keep down the postage on the letter.

Penelope and Lowis he did not read unless Margaret virtually ordered him to do so. They lay untouched in his pockets. The accumulated letters he eventually burnt. This attitude was matched by his insouciance with respect to his annoying habits, such as leaving hunks of plasticine sticking to furniture around the house and by other acts of self-assertion. Ben's behaviour forced Margaret into a moment of introspection about her role. People were not interested, her letter lamented, "in the poor neglected foster parent."

Margaret Penrose to Penelope Barman

1000 Wellington

London Ont

7th April 1942

[Added at the top of the letter:] My letter 9 in answer to your letters 8 & 10 which arrived together on 2nd April – both were air mail posted 12th and 18th March respectively.

My dear Penelope,

Thanks a lot for the March instalment for B. I've now had 3 months' worth. It is most useful for B., works out at $13.20 a month.

This typescript is the work of a whole afternoon on the part of your first-born. I gave him dictionary & typewriter. I had to tell him the first 4 letters of "conjurer" & how to spell "any" as neither began as he expected. The rest he looked up for himself – in fact I went out.

I quite appreciate your point about not bothering to make him write but I rather disagree. I think it is good for him — (a) from the literary & spelling point of view – he'd never write anything at all out of school if he didn't have this regular weekly assignment – & why, without it, should he ever improve? (b) because it reminds him of his family much more forcibly than receiving letters. He is liable to shove his mail unopened into his pocket whence it emerges weeks later in a horrible state of decay. I hope it doesn't hurt your feelings to hear this – but I generally have to ask him sev[eral] times whether he has remembered to read his letters! His idea of clearing out his desk or his drawer is to burn bunches of letters – unless I am in time to prevent him! Maybe this is partly because he has certain somewhat pyromaniac tendencies

– is this new? If I burn a few paper handkerchiefs or light a real fire he comes rushing from anywhere and can't take his eyes off the flame until it flickers out. I can't help wondering how he used to be in England where there used to be fires in sev[eral]. rooms quite a lot of the time. Did he rush from one to the other and feast his eyes on the flames there? Or is this something to do with his reaction to the different environment? He loves burning little bits of string and flipping lighted matches around the place – very dangerous in this dry climate! (We don't have safety matches here either). So I have to be rather fierce about it. But I can't control his activities when I am not at home. And there goes his complete correspondence as soon as I turn my back! This surprises me a lot as I still have the letters my father wrote to me when I was at school – tied up in bundles at Thorington! And I have also kept all your letters from England & lots of others. In fact I am rather a hoarder. He evidently is not – except as regards his <u>pockets</u>.

Plasticine has a great fascination for him & he never goes anywhere without a hunk of it – brings it out & squeezes it about at odd moments any time of the day. Moulds it round the sitting room furniture etc.! Is this new or old? You can't think how disgusting a pocket full of plasticine can be after it has been through the mangle (on the rare occasions when I have not emptied his pockets properly before washing his trousers). Luckily I am not very houseproud – but I did ask him today whether uncle Ross would be pleased to find chunks of plasticine firmly flattened round the arm of his best polished wood chair-arms etc. etc.! B. just grinned, peeled his latest production off & waddled away.

I like the way B says he doesn't know what his illness was this weekend! He went to the Harts for Easter & he & 3 other boys went a long expedition, with only a thermos of cocoa to quench their thirst (<u>very</u> unwise – but nothing to do with me!). So the little idiots (excuse my including your son in this category) drank quantities of <u>river</u> water from the famous "Thames"! Two days later all 4 of them were devastatingly sick with diarrhoea, tummy aches etc. etc. B was brought back here (2 days too soon) in a state of collapse & feeling extremely sorry for himself. We could only thank our lucky stars that they came off so lightly – they might have got dysentery or typhoid from the sewage – they were not far from the T.B. sanatorium. But I hope the purgative effects of the waters will have cleared these out of their systems – though why I speak so unscientifically I cannot tell. Of course typhoid would not come out for weeks & they may get it yet. No doubt I shall cable angrily if B. does! I asked him how the flavour of this Thames compared with that of Battersea reach – but he doesn't seem to have sampled the latter. I suppose that is one of the advantages of having a watchful nurse maid in tow. However I daresay he won't do this <u>again</u>!

I heard from S. Isaacs today. She thinks it would be interesting to get a collection of "normal, spontaneous letters of children" (evacuated to N. America) "to their parents – if they <u>could</u> be seen." Her idea is to try and trace "the changes of feeling & the attitude the children are showing to their parents & family at home." Also "How far they are affected by anxiety about bombings in England, recent events in Malay or of war coming to USA", etc etc. I don't know how far B's letters would come under the heading of "normal, spontaneous" ones. Yesterday's effort was certainly spontaneous, but was it normal? I have not kept track of them & I can't tell whether his attitude has altered much or not. I have been quite unable to detect a trace of anxiety about your being bombed. Though I admit that the first noise he makes when he wakes in the morning & the last before he dozes off at night is that of a dive bomber – a sound which punctuates his daily life as well. I am beginning to be able to deafen myself to the din. It is performed with enormous glee & gusto & as far as I can make out it owes its direct origin to the key signature of a daily radio serial, thriller "Captain Midnight" (which B. would rather die than miss). But it may have a deeper significance. Who can tell? Anyway if you feel like getting in touch with Dr Isaacs (30 Causewayside, Cambridge) on the subject – there is no reason why you shouldn't. I intend some day to concoct some sort of thesis on the subject myself (not only Benny but other evacuees that I have had the opportunity to observe). But I have no means of knowing what alterations take place in their letters home. And I can't help being more interested in the poor neglected foster parent & how her reactions vary – & no one cares about that! I reckon you're the person who knows as much about the latter as anyone. I use my weekly scrawl to you as a safety valve & it works wonders with my temper. I only hope it does some good to you. I'm afraid this waxes too long-winded.

I'm glad to hear that the fish that we are sending – <u>all</u> this year's tinned salmon and herrings & haddock – [as a present from Canada to "Old Grannie England"] will be welcome – as I judge from your last. Till I got your letter about the fish skins I was feeling rather indignant, as England used to be lousy with herrings. I shall miss the tinned <u>salmon</u> when it is over 90°, as most other things have to be cooked, & I hate cooking in this tropical summer. But your need is greater than ours. Here it is 7ᵈ big tin but sold out. What will you pay I wonder?

Much love from Margaret (Did I forget to sign my last typed letter?)

"Thorington" refers to the country property owned by the Penroses.

Ben's tendency to "burn bunches of letters" from his mother explains why only two of them (from 1940) still exist.

Despite Margaret's having saved "all your letters from England," none of Penelope's letters to Margaret appear to have survived.

"Plasticine" is a brand of modelling clay, invented in 1897, used for artistic purposes. The product has a slightly sticky touch and was sold in sets of different coloured sticks.

"S. Isaacs" is Susan Isaacs, the editor of the Cambridge Evacuation Survey, *mentioned in Margaret's letter of 3 March 1942. She was diagnosed with cancer in 1935, which may explain why the project that Margaret mentions in this letter never came to fruition.*

Ben vividly recalls the drama over drinking water from the River Thames mentioned in this letter. "We were very thirsty and the sulphurous water offered by a drinking fountain was to us quite unacceptable – so we mixed it with river water in the bottle assuming that it would sterilise it to some extent. Had we just drunk river water neat we would undoubtably been much worse."

Margaret's next letter, number 10, which followed in a matter of days is particularly informative about the clothes Ben wore and also about the clothing shortages, such as no woolen socks for sale, resulting from the war. What is surprising is that Ben's parents in England apparently still held a clothes ration card for him, despite his two year absence, and that they could buy and send clothing not available across the Atlantic.

Margaret Penrose to Penelope Barman

10

1000 Wellington
London Ont
16th April 1942

Dear Penelope

No letter from you since your 10 air mail of 18th Mar which arrived 2 weeks ago. Probably you've resorted to sea mail again & that certainly is slower though cheaper.

My last to you dated 7th April was so long that it practically gave me writers cramp. So I hope you received it. I don't mind if you don't get this one as I don't think I have much to say & I'd rather have a letter of yours to answer.

Benny is writing a (He will post later when snapshots are ready) perfectly "spontaneous" letter to you at this moment. He just came back from school & said "Margaret, do you know I've just thought of something, it's a long time since I wrote to my mother." So I said "go ahead & write then – typewriter & dictionary at your disposal." And this he did. So far he has come down to ask me how to spell "quarantine," "meningitis" & "Lionel." More doubtless to follow.

As I scribble on the porch (summer suddenly came yesterday – on Thursday & Friday we had snow storms!) the postman turned up & in his cheeky manner asked me to write <u>him</u> a letter, as he gets none himself! But he produced a letter for me at the same time – your 12 March 30th (airmail) which was doubly welcome as I was writing to you at the time. Usually your letter come just as I return from the postbox. Your 11 has not come yet, nor I think has your 9.

We went to Toronto for Thurs & Fri nights leaving a char in charge at home (Lionel & I & Jonathan). L & I stayed with one lot of friends & J with another. We almost got snowed in. But I enjoyed chatting with a number of my old cronies & I did a little shopping. The big stores there Etons & Simpsons beat Harrods (peacetime) & Selfridges hollow. I think they are wonderful places. We've nothing like that in London Ont though.

L & I go every where on bicycles since petrol has been rationed. It is very good for the lungs, the muscles & the nerves but I'm not so sure about the bottom! This is the right time of year. Later it is too hot & earlier it is too far too cold & snowy. There are fewer cars on the roads. We mean to get Oliver another 2nd hand bike (prices of bikes have gone rocketing up since rationing of petrol came). Oliver has so far to go to school. I won't get the smaller ones bikes yet as school is so near & they are completely satisfied with roller skates – in which they live! You said you didn't want B to bike. Of course it's safer now there are fewer cars. But he's rather a mut with traffic & often my heart is in my mouth when I see him crossing roads. I don't <u>allow</u> them to roller skate in the road. But of course they always do when I'm not looking. The road is so smooth & lovely. I should want to skate on it myself if I hadn't a bicycle.

I am so excited to have a letter from our old friend Oliver Strachey saying he will come to see us. Seems to be in Canada on business. It is such a thrill to see old English friends.

You ask about clothes for B – to be sent. Now that cash arrives it seems hardly necessary. But of course the cash only covers food so if you have clothes ration cards for B. which <u>don't deprive anyone else of anything</u> by all means send. The shoes you sent were too small for B. So I guess we'd better fit those here. Unless you want to send a pair of hulking

1. brogues – size seven or eight rubberized soles. He likes <u>brogues</u> best. Aunt Orion has hitherto got him shoes when he visited Montreal. They are supposed to be raised on inner side of instep as the Montreal doctor says his feet are flat & need support as he is so heavy. Slippers <u>not</u> wanted.

2. Then those lovely <u>woolen sox</u> – as many as you please. They are unobtainable here. One can only get the scratchy cottony kind that wear through in the wink of an eye & bind me to my workbox with bonds of steel. Cotton summer ones at 1/- a pair.

3. Another of gigantic <u>sweaters</u> if you like – though this one is still in constant use & being mended at only the elbows which doesn't show. I always pin it out to dry so it has lost none of its enormousness. (Try to avoid polo necks as I just have to alter them. They're too hot for these 80° houses.) Today I got B a <u>cotton</u> sweater for between seasons. He seems very pleased with it.

4. <u>Cotton</u> or <u>vyella</u> shirts or even flannelette are welcome. B insists on shirts with a <u>pocket</u> in them! One of those brown ones you sent had

no pocket so he won't wear it! (He keeps his money or his bus fares in his shirt pocket.) The vyella shirts he brought with him are still in use – in fact B. R & J have one on each at the moment. The flannel ones are too thick & too big. (They are size 14 – but sizes vary so) I shall adapt them next year. They were too long in the sleeve & (yes actually!) too bulky round the middle! & too scratchy to appeal to him. Size 7 or 8 shd be big enough. I think 8 is quite suitable. Cotton or vyella. Sorry to waffle so long before I decide. That's what comes of having diarrhea of the pen as I have!

B's underwear is still in perfect condition. He only wears the pants & he seems to have tons of pairs left intact. I may give him just a vest under his cotton sweater in future.

5. B's pyjamas are still O.K. Perhaps another pair or two would come in handy in due course. Those are v. good ones that you sent. He has worn them alternately ever since.

6. An outsize pair of grey flannel shorts would be useful in summer. B. has still been wearing his original ones & they keep busting in all directions. Of course he only uses them when he's not in winter breeches or midsummer cotton shorts & the interval is not very long!

7. If you've still got coupon cards to spare & room in the parcel what about another dressing gown. His old one is somewhat inadequate but it will do.

It never matters if things are too small as I can hand them on! You may not think so from the way I talk but everything you've sent has been a great success – one way or another. The lovely brown sweater was lamentably small but it will be lovely for R! R & J are in B's old grey school sweaters with the blue on the necks. They never wear out.

Summary

In order of importance

1 brogues – size 8
* 2 woolen sox
3 giant sweater – size 18 (age) size ?36 was it?
4 shirts (with pocket!) cotton or vyella not flannel or flannelette size 8
5 pyjamas – size 32 or 34
6 outsize grey flan. shorts

7 <u>winter</u> dressing gown (summer one still OK)

None of these are urgent & I really only care about the <u>sox</u>!

Much love Margaret

16th April

Copy of Benny's Report today

"Social Studies   43/50

Arithmetic   54/100

Nature Study   86%

Memory work – has learned 96 lines (they have to learn 200)

Did you get last times report? I will repeat some of it in case not.

"In our oral classwork in spelling B. seems to be getting the spelling idea & at times surprises me. Benjamin could work harder in school" but "spelling is still the problem."

Cramp doesn't permit me to write more. This seems to be the longest yet!

I will send complete report at end of school year if B is there to claim it. Last year he had chicken pox!

Mr Laidlaw goes off this week & B. couldn't go to him on Monday because they had cerebrospinal meningitis at Huron College where the man lives. Mr Laidlaw hopes to see you in England where he may eventually be stationed. He told me he would look you up.

Now I must stop

Margaret

"Char" is, as previously explained, the English word for "house cleaner."

"E[a]tons and Simpsons" are long gone from Toronto (1999 and 1991), but Harrods and Selfridges still flourish as high-end stores in London.

"Petrol has been rationed" refers to the rationing of gas on 1 April 1942.

"Mut" means a stupid or foolish person.

"Oliver Strachey" (1874–1960), the elder brother of writer Lytton Strachey, was a leading cryptanalyst during the two world wars. Seconded to the "Examination Unit" in Ottawa, he wrote to the Penroses on 14 April 1942 that "somehow we must meet," but "it's hard for me to get away." He returned to England in September 1942. His letter survives in the Penrose papers at University College, London.

"Clothes ration cards": Clothing was rationed from July 1941 in Great Britain through the issue of a set number of coupons for each person per year. The coupons

bought very little clothing. As the youngest son, I was forced to wear my older broth-ers' cast offs until, upon my surpassing them in height, new clothes were bought for me, to be passed on to them when I had outgrown them.

"Brogues" are low-heeled shoes with multi-piece leather uppers with decorative perforations and serrations along the uppers' dividing edges.

"Vyella," properly "viyella," is the brand name of a cloth made of a merino wool–cotton mix. The shirts and other clothing, manufactured in England, were synony-mous with quality and associated with the upper classes.

Ben persevered with typing his letters to his parents. The poorness of the spelling in his next letter, without date, may have been due to the departure of Mr. Laidlaw, by then enlisted in the airforce. The envelope is postmarked "Lon-don 12 AP 42 Ont."

Ben to His Parents [typed]

10

1,000 Wellington st.
London Ont.
[April 1942]

Dear Mummy & Daddy

The College [Added by Margaret: Huron College where Mr Laidlaw lived. Now, alas, departed.] was in quarantine for meningitis. At the college their was a snow house, I went to get in side it & it was just a piel of snow. hear [are] some snps of our hollow snow man, inside we can stand up. Margaret & Lionel went to Toronto. Margaret found my fountain pen to day. I have not got the READS (oboe reads) Silvia was goying to send.

LOVE FROM BENJAMIN

"Some snaps" refers to at least three photographs, stamped "224" on the back and now included in the envelope for the letter of 6 April 1942.

"Oboe reads": Ben meant the reeds used to play the oboe. As Margaret Penrose's letter of 16 May 1942 shows, the gift from Ben's aunt, Sylvia Anderson, was lost when the ship carrying it was torpedoed.

The following missive makes plain Margaret's desire to maintain close contact with Penelope through exchanging frequent letters and her renewed interest in assisting Ben to write to his mother and to be suitably dressed (she repeats the list of needed items given in her previous letter). The envelope for this letter bears stamps for thirty cents, ten times the cost of a letter sent by sea mail.

Margaret Penrose to Penelope Barman

11

1000 Wellington St
April 30th 1942

My dear Penelope,

I never sent you a record of music as the <u>copies</u> were frightful. I will if you like, shortly. Better to borrow my parents original, or swap for my original in B's.

8th April (airmail) to hand. It was just a short note to say you were writing sea mail at the same time. Latter not here yet. But I'm writing airmail myself this time as I see that the summer service (via <u>Newfoundland</u>) has begun. That really is worth doing – only supposed to take 2 two days if you hit the right day of the week to post. So I thought I'd try it out for your information. You can reach us far more quickly that way at the same price.

I've nothing much to say. B. has had a letter to you occupying the type-writer for two weeks! Every day or so he says – "I know what I'll do – I'll write to my 'muvver'" – & he proceeds to type a word or two. But he tires of the employment so quickly (now that it is no longer new) that he has not yet completed the second line & most of what he has written is scratched out or spelt queerly (despite dictionary) which is sad. I will try & get it finished in time to mail with this. But I'm determined that his writing should be "sponta-neous" & "natural"!!!! Did you get my letter number 9 about S[usan] Isaacs' letter to me – wishing she could get hold of such from children evacuated to North America! I don't feel that B's [letters] would be at all helpful to her. They don't really seem to say anything. Or do they? Maybe the Deweys are better? Anyway, now that Mr Laidlaw has joined up they are quite <u>unsolicited</u>! B. says his new teacher Miss Goodhue is a "really <u>good</u> teacher" & makes them "<u>work</u> hard". He says she's teaching him to spell & giving him the same work as the others. So we shall see what we shall see. I have not met her yet.

Mrs Hart's second son is about to go overseas so there will be another ("Ken") for you to meet & be kind to. Ken knows B. of course. Poor Mrs H was too het up to have B last Saturday but intends to resume her kindness to B as soon as she feels more composed. I am so sorry for her it must be ghastly. What am I to do about Mrs Flanagan. Of course B prefers to stay here but he loved his time there last summer. In my 10 I gave you a list of clothes for B. none of them urgent. But if you have coupons especially for him here is what I can remember of the (very unimportant-to-us) list

1. Black brogues, size 8, if poss. with instep support built into them

2. Lots of nice woollen sox

3. Cotton (or viyella) shirts with pocket if possible – size 8 according to one reckoning. [Those grey flan. 14s were too big & too scratchy] long & short sleeves welcome

4. One or 2 pairs of cotton pyjamas

5. A big winter dressing gown

6. Outsize grey flannel shorts

His suit & his underwear are still in the pink of condition. Really he doesn't need a thing except the shoes & those Aunt O[rion] buys in Montreal – or has the last two summers.

MUCH LOVE Margaret

From the "Roll" I see that Aunt Ursula Dewey is a fellow Newnhamite – greet her from me, please.

B's letter too heavy to include – three lines typescript. Post it sea mail.

The "Deweys" letters refer to those written home by Ben's cousins, Martin and Rosemary, who had come to Canada with him.

"The Roll" refers both to the listing of college graduates and to a newsletter of Newnham College for women at Cambridge, which was founded in 1871. It was not until 1948 that women were allowed to take Cambridge University degrees and their colleges (Girton and Newnham) allowed to participate in the governance of the university.

Margaret Penrose added the date to the following typed letter, which Ben signed. By sending his parents a photograph of his former teacher, Ben indicated the affection he had developed for John Laidlaw.

Figure 6.2 Ben's teacher John Laidlaw on his bicycle outside
Ryerson Elementary School

Ben to His Parents [typed]

10

1,000 Wellington St.

London Ont

30th April 42 [written in hand}

Dear Mummy & Daddy: –

Here is a snap of Mr. Laidlaw on a bicycle. I think J writing is very good. Miss Goodhue, our teacher, is good at teaching spelling. All the leves are out now & that's the spring. WE grade 5 are going to have a spelling test.

Love from

Benjamin

Added by Margaret: B. says: – "I've told them everything there is to say this time. I've said everything." My letter i going airmail – posted together M.P.

"J writing" must refer to a letter sent to Ben by his younger brother Jonathan.

The following two letters, sent in the same envelope, addressed by Margaret Penrose, show the continuing relationship between Ben and the Hart family.

Ben to His Parents

1,000 Wellington St
London Ont.
May 9, 1942

Dear Mummy and Daddy,

This Saturday I am over at the Harts, Donald and I have been playing catch this morning. I was not over last week as Kenneth was leaving and I hope sometime you will see him. I hope J[onathan] R[oderick] are better now. I am learning how to knit and it is quite easy. The weather is very hot so I have some of my warm clothes off.

Love from
A. Benjamin B

As to "J R are better now," I recall being sick in bed with my brother when at Twin Oaks. The doctor advised that we be fed from the food reserves (including some type of yellow cordial drink) that our mother kept in the cupboard under the dormer window in our bedroom.

Sent along with Ben's letter was one from Elsie Hart. It poignantly expressed the anguish that mothers face when their sons – two of them, in her case – went off to fight. The risk of their dying was considerable. No less worrying was the effect that life abroad – including exposure to a thousand temptations – would have on the young men.

Mrs Elsie Hart to Penelope Barman

68 Byron Avenue, London Ont
May 9th, 1942

Dear Mrs Barman: –

I will take this opportunity of enclosing a note in Benjamin's letter.

He came to us on the bus this morning and really have not seen much of him only at lunchtime; and then Donald helped with the dishes while Benjamin wrote his letter to his Mummy and Daddy; and now they have gone with Mr. Hart to see about some paint. This being Saturday afternoon he is going to paint our veranda floor, it seems necessary to do this job yearly but of course there are not so many feet leaping up on the veranda at present.

Now here I am rambling along and never to mention receiving your letter just this week; and also wish to acknowledge one from you some little time back and it was very kind of you to write; and I am afraid I have been lax in answering, but when I tell you we have said goodbye to our second son I know you will understand I have been busy.

I would like very much for Bev. to see you and I know he would like to; we have written your address to him. Letters from him this week tell us at the time of writing he had not had any long leave and would not be for a little time as he was starting some venture, probably some course. He is a very ambitious sort and would not care to miss an opportunity. He has enjoyed England to the utmost and his letters have been so interesting.

Now as I told you before Kenneth is with the Air Force and went over as a Sgt. Air Gunner and the last we heard of him was April 28th; so no news is good news. Kenneth carried your address with him and as he spent several Saturdays in the home with Benjamin it would be very interesting for him to contact you people; so who knows that may be the case sometime before too long. Our Kenneth is a real boy, of course he has just turned 20, over 6 foot and of course Mom thinks a grand looking soldier.

All this and nothing about your son – well he looks well indeed today and he and Donald seem to be very congenial companions. I had hoped to have Benj with us the Easter holidays, however, he did come on the Thurs. evening and stay until Sunday; and as Kenneth was on leave I wanted to be free to do things for him. However, Benjamin enjoyed his little visit I think and no trouble at all. He slept in Bev's room; I find it better if they sleep separately and get their proper rest.

Any hospitality shown to our boys would be indeed appreciated and I know they will look you up if the opportunity arises. I can fully realise the heartaches you people have; that we have to be good soldiers like our little sons and big sons. We like your Benjamin's accent.

With best wishes to all –

Sincerely Elsie Hart

"Embarking on some course" probably refers to Bev Hart's volunteering to serve in the nascent 1st Canadian Parachute Battalion, officially established on 1 July, 1942,

one part of which was being trained at the Parachute Training School at the Royal
Air Force (RAF) Ringway base near Manchester, England.

    "Benjamin's accent" must have continued to be noticeably upper-class British
to Canadian ears, even though, when he returned home in October 1943, his family
thought his accent Canadian.

Penelope and Lowis Barman did offer hospitality to Ken and Bev Hart, at Twin
Oaks and more so after the Barman family returned to their flat in Queen's
Gate Gardens in 1944. I recall their staying in the flat and remember them as
two lean, fit young men wearing bright blue uniforms. They both survived the
war. Bev Hart died in London, Ontario, 11 May 2011, aged ninety-two. No evidence has been found as to Ken Hart's life after 1945 or to the date of his death.
    Ben's letter from mid-May provides a good picture from a child's viewpoint
of what life was like in the Penroses' house.

Ben to His Parents

#12

1,000 wellington St
London Ont.
May 16\41

Dear Mummy and Daddy,
    Our cat has four kittens and two have their eyes open today. We worked
out the colour of the husband it was b[l]ack and worked out which ones were
male and female. Our cat is orange and it is one year old. Jonathan has had
his appendix out at eight o'clock on Tuesday night he was just in time. Oliver
gave Yunoshy the best game of chess and won the prize Lionel helped too.
To play pinball you roll a ball and try to knock down a wooden peg.

Love from
Benjamin B xxxxxxxxx

"Our cat" was Puskhin.

    "Yunoshy" is Ben's attempt to spell the name of Daniel Abraham Yanofsky
(1925–2000), who was Canada's first chess grandmaster and eight times chess
champion of Canada, beginning at the championship meet at Winnipeg in 1941.

Oliver Penrose recalls: "Abie Yanofsky, the youthful Canadian champion played a number of local players simultaneously, walking from board to board. I was one of those playing against him. I suppose I was about 12 or 13 at the time. My dad did not take a board because Jonathan had just had his appendix removed, so he (my father) stood behind me and gave advice, but then went off to see how Jonathan was. When he left I (that is, we) had a favourable position but without his help I faltered a bit and Yanofsky was able to draw the game (I think my father returned before the end of the game, otherwise I might well have lost). I had forgotten that there was any prize. About 10 years later I did play Yanofsky twice in one-to-one chess in Oxford v. Cambridge matches. The first time I drew (this was the important 'varsity' match), but the second time he thrashed me."[2]

As to "pinball," Ben is clearly referring to the game of pin bowling.

Ben celebrated his eleventh birthday on 22 May 1942. His next letter, dated 23 May, still shows the stain made by the piece of birthday cake he included. The bookmark he sent his parents also survives with the letter.

Ben to His Parents

13	1,000 Wellington
	London Ont
	May 23

Dear Mummy and Daddy

Here is a book marker I made for you. This is how it works you put the marker in the book like this [image of open page] and close the book. [image of closed book with marker visible]

I hate to make your mouths water but here is some of my Birthday cake. I will tell some of my presents a bow and arrow, compass 3 gliders, kite and handkerchief. Thank you fore the magnifying gass and thermoneter. It has been raining a lot recently and about 45 F. Yesterday I bourt a turtle it is very cute it tries to hibernate

Love from

Benjamin

2 Email from Oliver Penrose to Roderick Barman, 27 January 2015.

Figure 6.3 Ben with ice cream cone, June 1942

Margaret Penrose's letters numbered 12, 13, and 14 have not survived. The contents of the next missive, number 15, misdated July (it was sent in June), make clear the challenges that both women and men were facing during this period of the war.

Margaret Penrose to Penelope Barman

15   1000 Wellington

London Ont

Sun: 21st July 1942

My dear Penelope –

Ages since I wrote. But my intention has been to get Benny to dictate you a letter. He <u>never</u> seems to have time! I did expect to do it today as Lionel is on duty in the Hospital for the summer. But B. & R. were out all day (to my horror I afterwards discovered they were busy pushing the car of a neighbouring millionaire jeweller down a slope so that it crashed into a house!) But at the time I made use of the comparative household silence by painting the bathroom – walls & everything! – (with Oliver's help). We did the kitchen a few days ago & it looks lovely. Anyway no letter got written so I'll have to try & get B to do it tomorrow. I am quite alone in the house with the 4 children for the next few weeks.

If I was less worried about Jonathan's state of health I would enjoy it more. He continues to have headaches & vomiting attacks & feelings of dizziness despite the absence of his appendix & it rather frightens me especially as Dr Campbell has cheerfully suggested a tumour on the brain (don't tell the grandparents!!) But I hope to be assured soon that it is merely migraine due to his generally enfeebled state.

As I told you before the Flanagans can't have B. And I don't care to pay B's expenses to Montreal for a week or two's torture with Uncle Ross, as last year they only offered to have him for 10 days anyway – & it really isn't worthwhile to pay the fare for so long a distance and such a short time. So I am investigating neighbouring farms. Unfortunately we took all 4 boys to see the last one & when the farmer's wife subsequently telephoned on the subject of having one of the boys for the summer her husband was heard to remark as she spoke "it's Oliver we want not the fat one!!!!" So Oliver has made up his mind to be patriotic for the summer & work on that particular farm. Meanwhile the wife looks around among the neighbours for a place of B. I have offered to pay B's £3 a month to whichever takes him – if we like them & B agrees. They tell me O. will be free board and actually receive wages for his work. Probably he will be disgustingly exploited – though they seem v. nice people.

The labour shortage on farms here is extreme at the moment. But I shall miss Oliver if only on account of his lawn mowing & house decorating propensities. Not only that he really is extremely nice to talk to and so grown up! The other day he got a scholarship for being the best pupil year before last! I told you he had a girlfriend – he writes her long letters every day or two & takes her to the movies. I don't even know her name – he's very reticent about it, largely on account of being nagged by the other kids I imagine. He had his 13th birthday this month.

If the farms fail I shall send B to a camp for boys. I have him down for the Sunday School one but that only lasts a week June 27–July 4 on the shores of

Lake Huron north of Bayfield. There is also a Y M C A boys camp on Lake Erie which one can stay for as long as a month. I gather that the boys have a lovely time. But its more expensive. I shall be deciding within the next few days as soon as I hear from the farms. If Oliver overworks himself or wants to return early for any reason B. could go to the same farm after O & I could pay B's board <u>there</u>. They don't have room for more at a time.

We all six went up to Orillia (Lake Simcoe) last week for 4 days. L had work to do there. We had a cabin by Bass Lake & would have had a lovely time if Jonathan had not chosen that moment in the wilds to have one of his attacks. B. had a lovely time swimming & fishing – he bought Lionel (!) a fishing rod at Woolworths for his (Lionel's) birthday which happened to be just then! So B. spent his time asking <u>me</u> where he could find a worm! & how, where & why to fish. I've photographed him at it [Fig. 6.4]. But J was too ill for me to enjoy myself much. B nearly caught sev[eral] fish, luckily he didn't quite as it was against the law – the bass fishing season not having yet begun.

Have you got your washing machine yet? Washing day (Monday) is still my red letter day. I find it as satisfactory a safety valve as letter writing & weekly wash away the sins of the world in my rattley old machine.

Love from Margaret.

B will tell you of all his many picnics & hikes etc. I enclose a sample of his schoolwork. The letters you got were written with Mr Laidlaw <u>privately</u> – not at school.

Although Margaret wrote "Sun: 21ˢᵗ July 1942," the postmark on the envelope reads "London 14 JUN 22 1942 Ont."

Oliver would "receive wages" for his work on the farm but his hiring must have been unofficial, as he was just thirteen in the summer of 1942, and boys who enrolled in the government's Farm Cadet Brigade had to be at least fifteen.

Lionel's "work to do there" refers to his work at the Ontario Teaching Hospital in Orillia.

The "Sunday School one" can be identified from Ben's letters of 24 August and 10 September 1942, which mention his being at "Magog" and reading books at Bayfield.

The "YMCA boys camp" that Ben attended was not, as his letter of 24 August 1942 shows, the camp on Lake Erie but that of Kanawana at Saint Sauveur,

Figure 6.4
Ben fishing at Bass Lake,
Orillia, Ontario

Quebec, north of Montreal. His time at this camp was obviously in conjunction
with a stay with his uncle Ross and aunt Orion.

"Bass Lake" lies to the west of Orillia and is the site of a provincial park.

The "sample of his school work" has not survived.

In her letter of 21 June, Margaret Penrose promised that she would make Ben
write a letter. He did type the following long and informative missive, on which
Margaret wrote "? 13."

Ben to His Parents [typed]

?13 [by hand]
100 Wellington St, London, Ont.
22nd June, 1942.

Dear Mummie and Daddy,

Ten days ago we went to Toronto and then on to Orillia. At Toronto I
went to the Museum that interested me very much especially the prehistoric
animals. When we were in Orillia I bought a small fishing line in Woolworths
for Lionel's birthday. I tried to fish and I knew I wouldn't catch any fish.
Anyway it was quite fun trying. We spent the nights in a cabin by Bass lake.
Roger was sick on the way there and so were Oliver and Jonathan. But I
survived. We looked over the Institution at Orillia and their "cottages" were
more than twice as big as this house. Two raccoons dropped into a cage
there by mistake.

Last week our room at school went on a picnic at Springbank Park which
is four miles away from here. It was great fun. On Saturday when I was with
the Harts we went on a picnic there too down at St Thomas which is about 15
miles away. We had races and baseball at both picnics. At the Harts picnic we
had peanut scrambles and lots of new things. There weren't any peanuts so
we had a candy scramble.

In arithmetic my average was about 80. I don't know my spelling yet as we
may have another test. I had an oboe exam but my oboe wasn't working so
I had to take it to the shop and I am probably to have the test soon instead.
School ends this week and I am probably going to a farm for the holidays.

I have written to Bompa. I thanked him for putting my savings.

We have given all the kittens away. My watch hasn't come yet – have you
sent it? I hope it is a wristwatch [Added by Margaret: But if not] I can easily
sell it and get the money for it and buy a new one with a little extra I hope.

We haven't heard from uncle Ross yet. Do you think he will write?

Love from Benjamin

*The "museum" refers to the Royal Ontario Museum, Toronto, which had a fine
collection of dinosaur bones and models of other prehistoric animals.*

*The "cottages" at the Orillia Teaching Hospital were huge, each two or three
stories high and holding from 180 to 230 patients.*

*"St Thomas" is a small city about thirty kilometres south of London, Ontario,
well over half way to Lake Ontario.*

*"We haven't heard from uncle Ross yet" refers to Ben's possibly staying with his
uncle and aunt for a time during the summer vacation. He eventually did so, as
his letter of 24 August 1942 shows.*

*"Bompa" was a variant of "Bampa," the name for Ben's grandfather Leonard
Spencer.*

*"Putting my savings" must refer to Ben's grandfather putting money into a sav-
ings account in Ben's name.*

As the next letter attests, the end of the school year could not come a moment
too soon for Ben. He took a plethora of photographs at the term's close, two of
Ryerson School itself and several of his teachers – mostly of Mr Laidlaw and
Mr Durant, who had earlier roomed together at Huron College.

Ben to His Parents

15

1000 Wellington
London Ont
June 25 [1942]

Dear Mummy and Daddy

Yesterday I had a reading and writing test in reading I got 35 in writing I
don't now yet. I was going to hoe sugger beets but I am too young. On sat.
I'm going to a camp for the week. I think my writing teribul but yas [yours]
is good compard with mine!

The night before last I think that Margaret said to Roger "If Benjamin gets
in bed before you he can have 5¢, if you get into bed before him you can have
5¢." So Roger got into bed first and got 5¢ and I dent no anytheing about it
un till Roger told me about it. <u>This coming Friday</u> I get out of school!

Love from
Benjamin

The *"camp"* was clearly the one-week Sunday school camp on Lake Huron, north of Bayfield, mentioned in Margaret Penrose's letter of 21 June 1942.

Margaret received Ben's final report for the school year 1941–42, which she sent on to Ben's mother. The report, it should be noted, contained three earlier evaluations by Ben's teachers that had been sent to Margaret for her signature and then returned to the school.

Ben's School Report for Grade 5

27th of June 1942
London Public Schools
London Canada
PROGRESS REPORT

Name of Pupil Benjamin Barman
Grade V *School* Ryerson
For the School Year 1941 1942
Teacher J Laidlaw
Principal A P Silcox

Comment on the Pupil's Progress

It is my intention to give Benjamin a good trial – using his left-hand. He has a good vocabulary. Can think – reading quite average – arithmetic average – spelling does not spoil the whole of his written work.

His conduct is excellent.

Ben is doing good work in arithmetic. Spelling is still the problem. He is writing with his right hand. On account of the size of the class it is impossible for me to devote enough time to Benjamin during school hours to teach him to write with his left hand. I would be willing to give him extra time out of school hours and would welcome any suggestions.

In our oral classwork in spelling Benjamin seems to be getting the spelling idea. And at times surprises me. Benjamin could work harder in school.

Social studies 43/50; arithmetic 54/100; nature study 86; memory work lines learned 96.

"Promoted to Grade VI"

Bennie has worked hard and seems to be making considerable progress in spelling.

Month	Sept	Oct	Nov	Dec	Jan	Feb	Mar	Apr	May	June
Times late										
Days absent	4½	0	2	0	0	0	0	0	0	0

Date	Signature of Parent
4th Nov. 1941	Margaret Penrose
10th Jan 1942	Margaret Penrose
16 April 1942	M Penrose

Parents are requested to examine this report carefully and to acknowledge its receipt by signing above.

KINDLY RETURN PROMPTLY

The size and weight of the envelope containing the report, with the word "report" crossed out and stamps worth five cents instead of the usual three cents, may have been the reason it caught the eye of the censor, who opened it.

From 27 June to 19 August 1942, Ben lived an active life away from the Penroses. He first spent eight days (27 June to 4 July) at Camp Magog, then lived with a farming family, the Welds. Next, he attended the YMCA camp at Saint Sauveur, Quebec, and finally, in the first part of August, he stayed with his uncle and aunt in Montreal.

Judging from the enthusiasm with which Ben later discussed his time at Camp Magog, the week he spent there was a highlight, perhaps *the* highlight, of his time in Canada (Fig. 6.5). There is only one postcard, addressed to Margaret Penrose, from this period, but he took eight photographs of the boys, the staff, and the buildings at the camp. His hut contained sixteen boys under two leaders. His hut mates dubbed him "the professor," he recalls, since his conversation reflected the fact that "I was living with the Penroses who had IQs of 184 or 185" and with them "I was making the sort of remarks needed to keep my end up," but, at the camp, "I was making the kind of remarks I expected them [the boys] to understand and probably they did not do so."

Figure 6.5 Ben in a rowboat at Camp Magog, Lake Huron, Ontario

Postcard from Ben to Margaret Penrose

No address [postmarked July 1st 1942]

Dear Margaret,

I hope you are getting on all right. I am having a lovely time here doing <u>nothing</u>. Will you send me some paper and some thing to dour [draw] with.

Benjamin

Following Camp Magog, Ben moved on to stay on the farm of the Welds, at Mount Brydges, which lies to the west of London and is now part of Strathroy-Caradoc municipality. He took three photographs during his stay, of Fred W. Weld, his wife, and their two children; of their house; and of their barn. The tone of the letter that he wrote to his parents suggests that he enjoyed himself on the farm.

Ben to His Parents

F Weld
RR1 Mt. Brydges
Ont Canada
[postmarked 12 July]

Dear Mummy and Daddy

Here are some pictures which I took. To day I was picking berries here at the Weld's and having fun. Margaret said in the letter she sent "I think I will be comming over this weekend." Wed. we went to a garden party and had lots of fun.

Love from
Benjamin.

"F. Weld" was Fred W. Weld, born about 1898 in Ontario. In the voters list for 1940, he was listed as a farmer, residing at RRI Mount Brydges. He was still listed in the 1962 voters list. Typical for the period, his wife is given in the 1940 list only as "Mrs. Fred. W. Weld."

The envelope containing the above letter is addressed in Margaret's hand, so she must have made her weekend visit as promised and mailed the letter herself. Addressed to "Mrs Barman, Twin Oaks, Buckland Common, Tring, Herts, England," it was forwarded to "Shirley Tower Hotel, Torquay" and postmarked on the back "Tring Herts 9.45AM 11 Aug 42."

This circumstance has allowed Ben's brothers to date precisely their separate memories of their time at Torquay. Jonathan Barman recalls that his father, with his penchant for bending inconvenient rules, drove the family to Torquay, using gasoline allocated for business purposes only. One day, while the family was eating lunch in the hotel, the air raid siren sounded, followed by a loud explosion. Lowis and Penelope decided to take their sons to the hotel's air raid shelter. I remember that, as I climbed down from my chair (as five year olds do), I saw an elderly couple at an adjacent table maintaining a stoic mask of resolve: they were not going to move. When we got downstairs, to a room that oddly seemed to have a vast window overlooking Torquay bay, the hotel's manager explained that a German plane (probably a Focke-Wulf 1900) had been intercepted by a fighter and had escaped by jettisoning its bomb in the bay.

Jonathan recalls that Penelope, when at the hotel, wrote a letter to Margaret, probably informing her of this event and certainly commenting on military activities in Torquay. Margaret sent the letter back to Penelope because, Jonathan recalls, it "had been cut to pieces [by the censor], with every reference cut out so that it was unreadable."[3] Although some letters from Ben and Margaret were opened by the censor, none of them suffered any deletions, much less a virtual destruction.

While Ben was away, staying with his aunt and uncle in Montreal, Margaret Penrose and her family were enjoying a two-week vacation at Bayfield on the shores of Lake Huron. Pasted on the back of a postcard with a picture of Bayfield were three press clippings detailing the impact of the war on food supplies and daily life in Canada.

Postcard from Margaret Penrose to Penelope Barman

[Clippings:] "Prices Board Sets Ounce of Tea per Person Weekly, or 4 Ounces of Coffee, but not both." "Canadians now get less tea and sugar then the people of Britain, where their weekly ration bases per person is 2 ounces of tea and 12 ounces of sugar, against one and 8 ounces respectively in Canada. Coffee is not rationed for Britons, who are light coffee drinkers." "Ration cards issued for children under 12 cannot be used for tea and coffee purchases."

21   5th Aug. 1942

We' re having a pleasant two weeks holiday, thank you, despite the above which I send you to prevent you from feeling sorry for yourselves!

Love, Margaret

No news from Montreal since I last wrote to you.

"Prices Board" refers to the Wartime Prices and Trade Board, created by the Canadian government on 3 September 1939. As its name indicates, the board was given control of prices and sales of foodstuffs and other commodities in order to ensure fair profits and equal access to goods. On 3 August 1942, it set the weekly ration per person as either an ounce of tea or four ounces of coffee.

3 Jonathan Barman's communication to Ben Barman, 15 August 2014.

On the day he returned from Montreal to London, 19 August 1942, Ben sent his parents a short letter that included, unexpectedly, two .22 rifle targets and the pictures that he had meant to send when staying with the Welds.

Ben to His Parents

19 Aug. [1942]

Dear Mummy and Daddy,

Here are some photos. Uncle Ross was teaching [me] to shot a 22 rifle hear are 2 of my targets. as you can see, I [am] reddy for hitler.

Love from [no signature]

[On the back of the letter Margaret wrote:]

25   Undated

Dear Penelope

I wrote today but B wants to send you photos etc. Says he didn't write from Montreal.

The two targets have survived among the letters.

The photos include seven of Camp Magog and three of the Welds. The return address in Ben's handwriting on the back of the envelope of the letter, postmarked "London Aug 24 10PM 1942 Ont.," reads "B. Barman c/o F. Weld Mt. Brydges London."

"I wrote today": Margaret's letter of this date has not survived, nor have those numbered 16–29, from July–October 1942.

The following letter demonstrates that, following his time at Camp Magog, Ben finally found his own voice. The letter, which is typed, is long, and treats a variety of topics at length and in a systematic fashion. Above all, it shows that Ben, perhaps inspired by his time on his own, knew his own mind and was willing to express his views. The envelope containing this letter is addressed in a hand different from that of Margaret Penrose or Ben, with the address on the back being originally (in Ben's handwriting) "c/o F. Weld, Mt. Brydges, London."

Ben to His Parents with an Addition by Margaret Penrose [typed]

1000 Wellington Street,

LONDON, Ont.

24th August, 1942

Dear Mummie and Daddy,

Thank you for the nice clothes you sent me. They all fit perfectly. I hope you didn't have to use any of your own coupons on them. Do they allow me some of my own?

I wrote to Bampa today and thanked him for his letter and the news about the lodestone, which was very interesting.

I'm glad to be settled down here again. I got a new watch as soon as I came back on the 19th. It costs $3.50 cents with an 85 cent tax on it. It is a luminous wristwatch and I can tell the time in the dark.

I spent two nights at the Harts when I came back on Wednesday and I've played with Don there a lot. Mrs Hart got a telegram saying that Ken and Bev were O.K. after the Dieppe raid. When I came back from the Harts Roger and I have been playing lots of games in the house. We play a lot of make-up games. We invent them ourselves. Last night we all kicked [Added by Margaret: an old] Humpty around the grounds until most of its stuffing came out. It was great fun.

Just before I left Montreal Uncle Ross took the two coupons for sugar that I had saved up in camp (where we weren't rationed) off my card and got himself some extra sugar. But Margaret says she has more than enough anyway.

Mrs Hart read me her letter. I am so glad you like Bev a lot. I have not seen him but Ken is very nice and I think you will like him too.

Rosemary came back from boarding school and went to camp for the summer on the same day. Christopher and Martin are all going to the same boarding school next term. So Blair and Aunt Orion and the maid will be the only ones left in the house. I spent my last night in Montreal at Aunt Orion's sister's place and she is very nice. She looks more like Aunt Orion's mother and knows exactly how to take care of children very well.

I sent some of my hair in a letter to Jonathan as Margaret forwarded the letter with Rodericks hair to Montreal two weeks ago. I expect they will be sent back soon with all those Punches. I have not seen them yet. Thank you for sending them.

I have had quite a lot of swimming at Magog and at camp Kanawana. But at Magog I had an attack of dizziness so the doctor wouldn't let me swim much. There was an epidemic of this kind there. At camp there was an Indian of the Iroquois tribe who came and visited us for three days and showed how to make all sorts of things like bows and arrows, stone tomahawks. The ones that the real Indians used to make. And how to make tea out of different kinds of roots and plants. About half the camp learnt to smoke a pipe of peace, at least 2 or 3 people smoked it. He showed us how to do some Indian war dances and their hunting dances and a few other dances. Another event in the camp was Marcel, who is a great piano player who now is in the army, came with us for a week and played to us. When one of the camp chiefs gets up to speak the campers all sing "Why were you born so beautiful, why were you born at all? etc" and he has to stop them by sitting down and saying amen at the end. Then he gets up again and they begin saying "Speak, speak, speak" and when he does they all cheer for a long time, between his words, so that he doesn't get much said. We had a circus at camp and each tent put on their own booth. We had catapults and shot at Hitler and Mussolini and Hirohito.

Love from,
Benjamin

[Addition by Margaret Penrose:] Thanks a lot for the mass observation book. Much appreciated. B phoned from Harts Friday 8 30 AM to ask to come back here! So he did. He has moved around so much. MP

The "Dieppe Raid," on 19 August 1942, was a disastrous amphibious attack on the port of Dieppe, France, in which over half of the force, composed mostly of Canadian troops, was either killed, wounded, or captured.

"Humpty" probably refers to a cloth toy resembling the egg-shaped Humpty Dumpty, from the well-known children's song.

The taking of "two coupons for sugar" was not illegal until, in September 1943, the War Prices and Trade Board banned the use of an individual's food coupons by others.

"Rosemary," the only daughter of Norman and Ursula Dewey, and so Ben's cousin, was attending the Dunham School for Girls, in southern Quebec (now closed). She must have spent the months of July and August in camp.

"*Christopher and Martin*" *refer to the elder son of Ross and Orion Barman and to the youngest son of Ursula Dewey.*

"*Aunt Orion's sister*" *was Marion Costigan.*

"*Magog*" *was the name of the camp attended by Ben at the end of June, almost certainly the Sunday school camp mentioned in Margaret Penrose's letter of 21 June and Ben's letter of 10 September 1942.*

Kanawana Camp occupies a 550-acre site at the village of Saint Sauveur des Monts, now part of Saint Saveur, Quebec.

"*Iroquois tribe*" *refers to the Haudenosaunee First Nation, which lives in both Ontario and Quebec. The length of the Iroquois's visit suggests that it took place at Camp Kanawana.*

Ben's reference to "*tents*" *suggests that the activities he recounted took place at Camp Kanawana and not at Camp Magog, which housed the campers in huts.*

"*Mass Observation book*" *was probably* People in Production: An Enquiry into British War Production *by Mass Observation (1942). Mass Observation, founded in 1937, was a private undertaking that used volunteers to observe and report on the lives, culture, and views of ordinary people in Britain.*

The following letter marks Ben's return to everyday life in London, with daily school. The number of mistakes in the typing indicates that Ben typed it himself.

Ben to His Parents [typed]

xxxx

> 1000 Wellington St.
> London Ont.
> Sept. 10 [1942]

Dear Mummy and Daddy

On Sept. 8 I began school in grade 6 and I am doing fine. Miss Chapman is quit nice but the time goes very slowly. On my holidays I went in a canoe with 2 or 3 hols in it you could paddle 100 yards out and then sink. Our cat has 6 kittens, 4 black 1 yellow and 1 gray one. In my holidays at Bayfield I read 4 big little books they were quite exciting.

LOVE FROM BENJAMIN

[Addition on the back of the envelope:]
Margaret Penrose to Penelope Barman
That Mass Observation book you sent has been MUCH appreciated. Many
thanks. MP

"September 8" was, in 1942, the first day after Labour Day.
"Big little books" were first published in 1932 by the Whitman Publishing Com-
pany of Racine, Wisconsin. They were small, compact books designed with a cap-
tioned illustration on the right-hand page opposite a page of text on the left.

In September 1942, Ben began his third year of schooling in the Canadian ed-
ucational system. His adventures in July and August 1942 had enhanced his capacity to handle life outside of the Penrose family. Moreover, he had become
more accustomed to Canadian ways of life.

7

Ordered Home,
October 1942–April 1943

I am all right over here and I'd probably only see you for a few days and then
go off to a boarding school, which would be worse.
~Ben Barman to his parents, 15 October 1942

He is my one piece of war work and I should feel perfectly awful if he left me
and I had to start driving the salvage truck.
~Margaret Penrose to Penelope Barman, 16 October 1942

Studies of child evacuees agree that the fifth stage in the war guest experience,
the prospect and actual process of going home, was a deeply traumatic development for most of the children and also for their host families. On arriving
in North America, war guests had had to adjust to and settle into a very different
existence from the one they had left. Life in Canada, sometimes experienced
for as much as three years – an infinity for a child – became an established and
usually enjoyable norm. Most war guests had fading and at times ambivalent
memories of their original home and family. Moreover, listening to the radio
made many children conscious of the dangers and deprivations that life in
Great Britain entailed. Consequently, they saw little gain in leaving their safe
haven. Such was the case with Ben.

No evidence survives to explain why or precisely when Ben's parents resolved
to bring their eldest son back to England when they did. The reasons for the
decision are not hard to deduce. July 1942 marked the second anniversary of
Ben's departure. Correspondence and photographs provided no compensation
for his absence. He was already becoming a memory and so a stranger to his
parents. No good reason existed for his remaining in Canada, given that the
threat of a German invasion across the English Channel, the justification for
Ben's departure, had vanished. Ben, who had turned eleven in May 1942, was

close to the age when he would enter secondary school. As Anthony Bailey, an evacuee in the United States, has observed, "those who had put down their children's name for public schools saw the age of entry approaching and passing," with their progeny missing out "on what still seemed then the indispensable ladder of British education and success."[1] For Lewis, it was important that his eldest son enter Repton, the public school he and his uncle had attended. Another justification for Ben's parents' decision sprang from Ben's own statement "I suppose I'm beginning to become a good Canadian." If their eldest son did acquire a Canadian appearance, accent, and habits, he would be essentially "declassing" himself, ceasing to be an English gentleman.

The Penroses had no ability to block Ben's return, since his uncle Ross, not Lionel or Margaret, was his legal guardian in Canada. And, it would seem that their upbringing of Ben and the suitability of their household were both in question. In Ben's own words, "I subsequently learned that my parents had sent someone to visit me in Canada taking with them some extra money for the Penroses. They reported back that I should be removed immediately as the family were not satisfactory."[2] What makes a household suitable or unsuitable for raising a child depends a great deal on the perceptions and assumptions of the observer, yet the reasons that this person gave for this appraisal are not clear.

The Penroses' style of life was certainly not conventional. Writing about his father, Oliver Penrose observed, "My parents belonged to some kind of serious thinkers group in London, Ontario, and on one occasion the group asked my father to speak to them about mental illness. One of the symptoms of mental illness, he told them, was a lack of attention to one's own clothing and apparently they were very amused to note that the speaker's own trousers were not held up by a belt but by a length of string."[3] Possession of a private income meant, however, that Lionel Penrose could afford to disregard conventions. As for Margaret, the tone of her letters to Penelope indicates that she was inclined towards dramatic displays and making emphatic statements. Traits such as her having, in her own words, "pranced about all over the house waving a dish towel and a potato scraper" while listening to phonograph records, did not ac-

1 Bailey, *America Lost and Found*, 131.
2 The informant could have been the "Lt. Col. whatnot of Toronto" and his welcome "present," mentioned by Margaret Penrose in her letter of 11 January 1942.
3 Oliver Penrose, *Lionel S. Penrose* (1998), n.p.

cord with the accepted vision of proper behaviour by an upper-class wife. Given that Lowis and Penelope knew Margaret and Lionel well, the report they received as to the unsuitability of the Penrose household probably came as no great surprise. It may have contributed to their decision that the time had arrived for Ben to return to his own home and his own milieu, which demanded his entering a suitable English public school.

The next two letters show that the decision to bring Ben home was taken around the start of September 1942, being conveyed in letters to Ben, Margaret, and Ross Barman. Ross, as Ben's guardian, was put in charge of arranging the North American logistics of his nephew's return. As the following letter typed by Margaret Penrose shows, Ben was very unwilling to accept his recall home. He was happy where he was. A return to England would, he assumed quite correctly, mean going to a boarding school, which he equated with the hated Pinewood prep school he had attended in 1940.

Ben to His Parents [typed]

15th Oct. 1942
1000 Wellington Street, London, On

Dear Mummie and Daddy,

Uncle Ross says that he cannot get a place for me to come over till about next July. Anyway I am all right over here and I'd probably only see you for a few days and then go off to a boarding school, which would be worse.

Miss Chapman at school, I find, is an excellent teacher, and I have been getting on very well with the oboe.

Tomorrow all the bus routes will be changing and I am making a map of the bus routes. I am colouring them, one colour for each bus.

A few weeks ago I saw Bev Hart. He has come over here, as you probably know to take parachute training. I have just heard that Mr Laidlaw has gone to British Columbia. Miss Chapman hinted that he might be coming here tomorrow. I hope it will be him.

We are going to have a big project at school. There will be a big map of British Columbia on the floor of the auditorium. There will be pictures of real people on it. The pillars will be totem poles with great big pictures of mountain scenery behind them. We are the only class that knows about it.

We all went to see "Fantasia", Walt Disney's show, you know, have you seen it yet? A few days ago, Lionel showed us under a big microscope, some slides of normal blood, of T.B., tape worm's eggs, malaria, pneumococo and a louse that Lionel found on the toilet paper probably off the cat!! Margaret put some insect killing powder on the cat so thank goodness they're all dead.

Here are some photographs, as I said I was going to send you some in my last letter. We have not heard from you for a very long time. Your letter to Mrs Hart came today and was forwarded. We are all well here and getting along fine.

Love from,

Benjamin Barman

"Miss Chapman" was Ben's Grade 6 teacher.

"Mr Laidlaw" was Ben's former teacher.

Fantasia, released in 1940, was a Walt Disney film consisting of animated segments set to classical music.

"We have not heard from you": Penelope Barman's health problems may explain the lack of letters from her.

There is no way to identify the photographs to which Ben referred.

Penelope's letter of 15 September 1942, announcing the decision to bring Ben home, has not survived, but the reason she presented to justify the decision – that the Barmans wished to relieve the Penroses of the nuisance and expense of having Ben – can be deduced from Margaret's reply. The argument was intended to avoid giving offence with any suggestion that the Penroses' upbringing of Ben was in any respect deficient. As Margaret's letter number 30, the next one to survive, makes clear, this stratagem backfired. Her resentment was patent.

Margaret Penrose to Penelope Barman

October 16th 1942   30

1000 Wellington St, London Ont.

My dear Penelope,

Yours of the 17th Sept. has just arrived (32), since Benny dictated his letter. He has nothing to add except that it wasn't Mr. Laidlaw that gave them a

surprise visit today after all. Only some opera singer or other. He is disappointed.

I'm so sorry you've had such a time with your jaw. What about the innards?

I can't make out <u>how</u> you got the impression that I shall be in anyway re-
lieved if your plans for returning Ben mature. It is a complete misunder-
standing on your part. We should be very sorry indeed if he went. I didn't
argue more forcibly before because I naturally thought your main reason for
wishing to have him back soon was that you couldn't wait any longer. It is not
for me to interfere in <u>that</u> sphere, I suppose. But for God's sake don't let the
idea that he is in any way a nuisance to <u>us</u> influence you! What <u>can</u> I have
written "between the lines"? As a matter of fact he is my one piece of war
work and I should feel perfectly awful if he left me and I had to start driving
the salvage truck, day in and day out instead, to comfort my soul. He is such
a convenient piece of war work too – no inconvenience whatever. He is not
in the least bit difficult to manage or anything. He and Roger make a perfect
couple and are easier to cope with together than apart. We don't want him
to go for any reason whatsoever. So for God's sake don't send for him on <u>our</u>
account – or on his! You notice how he postpones the evil day, in his letter,
from April to July? Wishful thinking what? – (Uncle Ross said April was the
earliest possible to Lionel on the telephone). And incidentally my pet bêtes
noires, the Montreal Barmans, have been removed from me, because Lionel
says Uncle R[oss]. was as nice as he could be and told him that it was no use
writing him letters ever because he "always got hold of the wrong end of
the stick." He didn't approve of the idea of sending B[en] back through the
submarine blitz, either.

Please don't try to project your desire to have B. back on to <u>us</u> in any way!
The idea exists entirely in your <u>own</u> mind and irritates us not a little. <u>Do</u> let
well alone till the German war is over. It will be just as wonderful to see him
again whenever it is, you know. I shall probably be mortally offended if you
remove him forcibly despite my entreaties. And as far as I can see the removal
will have to <u>be</u> forcible if during the war!

LOVE from Margaret

*As to "your jaw," I cannot recall my mother having problems with her jaw during
the family's residence in Twin Oaks. Probably her complaint was never discussed
in front of the children.*

As to "your innards," it is clear that Penelope was having problems with her re-productive system. Late in 1942, she was in a hospital at Chesham, Bucking-hamshire, the closest town to Twin Oaks, almost certainly for a hysterectomy, an operation that was, as Jonathan recalls, "quite unmentionable in those times."

The "submarine blitz" refers to the Battle of the Atlantic, a key element in the Second World War, which was being fought unrelentingly during 1942, with the advantage shifting against the Germans (sixty-five U-boats sunk in the second half of that year compared to twenty-one in the first). A crisis in the Battle of the At-lantic came in the first months of 1943, starting with huge losses of shipping, but culminating in the destruction of forty-three U-boats in the month of May alone.

"Driving the salvage truck" involved picking up salvage items, such as metals, paper, and rubber, and carrying them for sorting at a central depot. The program started in Canada in January 1941.

The above two letters, placed in the same envelope, were not mailed until 23 October, which may indicate that Margaret had doubts about the suitability of her fierce response to Ben's parents' decision.

About the time that the two letters would have arrived in England, the Barmans received the following letter from Bev Hart. The missive provides insights into the mind and life of a young Canadian soldier. The hospitality shown to him in England provided him with a psychological refuge from the pressures of war. Various constraints, including military secrecy and respect for the proprieties, restricted Bev's expressions of gratitude.

The letter is typed on Department of National Defence letterhead, and the envelope bears the return address "Lieut BB Hart lst Cdn. Parachute Bn, Camp Shilo, Manitoba" and is postmarked "SHILO M.P.O 1001 PM OC 19 42 Manitoba."

Beverley Hart to Penelope Barman

October 18, 1942

Dear Mrs. Barman;

By now you will no doubt have heard that I am now in Western Canada and may shortly be going to Georgia 'way down south. My good fortune seems almost unbelievable as I did not leave England until the fifteenth of September and in the meantime I enjoyed quite an ocean voyage arriving in New York and spent two wonderful weeks leave at home.

You see I am now a qualified Paratrooper after taking the prescribed training with the RAF in England. It bothered me a great deal to have to leave without even so much as a "goodbye" and even my brother Ken did not know of my paratroop work or my departure for Canada and home.

I also miss my troop of tanks and all the officers and fellows in my old regiment but when opportunities present themselves for advancement, travel, greater experience and many other advantages one can't allow anything to block the way.

It was quite a thrill meeting Benjamin and what a fine looking boy he is – a credit to his home & country. Benjamin, Jim Collyer and Don have the time of their young lives and I'm sure your son will always look back upon these days spent in London, Canada as being among the happiest of his boyhood. We love to have him at our place and I'd told Mother that every little kindness she does for Benjamin will to some degree show her appreciation for the wonderful hospitality the Barman family showered upon me in England.

If you remember the beautiful weather of a Canadian autumn you can picture what a lovely day I am enjoying right now. The sun is warm and there is not a cloud in the sky with just enough breeze to carry away the gayly coloured autumn leaves as they float toward the ground.

I am sorry that I was not able to be in England for your fall but all the time I was in the southern part of the country the weather was very lovely indeed. While on my furlough I left a very favourable impression of England with all my friends and relatives and I can honestly say that I enjoyed every day of my service in your country.

I am now looking forward to the day when, with other Canadian Paratroopers I will set foot on England's shores again, perhaps early in the spring and of course I will see my brother then and also you.

Please give my best wishes to Mr. Barman and the boys and accept my thanks once more for all your kindness shown me.

Sincerely,

Beverly Hart

"Camp Shilo Manitoba" had been established for the military in 1910. In 1942, the training program of the 1st Canadian Parachute Battalion was transferred to Camp Shilo from Fort Benning, Columbus, Georgia, where Bev was probably going to receive further training.

"Jim Collier" must have been a friend of Don Hart's, the youngest Hart boy, with whom Ben played during his Saturday visits to the Harts.

"Furlough" in the sense of military leave.

Meanwhile, back in London, Ontario, life for Ben continued on its familiar course, unaffected, for the time being, by his parents' decision. The following note, clearly copied from a text provided by the teacher, was enclosed in Margaret's letter of 25 October 1942. Not too much should be read into Ben's use of the word "mother," since Ben introduced Margaret at the meeting as "my kind hostess," as her letter states.

Ben to Margaret Penrose

Ryerson School

Oct. 19th, 1942

Dear Margaret

Will you please come to our class room on Thursday October twenty-second at 2.45pm. Miss Chapman and the class want you to come and get acquainted and see our work. We want to show you that we all work together and we want one hundred percent of all the mother's here.

Yours loving, Benjamin B.

Ben was indeed becoming integrated into Canadian life and, in the following letter, he did his best to make a case to his parents against his being brought back (Fig. 7.1) to England. His handwriting shows the stress he was feeling.

Ben to His Parents, with an Addition by Margaret Penrose

> 1,000 Wellington St,
> London Ont.
> 23th Oct. 1942

Dear Mummy and Daddy

I hope you are getting on all right because I am getting on all right. It would be silly for me to come there and just because lots of people came over there safely. I dont want to be sunk in the St. Lawrence like other some people. Any how it would be a pity for me to change schools when I am getting on so well here. here is a leaflet that the plains dropped

> Love from
> Benjamin Barman

[On the reverse is an addition from Margaret Penrose]

> 23rd Oct 42

Dear Penelope,

I send you an absurd book "Thank You Twice" for Xmas. Probably you've read it. The Bell children's experiences were rather different from B's but may amuse you if new to you.

This letter of B's is entirely spontaneous – written on receipt of your number 33 to B. (? 25th Sept) which I have not seen. No letter to <u>me</u> so far. Uncle Ross told Lionel <u>he</u> didn't approve of sending B back through the blitz & hoped the idea would be dropped! No chance before April anyway. <u>Sorry</u>.

> Love M

"*Sunk in the St. Lawrence*": *German U-boats sank or damaged nineteen ships in the Gulf of St Lawrence from May to October 1942.*

"*A leaflet that the plains dropped*" *refers to leaflets promoting the purchase of Victory Bonds, part of an intensive government campaign promoting the November 1942 offering of the bonds.*

"*Thank You Twice*" *refers to Caroline and Edie Bell,* Thank You Twice or How We Like America *(1941).*

"*The Blitz*" *must refer not to the Baedeker Raids on British towns from April to October 1942 but to the Battle of the Atlantic, waged from 1939 onwards between the German U-boats and the Allied convoys and their escorts.*

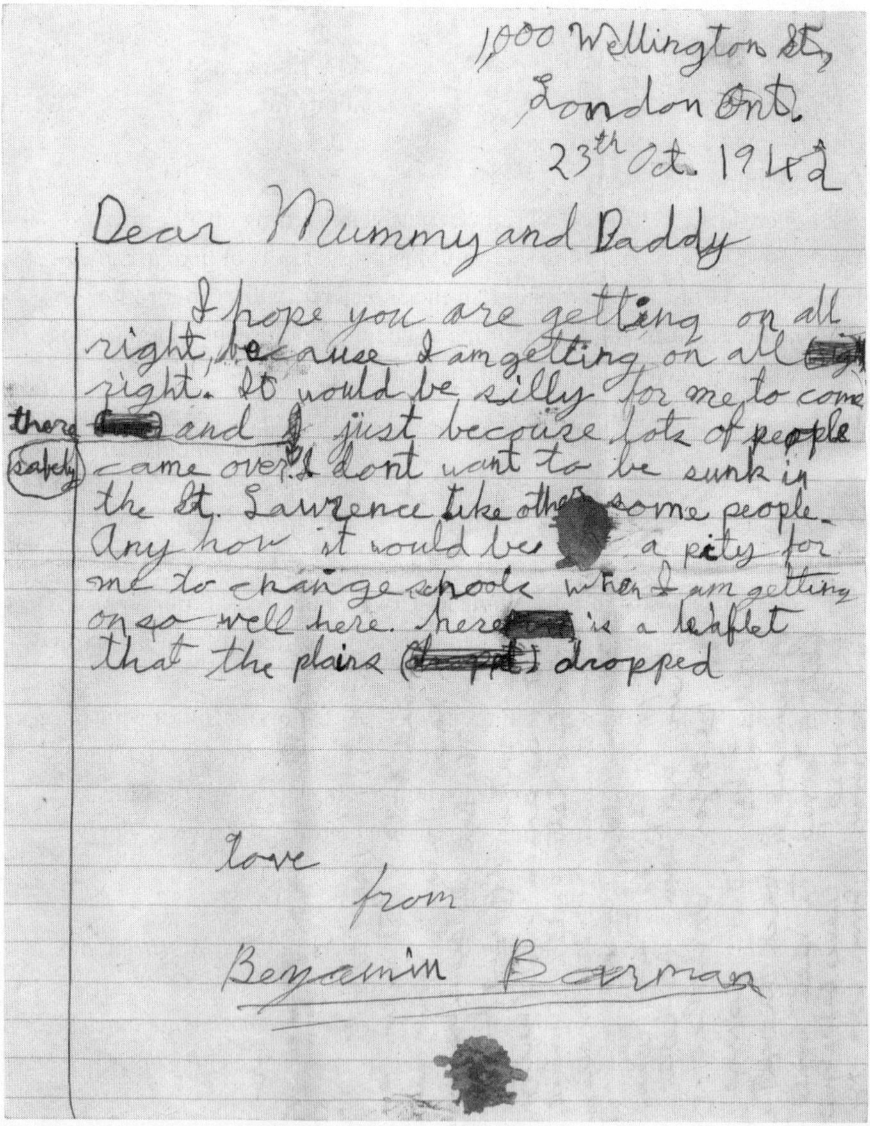

1000 Wellington St,
London Ont.
23th Oct. 1942

Dear Mummy and Daddy

I hope you are getting on all right, because I am getting on all right. It would be silly for me to come there ~~safely~~ and I just because lots of people came over. I don't want to be sunk in the St. Lawrence like ~~other~~ some people. Any how it would be a pity for me to change schools when I am getting on so well here. Here is a leaflet that the plains dropped

love
from

Benjamin Barman

Figure 7.1 Ben's letter to his parents, with a handwritten addition by Margaret Penrose, both dated 23 October 1942

Dear Penelope I wish you as
about look "Madelyn Two"
In Xmas. finally you've read
it. The Bell children's experience
were rather different from B's
but may amuse you if you ...
This letter of B's is actually
Spontaneous - written on ...

of your 33rd (?2.5 copy) which
I have not seen. No letter
to me sofa. Uncle Ross
liked the diary apiece
2) send me B check through the
felt + hoped the idea would
be dumped! No chance before April
answers. Love M.

Writing the above note, Margaret was clearly trying to use both Ben and his uncle Ross as weapons to persuade Ben's parents to drop their plans for their son's return.

The next letter, one of the few from Margaret to survive from the last months of 1942, is a vivid testimony to the central importance that food played in the lives of ordinary people in Canada and Great Britain during the Second World War. In Great Britain, the role of food parcels, both official and private, in providing variety and in supplying deficiencies was, as I well recall from my childhood, psychologically important for those who received them. Just how extensive was that receipt is difficult to judge from the literature on the subject.

Margaret Penrose to Penelope Barman

32   1000 Wellington St
                          Sun 25 Oct 42   London, Ont
                                              Canada

My dear Penelope,

I've just sent off six food parcels to England for Xmas & the one to you (from B) contains just marmalade, raisins and "jello." I searched the kitchen cupboard to fill it up as I was in the packing mood – it was Sunday – & that was all I could find after the ravages of the other parcels. First of all I'd tried putting in a pound of very strong smelly delicious cheese. But I decided that it would be phosphorescent before it reached you & might spoil the raisins so I replaced it with the jello that I know your children like (– ours don't much – so they won't mind the fact that it is getting scarce here. I'm just making a fat juicy "spotted dog" for supper which they much prefer – more filling & (I fear) more fattening.)

Anyway, I've been told you have so much cheese you have to put it in the pudding. I wish I knew more about the facts of the case. It would be nice to know (strictly in the abstract of course) what people are short of & what they are not. This simple instruction would save so much shipping space! One constantly hears of people packing up matches & lighter fuel & teabags (which you hate) tinned salmon and things that you have plenty of – and thus setting fire to the ship so well meaningly in their efforts to relieve you of "famine." Lots of parcels must be quite useless anyway. I know you need mar-

malade as you have no oranges. But I expect you don't need jam. Your sugar
ration is as big as ours (½ lb weekly) isn't it? And that is far more than we can
use. With our 12 lbs a month I bottle fruit, make jars & jars of applesauce,
grape juice and God knows what not & still have lots left over. As for sweets
perhaps you need those? But as you are rationed, I understand, to the ½ lb
weekly & I don't used ½ lb in a month for my family (except perhaps at
Xmas) – I've done nothing about sweets this time. Maybe that was a mistake.
Probably the shops don't stock that amount so your coupons are useless to
you? That is the kind of thing one wants to know. Also, do they remove
coupons from you if you receive goods (in parcels) that are rationed?? I never
can make out about that. It would be maddening to receive some filthy Lipton's tea when one was relying on one's coupons for Lapsang Souchong or
some such luxury. We can just manage on our tea ration ½ oz a week – as
Oliver is allowed tea coupons too. They are alternative to coffee is so we are
<u>worse</u> off than you on that score. Luckily Canadian coffee gives me indiges-
tion unless it is fresh ground so I've stopped buying it. Postum is unrationed.

As for meat we are sharing an ox with 3 other families! We keep it in a re-
frigeration plant which is kept below zero & my nightmare is to get locked
in there when I go to grab one of my joints of meat! It worked out at seven
pence a pound & is a wonderful economy! Liver, tongue, heart etc. thrown
in free. But I expect they will ration meat soon & stop this – probably not till
after our quarter ox is consumed. I hear that the Americans are to get 2 ½ lbs
meat each per week! How will they store all <u>that</u> away in their stomachs? It's
a funny life! There was a beef shortage a few weeks ago owing to a quarrel
between farmers & govt. But that seems to have been settled & beef abounds
once more. Baked beans & tinned fish are slightly scarce here as they are
being sent to England. I believe you get lots of Canadian cheese now? But
there's plenty left here.

All this peroration was meant to give me an opportunity to explain that
<u>tinned</u> marmalade is no longer on the market, so I poured a two lb jar into
an old treacle tin for you. As the tin had previously been used for water-pistol-
filling (by Roger & Benny) I poured some hot wax into the tin first & cooled
it off. So don't <u>scrape</u> the tin to get the marmalade out as it will be all waxy.
Anyway I'm afraid the marmalade won't keep, & I do want to know whether
it does or not, as if it <u>does</u> work I'll send more in this way to other people. If
it does <u>not</u> arrive in good condition I will save the time and energy! Will you

please tell me truthfully about this? One is not supposed to send marmalade
except in tins.

You've never told me yet whether you have clothes coupons for Benny in
England? Does he deprive you of clothing points by his lavish parcels? I've
just sent over 100 lbs of old clothes to Russia – many of them Benny's because
I feel their need is greater than ours. I even sent my old fur coat [Fig. 7.2] –
(bought just before I left England). Canadian moths are 100% bigger & worse
than English ones & it is impossible to keep clothes that are not in use here
anyway. B has lots & lots of clothes – shoes are his only shortage & I shall get
him some great boots for the snow when it comes, I think. [I can perfectly
well afford this out of B's board money!!]

The Ross Barmans gave him some white & fawn rubber soled ones this
summer, but they will be no good for the snow. And none of us know how to
clean them!! His others are all too small for him & too big for Roger. B wears
8s & Roger 4s, Oliver 8 ½. So that doesn't allow for cooperative shoeing yet!

What a dull letter – but I feel boring today & you never write now.

Much love Margaret

I enclose the invitation B sent me. He made a nice speech to the class &
introduced "my kind hostess" – all the children had to do this for their mothers. The class is "democratic" & has minsters of finance, interior, exterior etc.
etc. All made lovely speeches!! B happens not to be one of the "ministers."
But the show was first class. I took a friend who was most impressed. She
had never been into one of her own public elementary school classes
before – too snobbish!!

"Lapsang Souchong" is a smoke-dried black tea from China. Its very distinctive
taste makes it a connoisseur's tea.

"Postum" was invented by Charles Post in 1912 as a non-caffeine alternative to
coffee, although its taste was not the same. Postum was particularly popular in
North America during the Second World War, but thereafter fell out of favour.

Meat was exempt from rationing until 27 May 1943, when the weekly ration
was set at one to two and a half pounds, depending upon the type and cut. The
physical demands made by war work and the higher incomes the war generated
had actually increased the consumption of meat per capita between 1942 and 1943.

"Lipton's" were the first commercial teas, sold in packages at cheap prices for the
mass market, which made them "filthy."

Figure 7.2 Margaret in her "old fur coat," carrying Pushkin

"*Spotted dog*" *is an English pudding (alternatively known as "spotted dick")* *made with flour, beef suet, butter, and dried fruit (either currants or plums),* *wrapped in a cloth and then boiled. As Margaret Penrose notes, it is very fatten-* *ing.*

"*Sweets*" *is the English term for candy. Margaret Penrose's usage throughout her* *letters is uniformly English.*

"*Enclose the invitation*" *refers to Ben's letter of 19 October to Margaret Penrose,* *transcribed above.*

The fact that the ensuing letter from Margaret Penrose was not given a number suggests that the correspondence and therefore the relationship between the two women had become less close. Penelope's silence may have been, as Margaret surmised, due to ill health or, perhaps more likely, to Penelope's resenting Margaret's impassioned response to the decision to call Ben home. Margaret was clearly concerned to keep the friendship intact.

Margaret Penrose to Penelope Barman

1000 Wellington Street, Londn, Ont.
2nd Nov. 42

My dear Penelope,

I have given up the hope of having another nice letter from you. They used to be one of the bright features of the week. But now, though I get lots of English mail, there's never a word from you. Probably I had better not conjecture the reason. I'm sure to be wrong. I do hope it is not on account of ill health on your part. I have not heard since your operation, so you may well be suffering hell in hospital and in no fit state to put pen to paper. I also trust that you have not been so offended and horrified by B's eloquent outbursts on the subject of been transferred to Europe. [Added by Margaret in the margin in pencil: B is far better at dictating letters than I should be. It is difficult to type fast enough for him. He stands there with his hands in his pockets & his head on one side & criticises my efforts at getting down what he says in a most professional manner. Sometimes the results seem meaningless to me – but I leave them as he wishes!] We all get so horribly insular over here that it may be difficult for you to understand how he feels. Just as we often must miss the point with you. But maybe we shall have got B. toned down by April or whatever it may be. Up to the present I am afraid he will have to be made to embarque at the point of a pistol. And I'm hardly the person to do that. Or perhaps you will make the sensible decision of letting him wait a year or longer. He may get used to the idea of moving. At present he keeps saying that he wants money for Canadian Victory Stamps (most of the children get one a week at school price 1/- [one shilling]). They get a five dollar savings certificate for four dollars, when they have enough stamps, and these are repayable in 1957 or some such date. B. is convinced that he will be in Canada <u>then</u> to receive his award! But so far I have discouraged him from buying any. It really seems silly in his case. The others have them, of course, and it comes quite expensive. We ourselves blind all our spare cash, and much that is far from spare, in Victory Bonds, not to mention compulsory "savings" all of which will obviously have to be converted into something else when the fateful date arrives, or the country would go bust. So I shall concentrate on getting B <u>footwear</u> – (urgently required) – your kind quarterly instalment to hand, many thanks.

The purpose of this letter was to forward you Benny's report; –

"I think Benjamin's effort is improving. I wonder if more sleep would help him to pay attention without 'fiddling'.

Arith P   Social Studies P (P – 74 to 60%   U – 59 to 40%)
Spelling U   Writing U

H Chapman, Ryerson School

Grade VI"

I'm afraid this is not so encouraging as it might be. But Miss C. was very gloomy about Roger when he was in her class last year, and he (R) seems to be getting on like wildfire now he is in grade VII with Mr Wheeler. Incidentally, I provide the children with 11 hours sleep each night, but I don't seem to be able to increase the dose without more nagging than I care to provide. Lights are out at 8.30 or 9 and they all have to be woken at 8.15 except on Sundays when we all sleep till about 11, children included. I can't do more, though I wish I could get them practised, homeworked, bathed and bedded earlier so that I could go out to things in the evening on time myself. It is no good going out until they're settled. Miss Chapman is a very nice woman despite her gloomy report cards. She is an ardent Oxford Grouper (as most of the Ryerson teachers seem to be). The children are made to sit still for a few minutes each morning and "listen to God". They tend to say afterwards what God told them. Some of them are quite interesting. B. said God told <u>him</u> "always to be ready to try something new." Personally I have no objection to the system. Anyway with kids it only goes skin deep. So I hope you don't mind about it.

At last it has stopped raining and my sheets will begin to dry, I trust, in time to be ironed tomorrow. Monday's weather always seems desperately important. More so now as I've rashly agreed to drive the salvage truck on Mon. afternoons. But I think I shall resign at once, as I really seem to have quite enough to do. There must be lots of idler women around.

Love from Margaret

P. S. I wonder if you get enough sweets now that they are rationed? B wants to send J & R most of what he collected at Halloween – but if you get enough anyway it seems silly.

"Victory stamps" was a scheme to involve children in the war effort by enabling them to buy stamps in a booklet which, when full, could be exchanged for a Victory Bond.[4]

"P – 74 to 60%" and "U – 59 to 40%" on Ben's report card probably signified "Pass" and "Unsatisfactory."

"four dollars" then worth just under a pound sterling.

'Blind' is an English term that means "devote" or "lavish."

"Oxford Grouper" was a Christian movement, founded during the 1920s by Dr Frank Buchman (1878–1961), which emphasized absolute honesty, sincerity, unselfishness, and love as its goals. The movement was renamed Moral Rearmament in 1938.

In Great Britain "sweets" were first rationed on 2 July 1942, at seven ounces a week for children over five.

In the following letter, as Margaret Penrose commented on its back, Ben maintained his campaign against going back to England. His comments make clear that he not only listened to the radio but that he evaluated and so understood the significance of the news he heard.

Ben to His Parents, with an Addition from Margaret Penrose

1000 Wellington Street

6th Nov 42   LONDON, Ont.

Dear Mummie and Daddy,

I have just had your letter of 7th Oct. If you want me to come back in an <u>airoplane</u> as long as I don't have to go to boarding school immediately or in two or three weeks time, I wouldn't mind coming. I would like to come over and see you but I do think it is rather dangerous going over by ship and being bombed. And also when I'm in England I do not want to be bombed. I've often heard on the radio that a ship has been sunk and I've heard about the

4 Bailey, *America Lost and Found*, 131.

air raids. So I know it <u>is</u> dangerous. Margaret says that Mr Murray may be coming to see me. Why couldn't I go back with him in an AIROPLANE, provided I'm not going back to boarding school.

Just while I was in the middle of writing this letter, a travelling salesman came in and made a nuisance of himself by pretending to sell us a tin of moth ball crystals, and with it you get a comb and a bottle of window cleaner free, but really it cost twice as much as it would if you bought the things in a store.

They're going to get me a better oboe here. The oboe I have now is not on the conservatory system but the new one will be. I don't want to stop learning the oboe if I go back to England. As I'm going on so well at Ryerson School here it would be a pity for me to move and I think it will mess up my education.

We don't have to have coupons for clothes, so Margaret is just going out to get me a pair of boots. Is there really such a lot of food in England? I've always heard there wasn't hardly any at all. And you've always said you have to stand in queues such a lot. And I don't see why you've suddenly changed your mind. Has a lot of food suddenly arrived from here? If so will there still keep on being a lot more there? There's too much of everything here except tea and coffee which I don't drink, and we get along perfectly well. We have 3 or 4 quarts of milk every day so we're not at all short.

Love from Benjamin

[Margaret Penrose attached the following handwritten addition to Ben's letter:]

Dear P,

I think I may be able to get B round to the idea of going home if I'm given <u>time</u>. The idea was a shock at first as he is so well settled in. Of course whatever you think best will have to be done. Naturally we will welcome Mr Murray & invite him to anything he likes – if he ever materialises. Uncle Ross told Lionel that <u>he</u> might visit us. But I think it unlikely. He never asks L to see him (when in Montreal). But of course we'd invite him.

Much love, Margaret

B's letter is entirely spontaneous. Just the meanderings of his unprompted mind. I have never told him it was dangerous to sail the ocean. But not un-

Figure 7.3 Handkerchief printed with "Souvenir, London, Ont. Canada,"
enclosed in a letter Ben sent his parents, 6 November 1942

naturally he has got the idea from the news. Ten ships have been sunk in the
St Lawrence to date (Ottawa official.) But I don't expect the German war to
last ad infinitum.

Xmas present from B enclosed!

*"Mr Murray" cannot be identified, unless he was the Cmdr A.D.S. Murray, an em-
ployee of* BOAC, *mentioned in Lowis Barman's letter to Ben of 27 April 1943.*

*As to the "conservatory system," the standard oboe is the "conservatoire" or "con-
servatory" type developed in Paris in the nineteenth century.*

*"10 ships" were torpedoed in the St Lawrence by two U-boats between 27 August
and 7 September 1942.*

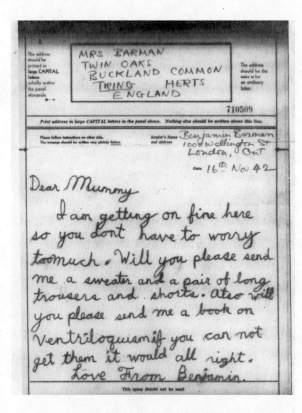

The address should be printed in large CAPITAL letters wholly within the panel alongside.

MRS BARMAN
TWIN OAKS
BUCKLAND COMMON
TRING   HERTS
    ENGLAND

The address should be the same as for an ordinary letter.

710509

Print address in large CAPITAL letters in the panel above. Nothing else should be written above this line.

Please follow instructions on other side. The message should be written very plainly below.

Sender's Name and Address   Benjamin Barman
1000 Wellington St
London, Ont
— 16ᵗʰ Nov 42—

Dear Mummy

I am getting on fine here
so you dont have to worry
too much. Will you please send
me a sweater and a pair of long
trousers and shorts. Also will
you please send me a book on
Ventriloquism if you can not
get them it would all right.
Love From Benjamin.

This space should not be used

Figure 7.4
Airgraph from
Ben to his mother,
16 November 1942

Margaret's addition to Ben's letter suggests that she was, by early November, beginning to accept that Ben would sooner or later return to England and that she must persuade him to accept the prospect of that return. The Christmas present sent by Ben to his parents survives. It was a souvenir handkerchief marked "Souvenir London Ont. Canada" with the picture of an Indian with a single feather in his hair (Fig. 7.3).

Ben's next letter (Fig. 7.4) is an interesting piece of evidence of the postal history of Canada. In 1941, the British General Postal Office began a system for mail between Great Britain and the troops stationed in the Middle East. Letters were written on special forms that were then microfilmed. The microfilm roll was then sent to Cairo, where the letters were printed out and mailed to the recipients. Soldiers sent home their letters by the same system. A roll of microfilm containing 1600 airgraphs weighed just five and a half ounces compared to five pounds for the equivalent letters on paper.

Canada started an identical system of airgraphs to Great Britain in November 1941. Airgraphs from Great Britain to Canada began in August 1942. The size of the printed out letter was three and a half by four and a half inches.

Airgraph from Ben to Penelope Barman

Benjamin Barman
1000 Wellington St
London, Ont.
16th Nov 42

Dear Mummy

I am getting on fine here so you dont have to worry too much. Will you please send me a sweater and a pair of long trousers and shorts. Also will you please send me a book on ventriloquism if you can not get them it would [be] all right.

Love From Benjamin.

Ben's grandfather Dr Leonard James Spencer developed, as the long-time editor of the *Mineralogical Magazine,* a network of professional and personal contacts with geologists around the world. Ben now profited from this network.

Arthur Leonard Parsons to Ben Barman

Royal Ontario Museum of Mineralogy
Queens Park
Toronto 5, Canada.
December 24 1942

My dear Benjamin,

I have just received a letter from your grandfather telling me of your address, and he had already told me that you had visited the Museum. I shall be glad if when you come the next time you would let me know so that I could see you.

Your grandfather tells me that you have a new cousin. Possibly you have not yet heard, because it arrived only a few days before he wrote his letter.

I would be very glad to show you some of the interesting things we have here, for your grandfather in the past has done the same sort of thing for me. I hope that you are going to have a most delightful Christmas and that I will see you before the New Year is very old.

Yours sincerely,
A. L. Parsons
Director

"A.L. Parsons" was Arthur Leonard Parsons, born in Mount Morris, New York, in 1873. He went to the University of Toronto in 1907, eventually became a full professor, and in 1935–43 served as the director of the Royal Ontario Museum of Mineralogy, now integrated into the Royal Ontario Museum.

As to Ben's "new cousin," the baby was Harriet Spencer (now Harriet Dashwood), born on 2 November 1942, the first child of Philip, Penelope's brother, and his wife, Barbara Spencer.

The following letter, which was typed, is notable for its display of Ben's interest in the outside world and for the beginnings of his acceptance that he had to return to England. It also reveals that his father rarely wrote to him.

Ben to His Parents [typed]

1000 Wellington Street, London, Ont.
29 Dec 1942

Dear Mummie and Daddy,

I got a letter from Mr Parsons the director of the Royal Ontario Museum of Mineralogy. He said that Bampa wrote to him telling him about me and how interested I was in the things that he had there. So he invited me to come and see him and he would show me all over the museum, which I'm sure is very nice of him.

Here it is thawing a lot and it is raining a little every now and again. It has been 15 below zero and daresay it will soon be again.

For Christmas, not counting my stocking, which I had a lot of things in, I got a fort, tool set, tie, two airoplanes, two jigsaw puzzles, "Hobbies and Sports for Boys", Bingo, a whirlaplane, Happy Hikers, Coast to Coast, a walkie toy, gloves, Bottoms Up, "Stories for Boys" (from Jonathan – one of the best). In my stocking some of the things were; – a pen (fountain) and a pencil on the other end. A puzzle that makes a butterfly when you put it together, an empty ink bottle with a trick artificial spill, a penknife, a note book, plasticine, and a key trick and three tangerines that were very good. There were other things that I have forgotten. I had a <u>very</u> nice Christmas with lots of turkey and Xmas pudding, and a lot of candy. Surprise to me, I wasn't sick.

Will you please tell me what you had at your Xmas, and what it was like. From the way Edward R Murrow talks on the radio from London, England I am afraid it must have been duller. He said it was the worst Xmas they had in a long time with last years Xmas cards and no excitements and not too much to eat. But yet you say there is plenty to eat and everything just going grand though you once told me a story about a lost onion and waiting in queues. How have you changed your mind so quickly?

Mrs Massy Beresford sent me $1 which I think was very nice of her.

I got Daddy's letter from the Grand Bristol Hotel and I was very pleased with it. It is the only one I have had from him for a very long time.

I began the holidays on 23rd Dec and we begin the school again on 4th Jan. You see here that we don't have such long holidays at Xmas and Easter, but 2 or 3 months in the summer. If I <u>do</u> go to England what school will I go to?

With love from Benjamin B

"Stories for Boys" has a title too general for the book to be identified.

"From Jonathan": the gift of "Stories for Boys" was from Ben's brother, as the next letter shows.

"Edward R. Murrow" (1908–65) was, during the Second World War, the CBS radio reporter in London. He was notable for the directness and vividness of his reporting, as Ben's comment attests.

Regarding "a lost onion," onions were in extremely short supply in Great Britain during the Second World War, so much so that losing one would be a cause for concern.

As to the "grand Hotel Bristol," hotels with this name were first class, but the location of this specific hotel is not clear.

The above typed letter continues:

Ben to Jonathan Barman

Dear Jonathan,

Thank you for the book you sent me it was one of my best presents. I hope you are having a nice time in England and having plenty to eat. How is Roderick getting on? Is he getting on too? I hope you don't fight and quarrel with each other. I suppose Roderick is now riding a bicycle that I used to have. I can just imagine you each day growing an inch higher.

Here Roger and I are having great fun playing, sometimes doing experiments, mostly making things out of cardboard and using up a tremendous lot of glue. Just after I got a tool set at Xmas, Roger and I made a wooden airoplane with a round piece of celophane for the propellor which makes it look as though it was buzzing around. Our landlord gave us a popcorn shaker and when you make the popcorn it tastes very nice and it is surprising how much the popcorn expands when it bursts. When I come back I might bring you some comic books of Superman and the Shadow, and some Biglittle books of Flash Gordon, Tailspin Tommy and 2 or three others. I will send you a comic book that I think you will like. These heroes are very tough. For instance if you shoot a bullet at Superman it bounces off him and usually hits the crook. He can jump amazing heights, more powerful than a locomotive and faster than a speeding bullet. He disguises himself as Clark Kent a newspaper reporter, who has a dumb girlfriend, Lois Lane.

Love from Benjamin B

"I hope you don't fight and quarrel" was a vain hope, thanks to my temper.

"Superman" began as a comic strip in 1938, rapidly gaining iconic status.

"The Shadow" started as a character on radio in 1930 and became the star of The Shadow Magazine *in 1931.*

"Flash Gordon," a science fiction hero, began as a comic strip in 1934.

"Tailspin Tommy," an airplane pilot, was the hero of a comic strip that ran from 1928 to 1942.

Included in the envelope addressed to "Mr. and Mrs. Barman and Jonathan" was a letter from Margaret.

Margaret Penrose to Penelope Barman

29th Dec 42

My dear Penelope.

Many Happy returns of the day. I must just thank you for all the lovely books you sent us. Bonamy Dobrée is a great friend of ours and Lionel knows E.M. Forster well. We had not got those books and it was a great pleasure to read them. The Sitwells I look forward to pursuing anon. You certainly are a genius at choosing us books. Unfortunately we already had 2 copies of the "Air and its Mysteries" so I handed that on to someone that we owed a present to. I think he enjoyed it. It is a lovely book and has been read with great enthusiasm. I did tell the children that the science encyclopaedia that I got 2nd hand from a friend was from you instead but I am not sure that they took me seriously as it was too big to post. This will explain their probable negligence in writing to thank you. I dont always have the energy to nag them to write as all suitable energy of that kind is absorbed by your son (forgive me). He has written 4 today. I like the one he composed to his younger brother – so elder brotherly!

I'm so tremendously impressed with the idea of your munition work. It makes me feel very insignificant in my small way. You certainly have plenty of energy and patriotism.

I think Benny is coming round to the idea of leaving Canada. I'm being as nasty as I can so I'm sure the prospect of leaving <u>me</u> will delight him. But his cheerfulness is irrepressible. I was slightly shocked by the way that he harps on food in his letters. Surely it can't be as important to him as all that? Probably a little less would improve his figure. There is no holding him where abundance reigns. They've just rationed butter to ½ lb a week each. But this is more than we are able to use up.

No proper letter from you for donkeys years. I suppose you're too busy now.

Much love from Margaret

By the way, the New Statesman is <u>such</u> a pleasure each week.

"Happy returns" refers to Penelope turning forty-one on 29 December 1942.

"Bonamy Dobrée" (1891–1974) was an academic and a prolific author on English literature and other subjects. The book sent was probably The Unacknowledged

Legislator: Conversation on Literature and Politics in a Warden's Post, 1941 *(1942)*.

"E.M. Forster" is Edward Morgan Forster (1879–1970), a leading English novelist of the twentieth century. The book sent may have been his Virginia Woolf *(1942).*

"The Sitwells" refers to Edith, [Sir] Osbert, and Sacheverell Sitwill, three aristocratic siblings who figured prominently in the literary world during the interwar period and after. The book may have been Trio: Dissertations on Some Aspects of National Genius *(1938).*

"Air and Its Mysteries" refers a book on meteorology by C.M. Botley (1938).

"They've just rationed butter": Butter rationing was introduced in Canada in December 1942.

Margaret Penrose to Penelope Barman

39 – I didn't start numbering mine till the end of Jan last year.

1000 Wellington St

London Ont

4ᵗʰ Jan 43

My dear Penelope

I forgot to thank you for the Osbert Lancaster. Of course that too was the immense success that he always is. Your presents to us all were extremely successful and well received. A thousand thanks.

It was funny how B. wrote last time saying that after all that food "surprise to me I wasn't sick"! On the very next day he complained of a Tummy ache & was lying down in the next room while we ate dinner. I kept asking how he felt & saying – no dinner for him while the pain lasted! After he had listened to us chomping away for a while he suddenly claimed that the pain had gone & came rushing in for some food. I warned him again, but he persisted that the symptoms had been "hysteria" so I served him. After one mouthful the worst happened all over the floor! So it was another example of the triumph of greed over nausea. It really was so funny that we couldn't help laughing.

B has been <u>so</u> good and charming since, he is an example to the others though I fear they are incapable of profiting from it. When my weekly char telephoned (as usual) – the "maid" took two weeks off at Xmas – to say she wasn't coming, B immediately, without a word from me, <u>went</u> up, &

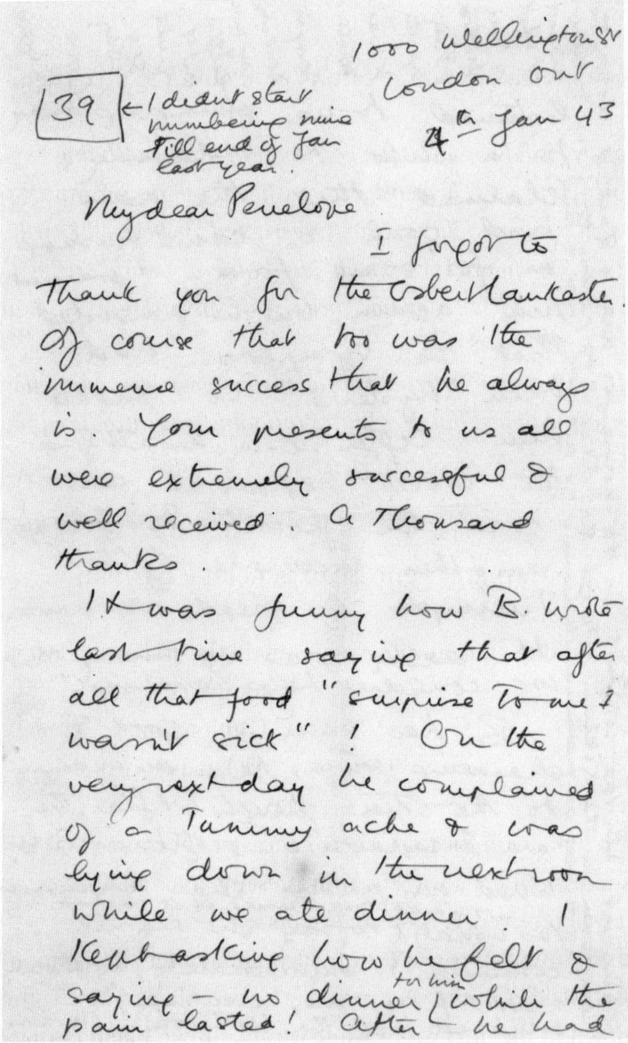

Figure 7.5 Margaret Penrose to Penelope Barman, 4 January 1943

scrubbed out the bathroom! He also removed all the cobwebs in the house for me & tacked down the linoleum in the kitchen. To get the other 3 to polish floors & dust I had to nag ad nauseum. However it is all done now & they are back at school. So I can set to & tidy up the Xmas mess.

Sorry you don't write any more letters but I quite see why.

Love Margaret

listened to us chumping away for a while he suddenly claimed that the pain had gone & came rushing in for some food. I warned him again, but he persisted that the symptoms had been "hysteria" so I served him. After one mouthful the worst happened all over the floor! So it was another example of the Triumph of greed over nausea. It really was so funny that we couldn't help laughing.

B has been so good & charming since, he is an example to the others though I fear they are incapable of profiting from it. When my weekly char telephoned *— The "maid" took 2 weeks off at xmas —* (as usual) to say she wasn't coming. B immediately, without a word from me, went up, & scrubbed out the bathroom! He also

---

"Osbert Lancaster" was Sir Osbert Lancaster (1908–86), a very successful cartoonist who invented the "pocket cartoon" appearing on the front page of several London newspapers. The book sent was probably Further Pocket Cartoons (London, 1942).

At the top of the following document, which is in Ben's handwriting, Margaret wrote: "4th Jan 43 School work"

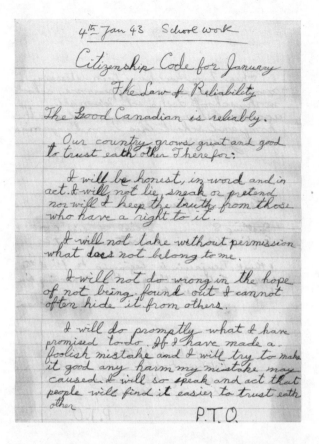

Figure 7.6 Ben's school work and report, 4 January 1943

Ben's School Work and Report

Citizenship Code for January
The Law of Reliability.

The Good Canadian is reliably.

Our country grows great and good to trust each other Therefor:

I will be honest, in word and in act. I will not lie, sneak or pretend nor will I keep the truth from those who have a right to it.

I will not take without permission what does not belong to me.

I will not do wrong in the hope of not being found out I cannot often hide it from others.

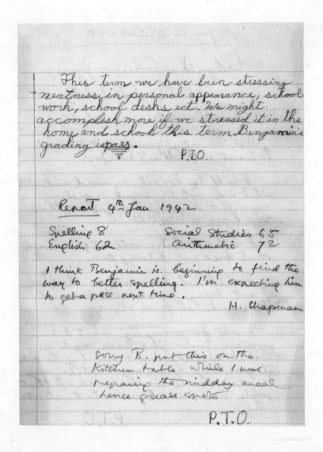

I will do promptly what I have promised to do. If I have made a foolish mistake and I will try to make it good any harm my mistake may caused. I will so speak and act that people will find it easier to trust each other.

This term we have been stressing neatness in personal appearance, school work, school desks ect. We might accomplish more if we stressed it in the home and school this term. Benjamin's grading is <u>pass</u>.

[Added by Miss Chapman:]

Report 4th Jan 1942

Spelling 8   Social Studies 65

English 62   Arithmetic 72

I think Benjamin is beginning to find the way to better spelling. I'm expecting him to get a pass next time.

H. Chapman

[Handwritten addition by Margaret Penrose:]
Sorry B. put this on the kitchen table while I was preparing the midday meal, hence grease spots.

The *"grease spots" remain very visible.*

In January 1943, although the surviving letters make no mention of the fact, a photograph was taken of the Penrose family and Ben in their home (see the frontispiece). Presumably the correspondence continued, but nothing survives until Ben wrote at the end of February.

Ben to His Parents

1000 Wellington St
London Ont Can
Feb 25 [1943]

Dear Mummy and Daddy
I hope you are getting on ok. because I had the "flu." I could not write a letter. The second day of my "flu" the temperature outside was -24 – or twenty-four below zero here is a picture of our thermometer with magnifying glass
At school we are having a chess tournament. I have not been able to play because I have been ill with the "flu" as I have told you.

Love from Benjamin.

Included in the letter was a piece of Ben's school work, on which Margaret had added a copy of Ben's most recent report from Miss Chapman, his teacher.

Ben's School Work and Report

The Law of Clean Play
The good Canadian plays fair. Clean play increases and trains one's strength and helps one to be more useful to one's country.

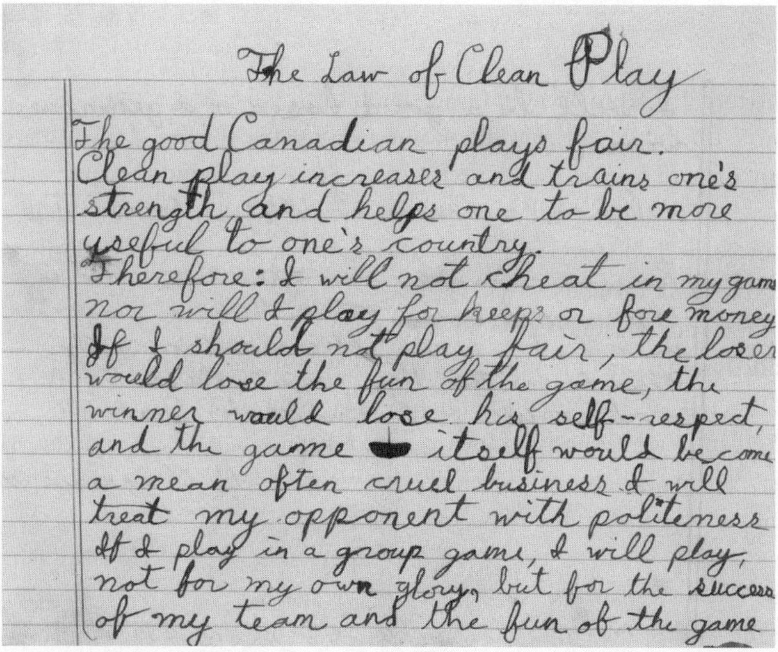

The Law of Clean Play

The good Canadian plays fair.
Clean play increases and trains one's
strength and helps one to be more
useful to one's country.
Therefore: I will not cheat in my game
nor will I play for keeps or for money
If I should not play fair, the loser
would lose the fun of the game, the
winner would lose his self-respect,
and the game itself would become
a mean often cruel business I will
treat my opponent with politeness
If I play in a group game, I will play,
not for my own glory, but for the success
of my team and the fun of the game

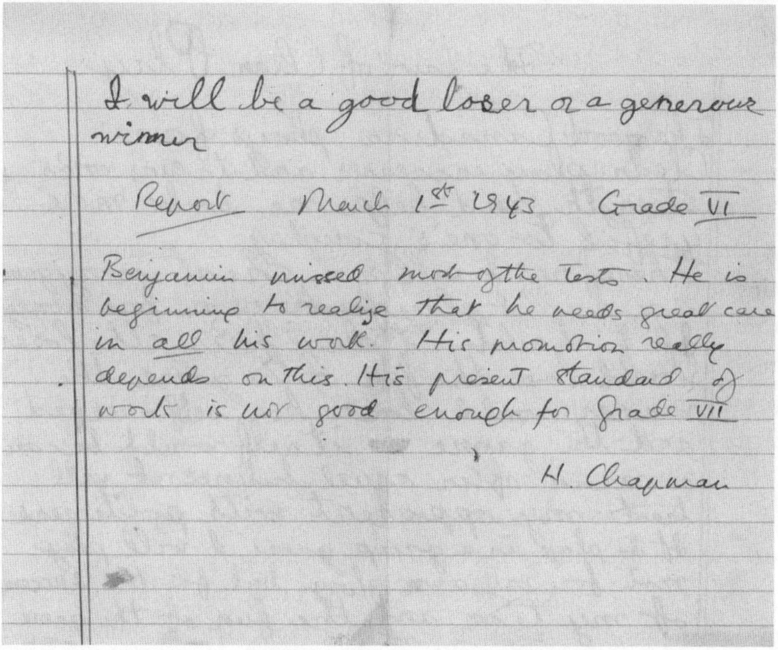

I will be a good loser or a generous
winner

Report   March 1st 1943   Grade VI

Benjamin missed most of the tests. He is
beginning to realize that he needs great care
in all his work. His promotion really
depends on this. His present standard of
work is not good enough for Grade VII

H. Chapman

Figure 7.7 Ben school work and report, 25 February 1943

Therefore: I will not cheat in my games nor will I play for keeps or for
money. If I should not play fair, the loser would lose the fun of the game, the
winner would lose his self-respect, and the game itself would become a mean
often cruel business. I will treat my opponent with politeness. If I play in a
group game, I will play, not for my own glory, but for the success of my team
and the fun of the game
I will be a good loser or a generous winner.
[Added in Margaret's handwriting was the report from Ben's teacher:]

<u>Report</u> March 1ˢᵗ 1943   Grade VI

Benjamin missed most of the tests. He is beginning to realize that he needs
great care in <u>all</u> his work. His promotion really depends on this. His present
standard of work is not good enough for Grade VII.

H. Chapman

On the back of the envelope postmarked "London Feb 27 PM 1943" and containing Ben's letter and school work Margaret Penrose wrote: "I think the scare
about having to move to Toronto has blown over so everything is okay. MP"

A passage in Oliver Penrose's 1998 tribute to his father throws light on Margaret's statement about the Toronto "scare": "After about three years [Lionel
Penrose's] job as a doctor in the psychiatric hospital was upgraded by giving
him the additional duties of Acting Director of Medical Statistics for the
Province of Ontario. A couple of years later he was made director of psychiatric
research for Ontario while still continuing his job in the hospital. One of his
duties in the new post involved sitting in an office in the provincial capital,
Toronto, answering letters sometimes even having to answer letters which he
himself had written a few days earlier in London, Ontario. Obviously, Lionel
Penrose's appointment (whether as acting director of medical statistics or as
director of psychiatric research) should have entailed his moving to Toronto
but various factors, including unwillingness to change his sons' schools in the
middle of the school year and the difficulties the war imposed on moving
house, determined him to remain in London."⁵

Ben's next surviving letter was not sent until a month later. The text expresses
contradictory feelings. By starting a "victory garden," Ben was anticipating, even

5 The informant could have been the "Lt. Col. whatnot of Toronto" and his welcome "present," mentioned by Margaret Penrose in her letter of 11 January 1942.

asserting his intent, that he would remain in Canada. But at the end he also voiced his desire "to see you and the family."

Ben to His Parents

1,000 Wellington St.
London Ont.,
April 25, 1943

Dear Mummy and Daddy,

For Easter we had a tie and a base-ball Ball. We have not had anything else yet because of the war but it has been a very nice Easter. I have started a victory Garden with some radishes and I hope the come up and are nice.

We think that our little kitten has got the mumps (that is our cat kitten).

On Good Friday we went on a hike which was great fun (that's is with the cups) near the spot where we went before and mummy I do want to see you and the family.

Love Benjamin

Canadians were exhorted to start "victory gardens" in their own backyards so that, by growing vegetables for their own consumption, they could boost food production.

"Cups" refers to Cub Scouts, the junior branch of the Scouting movement, which Ben joined about this time and which he much enjoyed.

The above letter was put into an envelope addressed by Ben "Mr. Barman, Twin Oaks, Buckland Common, Near Tring, Herts, England." However, it bears a British 2½ penny stamp and is postmarked "London S.W. 1 4 May 1943." The letter must have been entrusted to someone who travelled by air to England and who mailed it there. Sea mail sent from Canada to the United Kingdom normally took about a month.

The letter's contents attest to the severity of the war's impact on daily life in Canada, with Easter presents being restricted to a baseball and a tie. At the same time, it was clear by the end of April 1943 that, with the Germans' defeat at Stalingrad and their approaching expulsion from North Africa, the military advantage had passed to the Allied forces. The tide had finally turned both in the war, and for Ben.

8

Farewell to Canada, April–October 1943

I am arranging for you to come back to England on a Portuguese steamer, which sails from New York with lights shining, and is quite safe.
~*Lowis Barman to Ben Barman, 27 April 1943*

He also took a trawling line & hook in case he needed it to fish from the lifeboat (when wrecked!) and a few explosive caps to fire off as signals to passing planes and a book whereby to identify said planes. So he is well equipped. The axe in his trunk though he expects to use it to hack his way out of a sinking ship.
~*Margaret Penrose to Penelope Barman, 19 September 1943*

Thank you for lending him to us for 3 years.
~*Margaret Penrose to Penelope Barman, 19 September 1943*

To decide to bring a child back home, something that many parents resolved to do during 1942 and 1943, was comparatively simple. To implement that decision was quite another matter. Military advantage may have shifted in favour of the Allies, but the Nazis were far from defeated, precluding any early return to safe travel. The Atlantic route continued to be the site of a ferocious struggle with no fewer than 120 ships, amounting to 632,000 tons, being sunk during March 1943, the highest monthly total in the war. The balance in this contest shifted in May 1943 with the destruction of 41 U-boats, a quarter of those in operations. The Germans never regained the upper hand, with Allied shipping losses dropping sharply through the remainder of the war. Yet, this outcome could not be foreseen at the time and, even if it had been obvious, the risk of a ship with a returning child on board being torpedoed remained considerable.

Four means of crossing the Atlantic, three by sea and one by air, existed. Seaplane flights between Gander, Newfoundland, and Foynes in Ireland occurred during the war, a continuation of a commercial service that had begun in 1939.

Direct flights by land planes, mainly Liberators, began during the war, using the same routes.[1] However, passage was reserved for military and government officials, with just a few civilians. Some children may have flown this route but, if so, they would have been the offspring of the highly privileged.

Of the three sea routes, the most secure was provided by the two or three passage steamers of the Companhia Colonia de Navegação, which sailed between Philadelphia and Lisbon, a neutral port. These ships, which had to display the identification markings demanded by the German Navy, were small in size and with berths for fewer than 400 passengers. The price of a ticket was extremely high, £220 (over C$960) in August 1943.[2] The further drawback was that passengers were carried only to Lisbon, where they risked being trapped with no certainty of being able to complete the journey to England.

The second means of travel by sea was a service that the British government instituted in response to political pressure to bring children home. By 1943, a stream of naval vessels, constructed in the United States and lent to the British Navy under Lend Lease, was crossing the Atlantic in various capacities. For a fee of £10, young male evacuees were accepted as "messenger boys" on these ships, becoming crew members. In October 1944, Anthony Bailey, then aged eleven, embarked on the HMS *Ranjee*, an escort carrier loaded with seventy Corsair airplanes. The voyage was not without its perils. A crew member remarked, "These are coffin ships. If they're hit by a torpedo, they go down like a stone." There was one scare on Bailey's voyage – sonar contact with a U-boat – but Bailey along with a dozen other boys finally reached Greenock, Scotland, in safety.[3]

The third and by far the most dangerous form of sea travel was to book a birth on one of the cargo ships that, in escorted convoys, sailed from Halifax to England. "On 19 April 1942 I sailed on a banana boat from Halifax in a convoy to Britain. It was our second attempt. The first day out we had been attacked by a U-boat which was sunk by our accompanying destroyer. Then we developed engine trouble and limped back to port," recalled Negley Farson, who had

---

1 Smith, "Atlantic Journey."
2 In August 1943, the secretary at the London office of the American Office for the Evacuation of Children informed Anthony Bailey's parents that £220 was the cost of a passage for anyone over the age of twelve; see Bailey, *America Lost and Found*, 134.
3 Ibid., 134–5, 137–8, 140, 146–7.

come to Canada as part of an evacuated boarding school. "The dozen passengers grew to know each other quickly and too well. I was in a cabin with three other boys from Abinger [School]."[4] In 1943, a ticket for this type of passage cost about £35, a sum that Anthony Bailey's parents had been willing to pay before they learned of his selection as "a messenger boy."[5]

Lewis Barman did not move in the exalted circles that would have been required to obtain the return of his son by air travel. However, he did possess the wealth and the connections to arrange for Ben's travelling on one of the Portuguese steamers. As the following letter implies, he did not blanch at purchasing a first-class berth for his son, and he arranged, through the intervention of the Hon. Maurice Lubbock, the head of Production Engineering, his previous employer, for the necessary travel companions to look after Ben. Lewis used his contacts in BOAC, his current employer, to assure passage by air from Lisbon to England. Despite its genial tone, the letter, the only one from Lewis Barman that survives, is peremptory, and it contained a promise, perhaps sincerely made but certainly not honoured, that Ben would not be sent to boarding school following his return.

Lewis Barman to Ben

TWINOAKS,

BUCKLAND COMMON,

Nr. TRING, HERTS.

27th April. 1943.

Darling Benjamin,

I am arranging for you to come back to England on a Portuguese steamer, which sails from New York with lights shining, and is quite safe. You arrive at Lisbon and from there you fly back to England. So you should have no trouble and nothing to fear.

I am also arranging for you to be accompanied by a Miss Kate Ringling, [added in Margaret's handwriting: c/o Douglas Woods, 38 Avondale Rd.]

---

4 Farson, *Never a Normal Man*, 55.
5 Bailey, *America Lost and Found*, 134.

Toronto, Canada, who will be coming back to this country the same way. Miss Ringling was a nurse who took Mr. Lubbock's children to Canada, they are staying there but she is coming home.

At the present moment the bookings on the Portuguese ship are filled up until December of this year, but I am trying to arrange for you to come home earlier than this. We are all looking forward to seeing you again, it will be fun flying, especially the last piece.

In Lisbon I have asked Commander A.D.S. Murray, who is the British Overseas Airways Corporation Manager for Portugal, to look after you when you are in Lisbon. In New York Mrs. Lubbock will arrange for someone there to look after you when you are there. There are an awful lot of forms to fill in, passports, visas, etc. The shipping company are doing this, the shippers being J. Johnson and Co. who are working through Thomas Cook & Son.

[Margaret Penrose wrote in at this point in the letter: Mrs Gaynor, 23 Huntington Rd, Garden City, Long Island, New York.]

Jonathan and Roderick are getting very excited at the idea of seeing you. Roderick can now ride your little bicycle. I hope you will be able to ride mine, we can then all go for bicycle rides round the countryside. We are not going to send you to a boarding school when you get back [this first part of the sentence has been underlined by someone in dark ink] but will find somewhere nice for you to go.

Give my love to Margaret and Lionel. I am glad to hear that you play chess well. Jonathan is learning and longing to have some games with you.

Happy returns of the day and lots of love

Lowis

As to the "Portuguese steamer," Portugal remained neutral during the Second World War. The country was important to both the Allied and Axis powers in terms of trade and intelligence gathering. The Portuguese government was therefore able to arrange for its merchant vessels to sail without threat from the German submarines. In order to ensure identification, they had the name of the ship and the word "PORTUGAL" painted in giant letters on their sides and travelled fully lighted at night.

"Miss Rigling was a nurse": Kate Rigling (1875–1963) was a nanny, also called a children's nurse.

"Mr. Lubbock's children" were Alice and Eric (later the 4th Baron Avebury). The two came to Canada on ss Scythia in July 1940 accompanied by their nanny, Kate Rigling, and five cousins. The Lubbock children lived with the family of Douglas Woods, owner of Harvey Woods, a Canadian textile conglomerate, while their cousins lived with the Lawson family, the Woods' neighbours and business partners.

"Mrs. Lubbock" played no role in Ben's return journey.

"Mrs Angelica Gaynor" (1911–92) was the daughter of Cyril Edward Lloyd, MP, for Dudley, managing director of a steel company, and a director of Lloyds Bank. Lowis Barman's father, also in the steel business, probably knew Cyril Lloyd. Angelica's husband, John S. Gaynor, was a petroleum industry executive, working in Mexico, Trinidad, and the United States. Ben's mother must have sent Margaret Penrose the Gaynors' address in a letter that has not survived.

As to "come home earlier than this," Ben's father did manage to secure an earlier passage by purchasing a first-class cabin.

The words "Commander A.D.S. Murray" and "Lisbon" have been underlined in pencil.

The sentence "We are not going to send you to a boarding school when you get back but will find somewhere nice for you to go" was first underlined in pencil and then heavily in ink.

Early in May 1943, prior to receiving his father's instructions, Ben contracted mumps, although, as the following letter from Margaret Penrose shows, he suffered no long-lasting ill consequences. A passage in Margaret's missive makes reference to "oriental Jim," whom Ben remembers as Japanese. As Oliver Penrose recalls, "Oriental Jim must have been the young man known to us as Jim Kagawa. I never knew he was working in a factory ... My mother told me that he was of Japanese origin and came from British Columbia where such people might be unpopular because of the war." Oliver says that "Jim's sister Kazuko Kagawa also stayed with us for a while (a shorter time I think)," although Kazuko recalls that she never did so.[6] Wataru James Kagawa was one of five children of Shigetaro Kagawa and Uye Ishide Kagawa, immigrants from Japan

6 Letter from Oliver Penrose to me, 29 December 2014, and email message (forwarded to me) from Mariko Obokata, Kuzuko Kagawa's daughter, to Linda Kawamoto Reid, 15 December 2017.

Figure 8.1 The Kagawa family, with James Kagawa standing on the far left, January 1939 (reproduced by permission of the archives of the Nikkei National Museum and Cultural Centre, Burnaby BC)

who lived in Vancouver, British Columbia. In an episode that remains a disgrace to Canada, the Kagawa family was among the 20,000 Japanese, both immigrant and native born, who were forcibly "evacuated" in 1942 from coastal British Columbia to internment camps in the province's interior. What Margaret Penrose told her son was probably a widely held equivocation to avoid acknowledging the injustice of the Japanese expulsion. James Kagawa had been allowed to finish his junior year at Vancouver Technical School before joining his family in the camp at Creston, BC. The Kagawas moved to London, Ontario, in July 1942, residing at 194 Clarence Street, which runs parallel and to the west of Wellington Street. A lack of space in their own home may have caused Jim Kagawa to reside for a time in the Penrose household.

Margaret Penrose to Penelope Barman

                                        1000 Wellington
Sun   16 May 43   London Ont

My dear Penelope,

Bennie is in the pink of health & <u>very</u> talkative. He is not allowed back to school till Wed or Thurs but I am sure he isn't infectious any more. Anyhow I've given up the unequal struggle over keeping him isolated. B. has washed the car & several windows & seems to feel very energetic & busy. He dries dishes nicely too, & is a great help to me in his comic way. He was a <u>marvellous</u> patient. No trouble at all. Read 6 books and 1000 comics and listened to <u>all</u> the radio programmes. Roger & Jim [Kagawa] are the only two likely to get mumps from him & Lionel is almost perpetually away – this week Ottawa, Detroit, Toronto all in different directions with an occasional glance at the family on his way from one to the other. The trains are so full one can no longer get a sleeper so its a dog's life travelling 600 miles sitting on a suitcase and <u>living</u> that way. I'm sorry for him. Planes & <u>hotels</u> all full up too. One has to share a bed with a complete stranger!

The "toy dagger" duly arrived – sounds most suitable. It hasn't been opened yet. I got B's scout outfit for his birthday. Each thing I got was the "last" in the stock. So it's lucky I didn't wait till next week. I had to go to 7 shops to get an ordinary white shirt for Oliver (who needs it for cadets' parade tomorrow.) I wish we <u>were</u> rationed for clothes it's so silly being so short of everything in whatever size required, when one needs so little!

I couldn't get a scout hat or sox for B but maybe some will come in, or he will get them second hand at the scout headquarters.

Thanks for the second quarterly instalment – arrived punctually this time.

Our financial situation seems to have improved slightly partly on account of there being so little in the shops & partly because I dont have to pay for the occasional expensive charlady now that we have oriental Jim [James Kagawa] (he works at munitions 9 to 4:30 daily but helps in his off time in lieu of rent.)

Sorry about the reeds that Sylvia sent having fed the fishes. But B. has been playing less of late & spoiling fewer so I can rise to his demands. Scouting has absorbed much of his enthusiasm. And of course he has missed a good deal of practising over the mumps. He was very distressed to hear that 2 dozen reeds <u>had</u> got lost en route & said it was a pity Aunt S. had sent them all in one parcel – if she did. He hasn't used that many in his life.

Thanks for mumps telegram. It arrived about a week after I sent airgraph. Did you really get the airgraph so quickly? It <u>wasn't</u> reply paid so I didn't gather you wanted a reply. Did you? B is getting on splendidly & never was nearly as bad as Oliver, as regards a pumpkin countenance. [O will be 14 on 6ᵗʰ June]

Tunisia sounds hopeful, maybe the German war will stop soon.

Tho[ma]s Cook told me they had broached the subject of B.'s passport to Uncle Ross. They have not told me how successful they've been. I expect to have another battery of photographs demanded – I've only sent them six at different times so far and most of those they have lost. I shall recommend Thos. Cook to communicate with the uncle via the Montreal branch by telephone, when the matter becomes more urgent. I'm sure that will be the more efficient than the mail (if I know them). All I've got to do is to get B vaccinated again (for the sake of the susceptible Portuguese!) but the other red tape (re passport & permits) is extremely complicated & Thos. & Ross will have to get their heads together over it I fear.

Much love

Margaret.

Mumps involve a swelling of the neck and face, which explains Margaret's reference to the boys' "pumpkin countenance."

"His birthday" refers to Ben's twelfth birthday on 22 May.

"cadets" refers to the Cadet Services of Canada, founded in 1908 for the military training of future army officers. The cadets were important in the First World War and again in the Second. In 1942, King George VI made them the Royal Canadian Army Cadets. Oliver Penrose was then aged thirteen.

"Sylvia" Anderson was Penelope's younger sister and an oboist with the Hallé Orchestra, Manchester, England.

"Feed the fishes" means that the ship carrying the gift of the oboe reeds had been torpedoed and sunk, probably in March 1943, when 120 ships were lost in the Atlantic.

"Tunisia looks hopeful" refers to the surrender in Tunisia on 13 May 1943 of the remnants of the German Afrika Korps and Italian troops, numbering some 230,000 soldiers, thus bringing to an end the North African war waged since June 1940.

Whatever anxiety and unhappiness were inflicted on Ben by his proposed return to England do not seem to have affected his school work. As he reached his twelfth birthday, he had overcome many of the problems in spelling and writing that had previously held him back. He was promoted to Grade 7, but whether he would actually enter it depended on the timing of his departure from Canada.

Ben's School Report, with Comment by Margaret Penrose

London Public Schools PROGRESS REPORT
Name of pupil Benjamin Barman; Grade VI; *School* Ryerson For school year 1942 to 1943
Teacher H Chapman; *Principal* Mr A P Silcox
I think Benjamin's effort is improving. I wonder if more sleep would help him to pay attention without "fiddling".
Comment by Margaret Penrose
Benjamin has 11 hours sleep every night, I don't see how I can give him any more! MP
Jan. Spell 8; Social Studies 65; English 42; Arithmetic 72. I think Benjamin is beginning to find the way to better spelling. I'm expecting him to get a pass next time.
March. Benjamin missed most of the tests. He is beginning to realise that he needs great care in all his work. His promotion really depends on this. His present standard of work is not good enough for grade VII.
[The first part of the report consists of the information Margaret sent Penelope in her letter of 2 November 1942.]
May Benjamin has real arithmetic ability but he loses marks because of carelessness. *What marks correspond to "F"? MP.* F is below 40%
Benjamin still needs to fight with his spelling – particularly sounding carefully and writing as he sounds them. He is promoted to grade VII.

The following letter demonstrates Ben's increasing awareness of external events, particularly the ways in which the war affected everyday life in Canada.

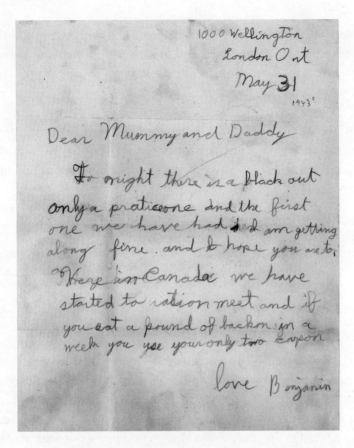

Figure 8.2 Ben's letter to his parents, 31 May 1943

Ben to His Parents

1000 Wellington
London Ont
May 31 [1943? added in hand]

Dear Mummy and Daddy

To night there is a black out only a practice one and the first one we have had. I am getting along fine and I hope you are to.

Here in Canada we have started to ration meet and if you eat a pound of backon in a week you use your only two coupon.

love Benjamin.

The "black out" was never imposed permanently in Canada during the Second World War. Practice blackouts were held in various cities from time to time, but, from November 1943, were permanently discontinued in areas to the west of the confluence of the St Lawrence and Ottawa Rivers.

Ben enthusiastically participated in the scouting movement. In a letter to his brother Jonathan, he enclosed a newspaper article reporting on his promotion from Cub Scout to Boy Scout, suggesting his pride in this accomplishment.

Ben to Jonathan Barman, with Enclosures

1000 Wellington
London Ont.
June 13 1943

Dear Jonathan

Here is a paper clippling about me in the Scouts. How are you and the family, I am O.K. Here. The night befor last I went and staded with the Harts and I had great fun playing kick the can, guns ect. When we were playing guns we were so hot that we had to stop the game. After that when I came home I found that we got an equarm wich has tadpoles, snails ect. To day I went on a pread to the church were Mr Mitchel funeral was held. Mr Mitchel was the president of the Scouts. Give my love to the family.

Benjamin

[An enclosed clipping, an article entitled "Boy Scout News," reads:]

12th Scout Group (St. Johns)

Nine cubs of the 12th London Pack were welcomed into the troop last Monday evening at a "Going Up Ceremony." The pack was in attendance to bid their chums goodbye and Akela. Bob Wallace urged those moving up to the troop to keep up the good work they had done as Cubs. After the last "Grand Howl" Troop Leader Stanley Stole took the nine new Scouts through the 10 Scout laws, a step at a time, and introduced them to the Scoutmaster. They were welcomed into the troop with three rousing cheers and a tiger. The cubs who came up were Brad Deslauriers, George Smith, Tom Neil, Tom Brown, Don MacArthur, Alan Robinson, James Talman, Ben Barman, and Paul Howson.

Although Ben does not mention a second press clipping in his letter, the following clipping among Ben's papers may also have been included with the above letter. The news of the shooting down of BOAC Flight 777 and the virtual marooning in Lisbon of a large number of evacuees returning to Great Britain can only have intensified his fears about leaving Canada.

Undated Clipping from Unidentified Newspaper

MAY MOVE EVACUEES IN PORTUGUESE VESSELS.
LONDON, June 3 – (CP Cable) – Great Britain may try to arrange to have Portuguese ships bring British evacuee children now awaiting transportation in Lisbon, it was reported here tonight.

Children returning from Canada and the United States have been flying a few at a time as space was found for them in planes leaving Lisbon but the loss of a passenger plane this week may necessitate a change.

There are an estimated 75 children at Lisbon at present.

"Loss of a passenger plane" refers to the shooting down over the Bay of Biscay of KLM/BOAC Flight 777, a Douglas DC3 aircraft, carrying seventeen passengers, including the film star Leslie Howard, during a daytime flight from Lisbon to England. Thereafter, flights were made at night to minimize the chances of attack.

The words "75 children at Lisbon at present" is underlined in ink and followed by an exclamation mark.

Ben's next letter, showing awareness of his imminent departure from Canada, attests to the deep and enduring trauma caused by the near torpedoing of the *Antonia*, the ship that had transported him to Canada in July 1940. As he later explained, "I don't think that the Penroses or my parents realised the effect that being torpedoed on the way over had on me. Seeing a torpedo passed by the stern, later that evening hearing a terrific bang whilst I was just going to sleep, Uncle Ross coming down in a flap and putting lifejackets on us and marshalling us upon deck. Because of censorship we couldn't divulge all this."

Ben to His Parents

1000 Wellington St
London Ont
July 31, 1943.

Dear Mummy and Daddy

I have got your lovely letter the one you sent on July 5. In a few days I will
be going to Montreal and I may be going on to New York, then to Portugal
then last of all to you. That is if I get started and not killed by a torpedo.
I will leave the rest to imagination.

I went to a scout camp and got all my tenderfot and second-class bages
except signalling in my second class.

Last Wednesday at bayfield there was a great show where there was Bingo,
hotdoges ect. I won one chicken, Oliver won one, and a laidy who is staying
with us one another, so altogether we had 3.

Love from Benjamin

*As to "Montreal," Ben went there in August for a final stay with his uncle and aunt,
Ross and Orion Barman, while he completed the formalities for his departure for
England.*

*Ben was vacationing with the Penrose family on a campground north of "Bay-
field" on Lake Huron, which had become the favourite vacation spot for Margaret
and Lionel. In 1946, the Penroses, despite being resident in England, purchased a
cottage in Bayfield, which they visited in 1964, when Lionel Penrose was in North
America to receive a Joseph P. Kennedy Jr. Foundation award.*

The envelope containing the above letter was addressed by Ben. It bears a British
2½ penny stamp and is postmarked "█Field Post Office Aug 1 1943." The letter
must have been transported to England by air and then mailed at a post office
on an air force base, the name of which was censored. The next letter, the only
one extant written by Lionel Penrose, reveals much about his character and
about the marginal role he played, as he with much honesty admits, in running
the household and raising the family. Lionel's comments speak to the gendered
division of labour existing in Canadian households at this period, no matter
what the family's social rank.

Lionel Penrose to Lowis Barman

Province of Ontario
Ontario Hospital
1000 Wellington Street, London Canada
16th August 1943

Dear Lowis,

Your letter arrived when I was away from home (which is not uncommon for me). Benny has certainly grown a lot since you last saw him and has obtained great prowess in many pursuits especially swimming, at which he shows quite remarkable facility. He has taken up Scouting this summer and seems to have enjoyed it very much indeed. He is a very determined character and absolutely fearless. All the time he has been with as he has been very healthy, I am glad to say, and his appetite is prodigious. He has been a most excellent companion for our boys and a very cheerful person to have with us. As you can well imagine, we are all very fond of him. He evidently feels himself very much at home here and when invited to stay away with the Harts recently would not remain there more than one night and then made straight for where we were, though it meant a 60 miles' bus ride. We were highly amused when he arrived at the door in his Boy Scout outfit in the middle of a rainstorm with his usual beaming smile. Margaret & I had both been under the impression that Mrs Hart was more indulgent than we were & that he would prefer to be with her but he had his own ideas. At present he has gone to his uncle Ross in Montreal whom, unfortunately, I have never succeeded in meeting though I have quite often conversed with him on the telephone.

All the arrangements with Thomas Cook & Sons are being made at that end; indeed this had to be so as Benny can only get his passport and papers in order there (formerly his passport was simply included on his uncle's). At the moment, I understand it is planned for Benny to come back to us in about 2 weeks and by then we will have got into touch with Miss Rigling & will either send him or take him to Toronto according to what we hear from Thos Cook & Sons. I make frequent journeys to Toronto on business for the Department of Health and expect to go there before Benny returns here probably taking Margaret too so that we will know exactly how the land – or rather the sea in this case – lies. At the same time, the prospect of having

Benny back with us again, for such a short visit as it is likely to be, causes me some misgiving because of the possibility of his making up his mind to stay with us. Not that we should not be very happy to have him at any time – in fact, he really has become for the time being part of the family –, but merely that having said goodbye to him, when he went off to Montreal, it will be hard to have to send him away again. However, quite probably by now he will have visualized his journey a little better and be eager to start as soon as possible. It is extremely difficult for a child to weigh in his own mind the pros and cons beforehand and he probably takes some time to adjust himself to the idea of seeing his small brothers and realising what fun it will be.

At first, when Benny came, as with other children, who came over in 1940, everyone was very anxious to keep him from feeling homesick; everything here was made as interesting as possible for them and their adaptation was made easier. I think Benny realises that he will now have to make a reverse adjustment and, though it actually will be much an easier one, he has not quite understood how pleasant and easy it will be.

I am writing at length partly because I have not had a suitable opportunity to write to you before (and Margaret's ability in letter writing makes me lazy) and partly to explain what may seem to you an apparent reluctance on Benny's part to take the initiative in going home but which I think is quite natural & arises from the unusual conditions under which he (& other children) came out to Canada. Children somewhat older (or younger) than Benny seem to make changes more easily either because they have grown up further or have not yet begun.

It has certainly been a great pleasure to have Bennie with us and has also been a privilege. For me, it has been a privilege obtained without any extra labour, which is an additional advantage not shared by Margaret, who has done all the letter writing, the cooking, the washing, the mending and so on, but nevertheless very happily. She even worked day and night to try and teach him to spell, but here, in the main, I'm afraid we must express that we have been failures.

With all best wishes,

yours

Lionel Penrose

Ben stayed with his aunt and uncle in Montreal for most of August 1943, as the arrangement of his travel documents was complex, in particular the is-suing of his own passport. The first travel document, a smallpox vaccination certificate, signed by Dr R.R. Struthers, is dated 24 August. The next day, Dr Struthers wrote out the following health certificate, using Ross Barman's headed writing paper.

Health Certificate

Nazing Lodge, St Bruno PQ August 25 1943
This is to certify that I have today examined Master Benjamin Barman and find him to be in good health and free from evidence of infectious disease.
Height 4' 10"
Weight 100 pounds
Vaccinated

R R Struthers MD
Montreal Canada

Ben returned to London, Ontario, in time to enter Grade 7 in September. He still needed to receive his boat ticket and to obtain his transit visa from the American authorities, as he informed his parents.

Ben to His Parents

September 10/43 1000 Wellington St
London Ont
Can.

Dear Mummy and Daddy
On the 19th (that is in 1 week 2 days from to day) I think I will be going to the USA. In 3 or 4 more days I am most likely going to Toronto to get my U.S.A. visa, that is when my protuguese one comes back from the protuguese people. Here are some pictures of me that I had got. I hope you like them. Tomorrow morning I am going taging, then to the movies with a friend. He

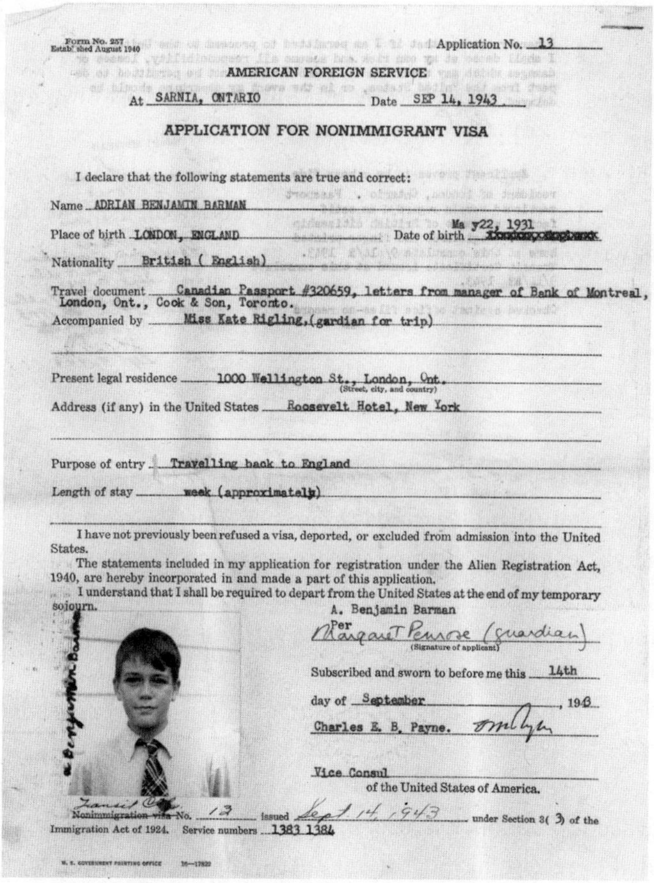

Form No. 257
Establ'shed August 1940

Application No. 13

AMERICAN FOREIGN SERVICE

At SARNIA, ONTARIO Date SEP 14, 1943.

APPLICATION FOR NONIMMIGRANT VISA

I declare that the following statements are true and correct:

Name ADRIAN BENJAMIN BARMAN

Place of birth LONDON, ENGLAND Date of birth Ma y22, 1931

Nationality British (English)

Travel document Canadian Passport #320659, letters from manager of Bank of Montreal, London, Ont., Cook & Son, Toronto.

Accompanied by Miss Kate Rigling,(gardian for trip)

Present legal residence 1000 Wellington St., London, Ont.
(Street, city, and country)

Address (if any) in the United States Roosevelt Hotel, New York

Purpose of entry Travelling back to England

Length of stay week (approximately)

I have not previously been refused a visa, deported, or excluded from admission into the United States.

The statements included in my application for registration under the Alien Registration Act, 1940, are hereby incorporated in and made a part of this application.

I understand that I shall be required to depart from the United States at the end of my temporary sojourn.

A. Benjamin Barman
Per
Margaret Penrose (guardian)
(Signature of applicant)

Subscribed and sworn to before me this 14th day of September, 1943

Charles E. B. Payne.

Vice Consul
of the United States of America.

Nonimmigration visa No. 13 issued Sept. 14, 1943 under Section 3(3) of the Immigration Act of 1924. Service numbers 1383 1384

U. S. GOVERNMENT PRINTING OFFICE 16—17822

Figure 8.3 Ben's visa from the American Foreign Service

is to meet me after I have lunch and then will go to the movies. After we will look around the shops and not by anything.

I am now in grade 7 Mr Wheeler room who is a good teacher.

Love Benjamin B.

The "pictures of me" may have included his visa photograph, although that is not in the envelope.

By his "protuguese" visa, Ben may have meant to refer to his boat ticket, which was issued on 14 September 1943. He did not receive the actual visa until 20 September 1943.

By "taging," Ben may have meant playing games of tag.

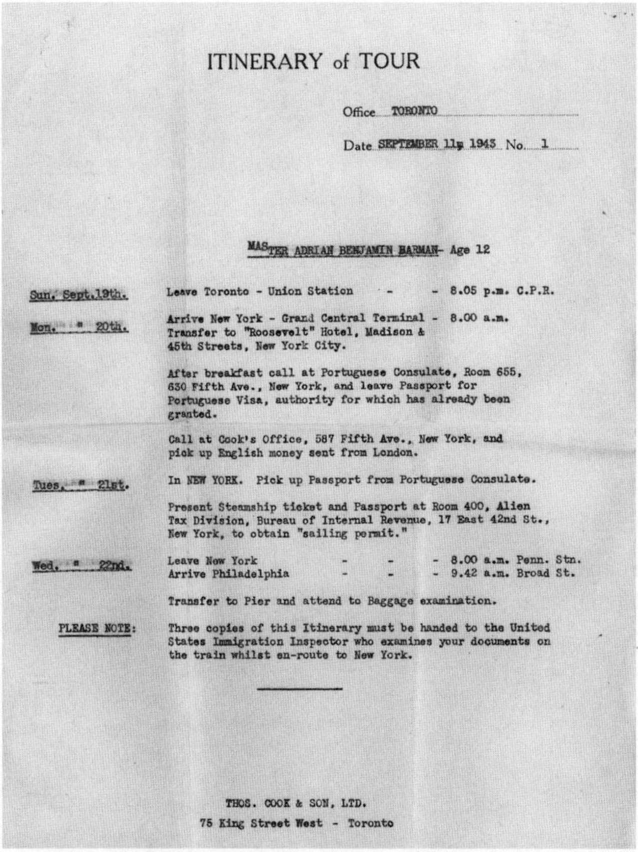

ITINERARY of TOUR

Office TORONTO

Date SEPTEMBER 11p 1943 No. 1

MASTER ADRIAN BENJAMIN BARMAN- Age 12

Sun. Sept.19th. Leave Toronto - Union Station - - 8.05 p.m. C.P.R.

Mon. " 20th. Arrive New York - Grand Central Terminal - 8.00 a.m.
Transfer to "Roosevelt" Hotel, Madison &
45th Streets, New York City.

After breakfast call at Portuguese Consulate, Room 655,
630 Fifth Ave., New York, and leave Passport for
Portuguese Visa, authority for which has already been
granted.

Call at Cook's Office, 587 Fifth Ave., New York, and
pick up English money sent from London.

Tues. " 21st. In NEW YORK. Pick up Passport from Portuguese Consulate.

Present Steamship ticket and Passport at Room 400, Alien
Tax Division, Bureau of Internal Revenue, 17 East 42nd St.,
New York, to obtain "sailing permit."

Wed. " 22nd. Leave New York - - - 8.00 a.m. Penn. Stn.
Arrive Philadelphia - - - 9.42 a.m. Broad St.

Transfer to Pier and attend to Baggage examination.

PLEASE NOTE: Three copies of this Itinerary must be handed to the United
States Immigration Inspector who examines your documents on
the train whilst en-route to New York.

THOS. COOK & SON, LTD.
75 King Street West - Toronto

Figure 8.4 Ben's itinerary, issued by Thomas Cook &
Sons, 11 September 1943

The letter, probably because of its bulk due to the photographs included, was
opened and resealed with the sticker "OPENED BY EXAMINER 736."

The next travel document is his instructions from Thomas Cook and Sons
for his travel within the United States (see Fig. 8.4).

On 14 September 1943, Ben's ticket was issued by James W. Elwell & Co, 17
State Street, New York, acting for the Companhia Colonial de Navegação (Colonial Navigation Company). It gave "Master A.B. Barman" a first-class passage
with *camarote* (berth) no. 12 on the ss *João Belo* (Fig. 8.5). According to the tour
itinerary (Fig 8.4), the ship was scheduled to depart New York for Philadelphia
and then Lisbon on 22 September 1943. The *João Bello* was a steamship, built
in Germany, acquired in 1928 by the Companhia Colonial de Navegação, and

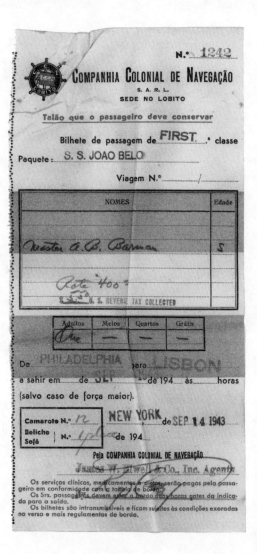

Figure 8.5
Ben's ticket on the ss *João Belo*,
dated 14 September 1943

employed during the Second World War on the transatlantic route. There is no record of what the passage cost.

Also on the 14th, Ben secured his transit visa, not in Toronto, but in Sarnia, Ontario, on the Michigan border. Margaret Penrose's final letter to Penelope Barman provides a graphic account of acquiring the visa and of Ben's last days in Canada, with his departure from Toronto for New York City on 18 September. Margaret includes humorous comments on Ben's acquiring an axe, fishing line, and other items he thought would be needed should his ship be torpedoed. She may have either underestimated or downplayed the deep trauma Ben's experience on the ss *Antonia* in July 1940 had inflicted on him.

Margaret Penrose to Penelope Barman

1000 Wellington St
London, Ont.
Sunday 19 Sept 43

My dear Penelope,

Thank you for lending him to us for 3 years – We've said goodbye to Benny once more – still half expecting him to come back to us again shortly – for some reason or other! B. was the tearful one this time. Last farewell I don't think he believed was serious. He gave me a nice little elephant as a parting gift & we gave him all sorts of things among them 2 pairs of underpants! – a luxury which had disappeared entirely from the shops for months until 2 days ago when a few put in an appearance. I was glad not to have to send him back in the rags he had had perforce to wear. I don't suppose you can get them in England either. He also took a trawling line & hook in case he needed it to fish from the lifeboat (when wrecked!) and a few explosive caps to fire off as signals to passing planes and a book whereby to identify said planes. So he is well equipped. The axe in his trunk though he expects to use it to hack his way out of a sinking ship. [Needless to say all these ideas are his own!]

But he is beaming at the prospect of the journey, nevertheless. He hopes to see Niagara Falls at midnight (I am sure it won't be illuminated these days!) & is thrilled at the prospect of New York skyscrapers. I hope the Gaynors will succeed in wresting him away from the watchful Miss R[igling]. to take him up the Empire State Bldg. It seems to be his main ambition in life. Mrs Gaynor has written to me 3 or 4 times & seems to be very nice. I think she is a bit ambitious to expect to get him to stay the <u>night</u> at Long Island. Thos Cook <u>would</u> object. But the Toronto Cooks told <u>me</u> that there would be no reason why he shouldn't go <u>out</u> with the Gaynors. The Woods (Toronto) thought otherwise & called <u>me twice</u> on the telephone to say that he was on no account to leave the hotel in New York. Maybe your cable will help. I sent mine partly to show you that he was on his way (in case you didn't know).

The worst tragedy (from B's point of view) at leaving was the fact that after having been allowed to spend most of his last day at school here in making a <u>teapot stand</u> (with a squirrel on it) out of wood in the school workshops – he brought it home triumphantly. It was to be for you. I told him to take it up &

put it into his bag safely. He was proud of it! But on his way by some freakish impulse he poked it into the cavity into which our sitting-room sliding door disappears & it vanished into thin air! He went around & fetched the land-lord who sadly confirmed my fears that there was no possible way of getting it out again except by "rippin' de joint apart" – an extravagance which he was not prepared to undertake. Luckily for us the door still slides & and hasn't stuck. L now suggests removing some wainscoting & angling for it – so May Be?? But I'm so sorry you can't have your squirrel teapot set. It was very nicely made. Not even ingenious Lionel can think of any way to get it out so far.

Lionel met B in Toronto last night & delivered him to Mr Woods. Mrs W. and Miss Rigling were in bed with colds. So it's lucky Lionel was there, as what B was sleepily looking for was a tiny little Miss R & a large Mrs W. (who was to wear a blue coat with a white gardenia on her bosom) B. wasn't quite sure what a gardenia was like. But luckily L's train from Kingston arrived in Toronto shortly before B's train from London. So L. was able to perform the introduction to Mr W. L. said Miss R. sounded nice on the telephone. He was not so sure about the Woods. Anyway, B spent the night with them & today is to go with Bampa's friend Prof Parsons to investigate the museum. Tonight they spend in the train to New York and after a few days move on to Philadelphia whence they sail.

I wonder if this will arrive as soon as they do? I won't send it airmail. Here is a spare visa photo in case you need help in recognising your son. He hasn't changed so very much but I see signs of his being about to become adolescent so it's as well you've got him before he makes the sweeping changes of 12 to 13 years (I found an old photo – nearly 3 years old – of the family and Oliver was quite unrecognisable – Benny & the others have hardly changed at all).

We may be going to live in London, Eng after the war. Lionel has been offered the job of his life there. My feelings are mixed & the children want terribly to stay on in this continent. It is so much more fun for them. I don't know what will happen in the end I'm sure.

I took B over to Sarnia last Tuesday to get his American visa & we had quite a trip (65 miles each way and we took the car without feeling guilty!) We gave a lift to some boys who (it turned out) were also going to Sarnia &

also to the consul! –they "thumbed" a ride on the road. So after transacting the business which took 3 or 4 hours (the consul being ill in bed & the office girls quite inexperienced) B was made to give 10 fingerprints 4 or 5 times each! We all came back to London together. It was certainly more fun than spending all day in a crowded train. I wonder if B. will be very jealous of your R[oderick] and J[onathan]. He shows a marked tendency that way with our J. Just curiosity on my part.

Love M.

I suppose you've stopped factory work pro tem? Your life will be more like mine. All you need is one more boy after B. to complete the family picture.

As to Lionel Penrose securing "job of his life there," Ronald Fisher, a leading statistician and eugenicist, resigned in 1943 from the Galton chair at University College, London. J.B.S. Haldane sounded out Lionel, through a letter to his brother Ronald Penrose, as to whether the post interested him.[7] Lionel's response was, as Margaret's comment indicates, enthusiastic, and Haldane pushed his candidacy. Although administrative questions delayed a decision, the post finally was offered to Lionel in December 1944. He did not occupy the chair until after the family's return to England in 1945.

"One more boy after B.": Margaret had clearly become accustomed to managing four children, so that Ben's departure left a psychological gap. It is perhaps significant that in the middle of 1944, at the age of 44, she became pregnant again, giving birth to a daughter (Shirley) on 22 February 1945.

The following letter, dated 1 December 1943, from Hugh Lawson, friend and neighbour of the Woods family in Toronto, is placed here, out of strict chronological order, since it describes Ben's trip from Toronto to New York City in late September.

---

7 In a letter to Lionel Penrose, Chisbury Manor Gt. Bedwyn Marlborough Wilts, 18 March 1944, his brother Alexander Penrose enquired "Bye the bye what happened about the professorship which Haldane suggested through Roland you might apply for?" See University College, London, Science Library, Special Collections, Penrose Papers, 3/16/7.

Hugh Lawson to Lowis Barman

York Knitting Mills
170 Crawford Street
Toronto, Ont

December 1, 1943

Dear Mr Barman,

Your letter of October 26 with respect to Benjamin's New York sojourn. Your letter was addressed to my brother, L.W., by mistake.

Katherine Bruce, and Benjamin, Nan Riggling and I went to New York together. I went along to see them safely off, or at least safely through the various visa offices, etc. I was not able to stay with them until they sailed because the boat was delayed for a number of days.

When Benjamin arrived in Toronto to join our little party, I was sorry to see he had a jacket and trousers which obviously were several sizes too big for him. I was very much taken with Benjamin who is most manly little fellow, and by the time we parted in New York I had developed a real appreciation of his behaviour and good qualities. I felt that he himself might feel somewhat conscious of wearing clothing obviously too big, and in addition I felt that you would certainly want him outfitted with his proper size. So, I bought him the best quality boys' suit which they had at the time at Macy's in New York. I also bought him two or three pairs of socks for good measure because he did not seem to be sure as to how many pairs were in his personal kit which, as you know, had to be a minimum weight on account of the aeroplane restrictions.

It so happened that after we had finished going through the necessary official New York offices, we discovered that our little party had more English money than they were allowed to take out of the States, according to the regulations as laid before us. As it was Kate Riggling who had some 10 pounds more than was allowable, we decided that whereas I had paid for Benjamin's suit, she would give me some of her surplus English money, and would collect the price of the suit from you when she got to England.

As it stands, therefore, you owe Kate Riggling seven pounds sterling, which is the figure she turned over to me, and which in English money represents what I paid for Benjamin's suit and other odds and ends in New York. You probably know that Kate Riggling has been Nannie in the Lubbock family for

COMPANHIA COLONIAL DE NAVEGAÇÃO

Paquete «João Belo»   Tonelagem bruta 6.365

Figure 8.6 Postcard view of the ss *João Belo*, owned by the
Companhia Colonial de Navegação

many years so you will have no difficulty in locating her through Maurice,
when she lands.

It was particularly pleasant for me to meet your young son, as I do remember having met you in London on one of my trips. It also gave me a good
deal of pleasure to have Benjamin with us in New York because we enjoyed
our brief stay there very much indeed. I would like you to give him my
salutations.

Kind regards to you.

Sincerely, Hugh Lawson

*"Katherine Bruce" cannot be further identified, but Ben thinks that she may have
been related to the Lubbock family.*

*"Hugh Lawson" was a business partner and neighbour of the Woods family,
both living on Avondale Road, Toronto.*

Kate Rigling's transit visa records kept by the US Immigration Service show
that she, Ben, and Katherine (or Catherine) Bruce finally sailed from Philadelphia on 26 September 1943, on the *João Belo*. Ben does not recall much about

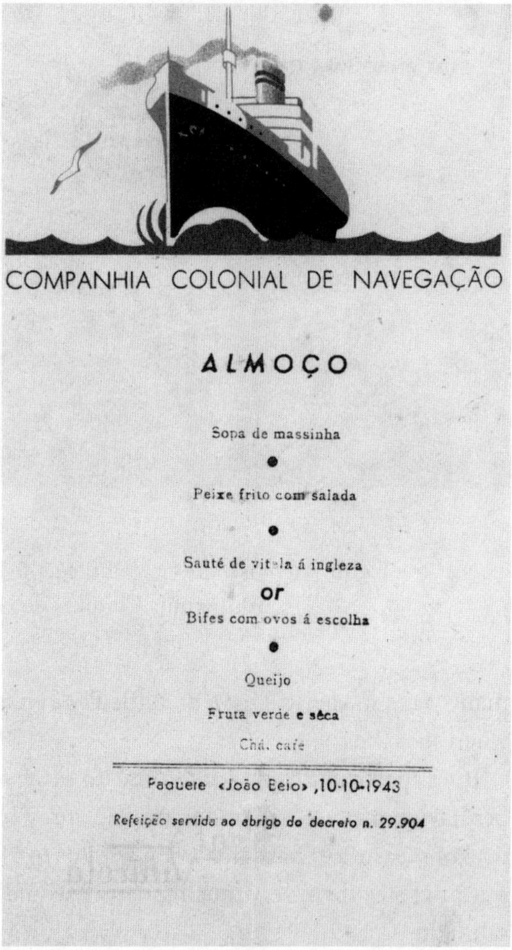

Figure 8.7
Printed lunch menu, ss *João
Belo*, 10 October 1943

COMPANHIA COLONIAL DE NAVEGAÇÃO

ALMOÇO

Sopa de massinha

•

Peixe frito com salada

•

Sauté de vitela á ingleza
or
Bifes com ovos á escolha

•

Queijo

Fruta verde e sêca

Chá, café

Paquete «João Belo» ,10-10-1943

Refeição servida ao abrigo do decreto n. 29.904

the voyage except that the ship was lit up at night and that Kate Rigling did not
approve of his table manners. He did, however, keep the menu for one of the
lunches (Fig. 8.7).

The passengers were offered vermicelli soup, fried fish with salad, sautéed
veal English style, or beef with eggs any style, cheese and fresh and dried
fruits, and coffee and tea. The wine list was extensive, including aperitifs,
port, and brandy.

The *João Belo* finally docked at Lisbon in the middle of October 1943. As
a telegram from Kate Rigling showed, there was no certainty of any rapid
return to England.

Cable (via Cable and Wireless Limited)
Kate Rigling to Lowis Barman

Office of Issue: Stamp "W. C. &W. LTD 13 OCT 43 CENTRAL STATION"
Stamp "Passed by Censor No. T35"
Number of Message: 289 Office of Origin: ESTORIL Number of Words: 32
Date 12 Time Handed In: 1714
ELT BRUCE BARMAN 14 LOWNDES SQUARE LONDON SW ONE ENGLAND
ESTORIL HOTEL LISBON GOOD JOURNEY ALL WELL HAPPY LOVE TO ALL
OWING TO NO TRANSPORTATION MAY BE HERE 3 MONTHS BARMAN
BRUCE KATE RIGLING

*As to "Bruce Barman," Ben notes that "many people, not just Kate Rigling, were
confused by my father's unusual name Lowis, that confusion explaining why he
frequently went by his actual first name, Harry. The address on the telegram is
that of the Maurice Lubbock household."*

As soon as Ben's parents learned of his safe arrival in Lisbon, they informed the
Penroses by cable of the fact. As Margaret Penrose's response indicates, there
was some concern about the next stage in his journey, that of reaching England.

Airgraph from Margaret Penrose to Penelope Barman

1000 Wellington St London Ont. 19 Oct 43
My dear Penelope,
    Thank you for the cable that arrived several days ago. I did not answer
sooner as Roger wanted to write again to Benny & convey my message. But
pressure of events have proved too great for him. There are so many urgent
occupations for the young here. Anyway we await the cable from <u>England</u>,
when B gets there, with great excitement, if not anxiety. I do hope he does
not have to kick his heels in Portugal for too long. But events seem to be
moving there apace & that may make for extra delay. Uncle Ross has very
kindly given me a completely unexpected present (!) for which we are pro-
foundly grateful. Mrs Gaynor wrote from New York & said B was "a credit to"
us which surprised & pleased us much. She commented on the fact that he

was not exactly fading away & that he seemed to find American rationing less
generous than Canadian! So I wish you luck with your food coupons. Probably Lisbon will not be very lavish (I read of bread queues there) so I am
afraid he may look less buxom when he reaches you.

. Love to you all Margaret.
P.S. I have dispatched a meager parcel of food to you.

Ross Barman's "present" was likely a sum of money.

Ben and his two companions stayed at the Hotel Estoril, a seaside resort lying
to the west of Lisbon. Ben's father must have pulled strings through his BOAC
connections to ensure that his eldest son did not spend the next three
months in Lisbon, as Kate Rigling had been told. Ben describes the last leg
of his journey:

I waited about two weeks in Estoril before flying to the UK. Because of
enemy action it was a night flight to Bristol …

Catherine Bruce, who travelled with me and Kate Rigling, was not
pleased that I got on a plane before her. The plane I travelled on was full of
pilots and I was probably the only child. On arrival at Bristol Airport I was
transferred to Temple Meads railway station for the journey to London
Paddington. Other passengers in my compartment were quite amazed
when on asking me where I came from I replied "Estoril." I was met in
London by my father. This was late October 1943.

The date was probably 27 or 28 October.

One of my most vivid memories from childhood is sitting on a sofa in the
lounge of a London hotel (looking out onto a busy street) with my brother
Jonathan ensconced next to me and our mother seated in an armchair to our
left. Suddenly there appeared our father accompanied by a boy, plump, with
black hair cut in bangs, flashing blue eyes, and a broad smile. He talked with a
strange accent, though what he said was entirely understandable. Our mother
went into raptures as she greeted him. Lowis looked like the cat that had swallowed the canary. What can be deduced in retrospect from this visual memory
of Lowis's facial expression is the obvious pride that our father felt in having
regained a son and heir who was so good looking and so healthy.

Ben was finally back home with his family.

9

Aftermath: Reintegration and Impact

For behaviour I give him full marks (10 out of 10!) His easy friendly courteous
manners could hardly be improved upon.
~*H. Stafford Webber to Penelope Barman, 16 December 1943*

After the reunion in London, Ben went with his family to their rented house at
Buckland Common, Buckinghamshire. The journey marked the start of the
process of his reintegration into British life, the sixth and final phase in the war
guest experience. Change was the order of the day. Ben took over the front upstairs bedroom, previously his father's workroom, and adjusted to living with
the family he had left three and a half years earlier. In place of the companion-
ship of the Penrose sons, close to him in age, he had to deal with his two
brothers, both younger than he. I was not only six years his junior but prone
to prolonged temper tantrums. Ben recalls that, during one of these fits, our
father, taking a newspaper to read, locked himself in a bedroom with me, remaining there until the tantrum was over. Ben could not seek company outside
the house. Whereas London, Ontario, was a considerable town with shops and
means of entertainment all around, Buckland Common and its neighbour,
Cholesbury, were hamlets, two handfuls of houses each with a single shop. Visiting Chesham, the local town, required a twenty-minute bus ride.

During his three and half years in Canada, Ben had gradually developed
a life that suited his disposition and outlook. His major challenge, dyslexia,
had largely been ameliorated, thanks to the efforts of his teachers, above all
John Laidlaw, and of his foster mother, among others. His fairly free-wheeling
life in Canada had allowed him to acquire a degree of social autonomy and
self-confidence.

In England, he found that his parents held a very different set of assumptions and priorities both about everyday life and about his future. His time in

Canada, necessary as it was, was, from their perspective, an unproductive diversion from the course marked out for an eldest son. After closely interrogating Ben about the nature of his education in Canada, his grandmother, Edie Spencer, pronounced it as being both inferior and deficient. His parents viewed his time at Ryerson School as a hindrance to his catching up with and advancing in the schooling, both academic and social, required of an upper-class boy. Ben knew no Latin, command of which served as the identifying mark of a gentleman. He did not possess the outlook and manners that attending a boarding school inculcated. To enrol their eldest in a state school was for Lowis and Penelope unimaginable. Sending him to a progressive boarding school such as Dartington Hall (founded in 1926) or, worse yet, Summerhills (founded in 1921) was no less unthinkable, as they flouted the established conventions: they were coeducational, refrained from discipline, and often had scandalous reputations.

With his eldest son safely back in England, Lowis reneged on his promise, made in his letter of 29 April 1943, that "we are not going to send you to a boarding school" and reverted to his original intent – enrolling his eldest son to Repton School, which he, and his uncle before him, had attended. Boys entered public school at the age of thirteen, which Ben would become in May 1944, a few months before the start of the school year. The first step towards Ben's attending Repton was for him to pass the entrance exam.

Ben takes up the story: "On my return one of the first things I had to do was to have coaching for the Common Entrance Exam since the North American education system was so very different to the British: no Latin, with the emphasis on Art etc. Arithmetic was also different. I remember going around with my mother interviewing different coaches and we settled on Mr. Webber of Little Cartridge Chesham. I cycled the 5 miles from Twin Oaks at Buckland Common where we lived." Ben began work with his new tutor on 22 November 1943. The following letters record his progress.

H. Stafford Webber to Penelope Barman

November 29, 1943. Little Cartridge, Chesham, Bucks
Dear Mrs Barman,

Very good work for the first week. Another boy (whose standard of work is about the same as Benjamin's) will probably be coming to me on January 3, but in any case, as Benjamin is such a good boy to teach, after this four weeks I should be glad to have him for three guineas a week instead of four.

If you find this too much in view of your other commitments I quite understand.

Yours sincerely,

H Stafford Webber

B is inclined to be a little untidy and "slapdash" over his arithmetic, but he will have no difficulty in passing the Common entrance in maths when the time comes. HSW

"H. Stafford Webber" was Henry Stafford Webber, born in 1862, and a long-time private schoolmaster. He died on 25 November 1945 at his home.

The "guinea" was part and parcel of the English class system in respect to money. Ordinary businesses used pounds, shillings, and pence, but any business with class pretensions charged for their services in "guineas," worth a pound and one shilling. The practice did not long survive the decimalization of British currency in 1971.

H. Stafford Webber to Penelope Barman

December 16, 1943. Little Cartridge, Chesham

Dear Mrs Barman.

On the whole I am quite satisfied with the progress Benjamin has made during these four weeks. Mathematics will give him little trouble, though there is, of course, a lot of ground to be covered before he reaches the Common entrance standard. His French is not unpromising for a beginner – but in Latin he is rather slower than I expected. His trouble at present seems to be an untrained memory and a definite lack of concentration, but I feel very confident that these disabilities will vanish in time.

Since writing the above I had a word with you on the telephone. For boys like Benjamin I am a great believer in what we used to call at Cartridge "four lines" (of poetry). He might copy out the four lines with absolute accuracy. If he makes the slightest mistake (e.g. missing even a comma, putting a small letter instead of a capital etc. etc.) or makes any correction he should write it all out again from the beginning. He should then learn and say it by heart (again without any mistake) and finally write it down without a blemish.

If there is the least error he should rewrite (by heart of course) the whole thing again. It is tedious work but in my opinion most salutary! I don't suggest he should do much work; one page well done is worth 20 covered with red pencil corrections.

For behaviour I give him full marks (10 out of 10!) His easy friendly courteous manners could hardly be improved upon.

Believe me. Yours sincerely

H Stafford Webber

I vividly remember Ben industriously doing his homework in the living room at Twin Oaks, carefully using correcting fluid to remove mistakes in his marked exercises. Ben informed me that his tutor knew exactly which Latin words a pupil had to know in order to pass the Common Entrance exam. It was a matter of how many and no more.

Late in the first half of 1944, Ben and his family moved from rural isolation at Twin Oaks to the family's flat at 42 Queen's Gate Gardens, London, a quite large but extremely gloomy ground-floor apartment. Ken and Bev Hart, the sons of Mrs Elsie Hart, who had given Ben care and attention on Saturdays in London, Ontario, often stayed with the Barman family during their leaves from the war, which, following Operation Overlord in June 1944, was being fought in France. I remember well the visits of the young men with their flat North American accents. A relatively worry-free existence for Londoners was ended by the onslaught of the "flying bombs" (V1s) against London from June to September 1944 and later by the V2 rockets (much less horrible, because if one one heard them explode one knew that one had survived) from September 1944 to March 1945.

The occasional presence of the Hart brothers was, by 1944, the only reminder that Ben had of his years in Canada. Every month of life in England made his Canadian experience more and more distant and less relevant. When in London, his mother took him, with Jonathan and myself as spectators, to an ice skating rink. Ben did not display any zest or much confidence on the ice. The experience was never repeated.

Ben's closest friendship in Canada had been with Roger Penrose, three months his junior, a friendship based on shared activities to which Roger contributed the intellectual and Ben the practical and down-to-earth element. Separated by the Atlantic, which letters took a month to cross, and given that writing did not come easily to Ben, the two boys, now in adolescence, drifted apart. One letter from Roger to Ben, dating from the last months of 1944 and mainly devoted to spacecraft and chess, survives. Roger sent Ben, as a Christmas present, a jigsaw puzzle made of cardboard pieces. I vividly remember my eldest brother, after opening the present and examining the puzzle, remarking "That will be easy to solve. I know Roger. He will have forgotten to smooth the edges of the pieces which form the outside." Such was indeed the case and, after finding the pieces with rough edges, Ben rapidly put the puzzle together. He still possesses and treasures Roger's gift.

Ben passed his Common Entrance exams and gained admittance to Repton School, which – fortunately for him – lay in central England, far outside the range of both flying bombs and V2 rockets. His former tutor was proud of Ben's achievement, as the following postcard attests.

Postcard from H. Stafford Webber to Ben Barman

19 September 1944. Hill House Cartridge
Just a word to wish you good luck in your first term. Victor had a day off this morning, so I bicycled to Leyshed and played golf. All good wishes from everybody. I shall miss you in that corner!

"Sir"

Ben's entrance into Repton School, which inculcated the ethos of the upper classes, signalled his reintegration into British society. He found Repton to be a near repetition of Pinewood, the boarding school he had attended in 1940, prior to going to Canada. He did have one brief consolation after arriving there. In a classroom, he came across an ancient oak desk with its lid inscribed "H L Barman," carved by his father a generation previously. The antiquated plant was not the only problem that marred the school. Its teaching facilities were inadequate, its teachers (all male) aged and untrained, and its curriculum utterly traditional – the inculcation of facts through rote learning. While the height of academic achievement was to learn ancient Greek, the boys' lives revolved around sports, known as "games." Those who lacked the physical prowess that games required were consigned, as I discovered to my cost, to the outer darkness.

On 8 September 1945, the month Ben entered Repton, the Penroses arrived in England on the ss *Samaria*. The family included a baby daughter, Shirley, born in February 1945. Lionel and Margaret purchased a house and the family adapted to life in London, England, with no difficulty, in part because the family had always set its own course in life with scant regard for accepted conventions. As Galton Professor at University College London, Lionel Penrose held a secure position in the academic world, while the three sons' intelligence meant that adapting to English education presented no challenge.

Inevitably, the diverging trajectory of the two families' existence meant that the close bonds established with Ben during his four years in Canada slackened somewhat, especially after the Barmans' move to Birmingham in 1947, when Lowis Barman took up a senior post at Chance Brothers, managing their lighthouse division. The ties endured nonetheless, with Oliver Penrose helping Ben when he prepared for his entrance exams to Cambridge University. Margaret's continuing affection for Ben and her desire to maintain the relationship is evident from the surviving letter she wrote him in May 1953 (Fig. 9.1), almost exactly ten years after Ben's return to England.

Margaret Penrose to Ben

1 Rodborough Road
London
N. W. 11
Friday 29 V 53

My dear Benny,

I will try & phone you this evening but you or we may be out. We all want to see you so much. Can't you please come out to Thorington with Oliver & spend Sunday night with us out there? It is so much nicer. Roger will be there too & Shirley.

[Added on the page top:] We're going to watch the coronation on T.V. at Thorington & see the queen at U.C. [University College] on Thursday

London is horribly full & I think the decorations rather disappointing. Then you can get back to town in time to see the coronation. Have you got seats? You can sleep here Mon. night & any of your friends too if you like.

There will be seven empty beds! Audrey will be in residence & would get you breakfast or whatever.

Do <u>please</u> come to Thorington for Sun. night.

Much love from us all

Margaret

"Thorington" Hall was the large farmhouse that Lionel Penrose purchased in 1937, restored to its original condition and gave to the National Trust in 1940, reserving a right of residence for his family.

"The coronation" refers to the crowning of Queen Elizabeth on 2 June 1953. The Barman family viewed the coronation on a large screen in the London offices of Messrs. Chance Bros., glass manufacturers and Lowis's employer, which stood on the route of the coronation procession. Sixty-five years later, I retain vivid memories of that day, including the queen's beauty and dignity, Richard Dimbleby's masterly commentary on television, and the exuberant personality of Queen Salote of Tonga.

Ben turned twenty-two a few days before he received Margaret's 1953 letter. While he had survived his years at Repton, he had also suffered in late adolescence from the "first son" syndrome. His parents expected that he would, as their eldest son and heir, secure entry into Cambridge, the elite university attended by his father. The pressures of these expectations contributed to inducing a duodenal ulcer. Fortunately, Ben's health recovered. In place of entering university, he took evening courses in engineering. Marriage offered Ben, as it did for his two brothers, the means of securing autonomy. Ben and his brother Jonathan courted and wed Quaker cousins who, while of suitable lineage, had much simpler outlooks on life and more open dispositions than did Lowis and Penelope. Ben made a career as a production engineer with Cadburys, the premier chocolate manufacturers, while Jonathan became a chartered accountant. I, their youngest son, took a different route. After fulfilling my father's expectations in respect to higher education at King's College, Cambridge, I married an American, escaped to the University of California at Berkeley for my doctorate, and pursued an academic career at a Canadian university. By a twist of fate, my introduction to Canada, and to British Columbia where I would teach, was occasioned by a visit to the same uncle Ross who so many years before had facilitated Ben's evacuation to Canada and who subsequently left Montreal for

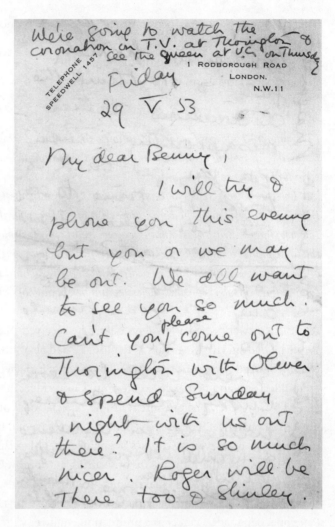

Figure 9.1
Letter from
Margaret Penrose
to Ben, 29 May 1953

retirement at Oak Bay on Vancouver Island. Lowis Barman died of cancer in
1972 while Penelope Barman survived, in discontented widowhood, until 1993.

As to the Penroses, their new home in London, 1 Rodborough Road, has been
described as "a tremendously large, old and extremely cold house."[1] Lionel held
the Galton Chair at University College until his retirement in 1965. He then
founded the Kennedy-Galton Centre at St Albans, using the moneys from the

1 Renata Laxova, "Lionel Sharples Penrose," n.p.

> London is horribly full & I think the decorations rather disappointing. Then you can get back to town in time to see the coronation. Have you got seats? You can sleep here ρ mon. night & any of your friends too if you like. There will be seven empty beds! Audrey will be in residence & would get you breakfast or whatever. Do please come to Thought for Sun. night.
>
> much love from us all Margaret.

award he received in 1964 from the Joseph P. Kennedy Jr. Foundation. He remained active until his death in 1972. Margaret found happiness in a second marriage to Max Newman (1897–1984), a leading mathematician, former code breaker at Bletchley Park, and pioneer computer scientist. She died in 1989, four years prior to the decease of her childhood friend Penelope Barman.

All of Margaret and Lionel's four offspring have had outstanding careers. On returning to England, Oliver gained accelerated entrance to University College, London, from which he received his BA. His brothers both attended

University College School in London. After gaining his doctorate at Cambridge University, Oliver taught mathematics first at Imperial College, then at the Open University, finally moving in 1986 to Heriot-Watt University, where he retired as professor of mathematics in 1994. His prowess in research on statistical mechanics and other subjects secured him election as a Fellow of the Royal Society. His second brother, Roger, after gaining his doctorate at Cambridge University in 1958, occupied positions, both permanent and visiting, at many different universities on both sides of the Atlantic, ending as Rouse Ball Professor of Mathematics at Oxford (1973–99). He achieved renown for his research and his theoretical innovations in mathematical physics, becoming a Fellow of the Royal Society in 1972, receiving a knighthood in 1994, and being appointed to the Order of Merit in 2000. The youngest brother, Jonathan, secured a degree in psychology at University College and became a lecturer in that subject at Middlesex Polytechnic. He made his mark as a chess prodigy, a game he learned at the age of four. He won the British Chess Championship ten times between 1958 and 1969, a record that still stands. He beat the world chess champion, Mikhail Tal, in 1960 and became an International Grand Master in the 1990s, being also a Grand Master in correspondence chess. He received the Order of the British Empire for his achievements in the game. The youngest sibling, Shirley Hodgson, followed both of her parents in her chosen career. After studying medicine at University College, London, and Somerville College, Oxford, she gained her medical doctorate, first practising as a general practitioner and then in paediatrics. In 1971, she wed Humphrey Hodgson, also a medical doctor. Becoming a specialist in cancer genetics, focusing on the inherited aspects of colorectal and breast cancer, she served from 2013 until her recent retirement as a professor of cancer genetics at St George University, London.

After the return of the Penrose family to England, the two families kept in touch, but on an individual rather than a group basis. Shirley Penrose stayed with the Barmans at their home in Melbourne, Derbyshire, in the mid 1950s, and Ben attended Roger Penrose's marriage to Joan Wedge in 1959. All the Barman and Penrose offspring are alive at the time of writing.

The six phases of life for the war guest – decision, transit, reception, living, going home, and reintegration – had a diverse impact on each child evacuee and a different influence on their ensuing lives. In Ben's case, the impact and influence can, for a number of reasons, be termed mixed. The ample means possessed by both his parents and the Penroses meant that he never suffered financial constraint or deprivation during the phases of his war guest experience. He was young, just over nine years old at the time of his arrival, and he left Canada before fully adolescent. His brush with death by torpedo in the *Antonia* induced a profound trauma that did nothing to build his self-confidence. In Canada he lived with a family that, for all its nonconformist aspects, was British in behaviour and outlook. Much as the Penroses enjoyed life in London, Ontario, they had no hesitation in later opting for England over Canada. Ben found in Margaret a very acceptable alternative to his birth mother and in Roger Penrose an excellent and very compatible brother. In his own words, he did not make a circle of friends outside of the family.

Once Ben returned, his parents simply assumed, as did so many other parents of wartime guests. that he would easily resume the existence he had for three years left behind. The elements of life, such as swimming, which had made his life interesting and distinctive in Canada were not generally available in England. The difficulties of communication across the Atlantic, especially after the Penroses' return to England in 1945, meant that Ben had little to keep him in contact with Canada. To this day, the British press and the public discourse pay little or no attention to Canada. For Ben returning there on becoming an adult would have required an uprooting of his life and the exercise of qualities not foremost in his character. It is not at all clear a return to Canada would have served any purpose.

Canada had provided a safe haven for both Ben Barman and for Margaret Penrose and her family in a time of great danger. Ships seek secure harbours during threatening weather and during hostilities, but such safe havens are no more than interludes: vessels' purpose is to undertake longer voyages. So it was for Ben and Margaret. Canada provided a refuge. Their lives lay in England and in undertaking there the journey of life.

The events narrated here now belong to history. The eightieth anniversary of the outbreak of the Second World will soon be upon us. Knowledge about "the war," as those who lived through it still term it, is rapidly fading from popular consciousness, arousing little interest. The letters and recollections included here, recounting the disrupted childhood of a young boy, and the challenges faced by the foster parent who cared for him along with her own children, will hopefully possess meaning and appeal for a new generation.

Appendix:
Annotated Bibliography
on Child Evacuation

Bailey, Anthony. *America Lost and Found*. Rev. ed. Chicago: University of Chicago Press, 2000.
A memoir of an evacuee's years in the United States, a time that brought the author more happiness and content than he could have expected in England and that set him on the path, equipped with the right connections, to becoming a successful journalist for the *New Yorker*. The author's very upbeat and nostalgic approach does not preclude his providing many shrewd insights, including the allure of summer camp. The original edition appeared in 1981.

Bell, Caroline, and Eddie Bell. *Thank You Twice, or How We Like America*. Edited by Alden Hatch. New York: Harcourt, Brace, 1941.
The account by two children, as filtered through their elder sister and an editor, of their voyage to Canada and subsequent move to live with that sister in New England. Their father, who organized their evacuation along with several others, was Kenneth Norman Bell (1884–1951), a historian and fellow at Balliol College, Oxford. The purpose of the work was to justify to the influx of British children and to reconcile Americans to their presence.

Bilson, Geoffrey. *The Guest Children: The Story of British Child Evacuees Sent to Canada during World War II*. Saskatoon: Fifth House, 1988.
That the work was published posthumously probably explains why it is not as developed as it could be. The experiences of eleven children are told in segments and are not integrated into well-organized sections on the different aspects of

the evacuees' life. All but one of the eleven were sponsored by the Children's Overseas Reception Board (CORB), providing some insights into the experience of that segment of the war guest population.

Farson, Daniel [Negley]. *Never a Normal Man*. London: HarperCollins, 1997.
In 1940, forty boys from Abinger Hill boarding school were evacuated to Ontario, where they were incorporated into Ashbury College. The author, anything but orthodox in his later life, recalls his experience at Ashbury and with relatives in North America with cynicism and displeasure. He returned to England on a banana ship in April 1942.

Fethney, Michael. *The Absurd and the Brave: CORB – The True Account of the British Government's World War II Evacuation of Children Overseas*. Lewes, Sussex: Book Guild, 1990.
An exhaustive recounting of the formation, activities, and demise of the CORB, written without much imagination or verve. Its main attributes lie in the author's use of the official files, his listing of the children and adults involved, and his interviews with those involved, notably Geoffrey Shakespeare, head of the program.

Halstead, Claire L. "From Lion to Leaf: The Evacuation of British Children to Canada during the Second World War." PhD dissertation, Western University, 2015.
This broad-ranging work contains a wealth of information on child evacuees, both public (CORB) and private. The recognition of the latter group is a welcome innovation, as is the pioneering use of the Immigration Branch files held in Library and Archives Canada. The author's concern to be inclusive shapes the dissertation's structure.

Horne, Alastair. *A Bundle from Britain*. London: Macmillan, 1993.
The offspring of a dysfunctional marriage, the author time in the United States, from his dispatch in 1940, provided him with a stable, secure environment. His American boarding school experience contrasted starkly with what he had suffered at such schools in England.

Inglis, Ruth. *The Children's War Evacuation, 1939–1945*. London: Collins, 1989.
The bulk of the work, which is clearly written but not profound, deals with evacuation within Great Britain, save for chapter 7, "Evacuation Overseas: Some Succeeded, Others Not."

Jackson, Carlton. *Who Will Take Our Children? The British Evacuation Program of World War II*. Rev. ed. Jefferson, NC: Macfarland, 2008.
A fairly simplistic, if clearly written, retelling of the evacuee experience, which recounts what others had also concluded (a trait especially evident in the overview of the post-1985 literature). The original edition appeared in 1985.

Keshen, Jeffrey A. *Saints, Sinners, and Soldiers: Canada's Second World War*. Vancouver: UBC Press, 2004.
Given the importance of the Second World War in shaping the development of Canada as a nation state, the literature on the subject is very limited. This work provides excellent background information on the experience, with some emphasis on the negative aspects of "the good war." The author provides a succinct but balanced and acute account of the experience of the "guest children," making good use of Geoffrey Bilson's data.

Mann, Jessica. *Out of Harm's Way: The Wartime Evacuation of Children from Britain*. London: Headline, 2005.
The author, the child of a refugee German Jewish couple, was sent to Canada and on to the United States, returning in 1943. Instead of concentrating on that experience and that of others in the same situation, the study includes every aspect of the child refugee experience and provides a plethora of quotes from evacuees, depriving the book of focus and power.

Welshman, John. *Churchill's Children: The Evacuee Experience in Wartime Britain*. Oxford: Oxford University Press, 2010.
The study is innovative in that it pays as much attention to the bureaucratic and logistical dimensions of the war evacuation as it does to the experience of the evacuees, both children and adults. The second half of the work focuses on the impact of evacuation on all those involved.

Wicks, Ben. *The Day They Took the Children*. Toronto: Stoddart, 1989.
The strength of this brief work lies in its excellent pictures and in its use of the
memories of a limited number of individuals to record each stage of the evacuee experience within Great Britain. It is admirably focused, if overly brief.

Works Cited

Bailey, Anthony. *America Lost and Found*. Rev. ed. Chicago: University of Chicago Press, 2000.

Bell, Caroline, and Eddie Bell. *Thank You Twice, or How We Like America*. Edited by Alden Hatch. New York: Harcourt, Brace, 1941.

Bilson, Geoffrey. *The Guest Children: The Story of British Child Evacuees Sent to Canada during World War II*. Saskatoon: Fifth House, 1988.

Board of Governors Minutes. Western University Archives, London, Ontario.

"Britain Declares War on Germany." http://www.bbc.co.uk/archive/ww2outbreak/7917.shtml.

Cooke, John. *Safe Keeping: Voices from a Vanished World*. N.p.: Arachne Enterprises, 2015. https://issuu.com/footenews/docs/safekeeping

Farson, Daniel [Negley]. *Never a Normal Man*. London: HarperCollins, 1997.

Fethney, Michael. *The Absurd and the Brave: CORB – The True Account of the British Government's World War II Evacuation of Children Overseas*. Lewes, Sussex: Book Guild, 1990.

"G7e Torpedo." http://en.wikipedia.org/wiki/G7e_torpedo.

Garnett, David, ed. *Letters and Extracts from the Diaries of Carrington*. Oxford: Oxford University Press, 1970.

Halstead, Claire E. "From Lion to Leaf: The Evacuation of British Children to Canada during the Second World War." PhD dissertation, Western University, 2015.

Haskell, Arnold L. *Penelope Spencer and Other Studies*. 2nd ed. London: British Continental Press, 1931.

Hogben, Adrian, and Anne Hogben, ed. *Lancelot Hogben: Scientific Humanist, An Unauthorised Autobiography*. Rendlesham, Surrey: Merlin Press, 1998.

Horne, Alastair. *A Bundle from Britain*. London: Macmillan, 1993.

Inglis, Ruth. *The Children's War Evacuation, 1939–1945*. London: Collins, 1989.

Jackson, Carlton. *Who Will Take Our Children? The British Evacuation Program of World War II*. Rev. ed. Jefferson, NC: Macfarland, 2008.

James, Robert Rhodes, ed., *The Diaries of Sir Henry Channon*. London: Weidenfeld and Nicolson, 1967.

Keshen, Jeffrey A. *Saints, Sinners, and Soldiers: Canada's Second World War*. Vancouver: UBC Press, 2004.

L.S. Penrose Papers. University College, London, Science Library, Special Collections.

Laughton, Sir Anthony. "Sir Anthony Laughton Interviewed by Dr. Paul Merchant." http://sounds.bl.uk/related-content/TRANSCRIPTS/021T-C1379 X0029XX-0000A0.pdf.

Laxova, Renata. "Lionel Sharples Penrose, 1898–1972: A Personal Memoir in Celebration of the Centenary of His Birth." http://www.genetics.org/content/150/4/1333.full.

Massy-Beresford DS MC, Brigadier T H, Private Papers. Imperial War Museums. http://www.iwm.org.uk/collections/item/object/1030014283.

Mosby, Ian. *Food Will Win the War: The Politics, Culture, and Science of Food on Canada's Home Front*. Vancouver: UBC Press, 2014.

Nedelchev, Nicolay. "The Norwegian Operation and the Torpedo Crisis." http://www.uboat.net/history/torpedo_crisis.htm

"Obituary: Margaret Penrose MA MRCS LRCP." *Medicine and War* 5 (1989): 204–8. http:www.tanfonline.com/doi/pdf/10.1080/08748800890840888q

Overseas Evacuation Remittances. 2323ttp://hansard.millbanksystems.com/sittings/1942/jan/08 Commons Sittings 7 January 1942 Series 5 vol. 377.

Penrose, Margaret. "Reminiscences." Unpublished typescript in her family's possession, n.d.

Penrose, Oliver, *Lionel S. Penrose: Human Geneticist and Human Being*. Peterborough, UK: Effective Print, 1999.

– "Lionel S. Penrose: Human Geneticist and Human Being." *Penrose: Pioneer in Human Genetics. Report on a Symposium Held to Celebrate the Centenary of the Birth of Lionel Penrose, Held 12th and 13th March 1998*. London: University College, London Centre for Human Genetics, n.d.

Penrose, Roger. "Lionel Penrose: Colleague and Father." *Penrose: Pioneer in Human Genetics. Report on a Symposium Held to Celebrate the Centenary of the Birth of Lionel Penrose, Held 12th and 13th March 1998.* London: University College, London Centre for Human Genetics, n.d.

Ritchie, Charles. *The Siren Years: A Canadian Diplomat Abroad, 1937–1945.* Toronto: Macmillan, 1974.

Smith, Thomas, "Atlantic Journey: Impressions of a Constellation Proving Flight – To New York, with B.O.A.C." *Flight,* 11 July 1946. https://www.flight global.com/pdfarchive/view/1946/1946%20-%201325.html

Thomas, Pat. "Memories of My Childhood at the Lakehouse." James Luther Lakehouse Club. https://sites.google.com/site/jameslutherlakehouseclub/the-first-100-years/childhood-memories-pat-thomas

– "Saturday 14 April 2014 Notes." http://coolgreenyfarm.blogspot.ca/2014/04/notes-from-pat-thomas.html

"Thorington Hall." http://en.wikipedia.org/wiki/Thorington_Street

Titmuss, Richard M. *Problems of Social Policy.* London: HMSO and Longmans Green, 1950.

"Uboat.net." http://www.uboat.net/allies/merchants/losses_year.html?qdate=1940-07

Wargon, Sylvia T. "Enid Charles: One Hundred Years, 1894–1972–1994." *Canadian Studies in Population* 21, no. 2 (1994): 181–5.

Wicks, Ben. *The Day They Took the Children.* Toronto: Stoddart, 1989.

Index